Geology and Virginia

Geology and Virginia

Richard V. Dietrich

Professor of Geology and Dean
School of Arts and Sciences, Central Michigan University

The University Press of Virginia
Charlottesville

THE UNIVERSITY PRESS OF VIRGINIA
Copyright © 1970 by the Rector and Visitors
of the University of Virginia

First published 1970

Standard Book Number: 8139–0289–4
Library of Congress Catalog Card Number: 76–110752
Printed in the United States of America

To
Frances,
Rick,
Kurt,
Krista,
and
Virginia

THIS book has been prepared for young students and laymen—both natives of Virginia and visitors to the Commonwealth—who are interested in geology and in Virginia. It attempts to answer such perennial questions as: How was Natural Bridge formed? Why are there so many caves in Virginia? What is the Fall Line? Why is central Virginia called the Piedmont? Why is the Coastal Plain so flat and the Blue Ridge and western Virginia so rugged? It reviews each of the major branches of geology, with emphasis on minerals, rocks, fossils, and diverse geological features that may be found and observed within the state.

To some, this book will be a recitation of facts and fancies, most of which they have heard before; to others, it will offer much that is new. As already mentioned, it is the latter group for whom the book has been prepared—to serve, it is hoped, as a mind stretcher. The writer has a predilection for promoting mind stretching; he is a firm believer in the advantages implied by Oliver Wendell Holmes's aphorism, "A man's mind, stretched by a new idea, can never go back to its original dimension."

In order to make the book easier to read, references have generally been omitted from the text, and technical terminology has been kept to a minimum. Supplementary readings and a glossary are, however, given in the back of the book.

Although this book was not written primarily to serve as a textbook, it has been prepared so that it will adequately fulfill the requirements of an introductory earth science course for either high school or college students. It also could serve as the basic text for a more specialized course dealing with the geology of Virginia. It should not, however, be considered a comprehensive account of the geology of the state: with the current shortage of pertinent information any serious attempt to prepare such a volume would be presumptuous.

Nearly all the data and concepts presented herein were introduced by other geologists. To all the scientists who have made the results of their studies available either directly or indirectly, through publications, the author gratefully acknowledges his indebtedness.

Some of the text and several of the tables and figures have appeared in bulletins by the writer previously published by the Virginia Polytechnic Institute. The university's Information Service kindly released them for inclusion in this book. Although credit lines are given with each table and figure, it seems only proper also to acknowledge here the contributions of the photographers G. K. McCauley and H. C. Porter of V.P.I., T. M. Gathright, Jr., of the Virginia Division of Mineral Resources, P. Flournoy of the Virginia Chamber of Commerce, J. D. Kanode and W. F. Rader of the Norfolk and Western Railway; of G. A. Cooper, P. E. Desautels, Clayton Ray, and George Switzer, each of whom arranged for some of the pictures credited to the Smithsonian Institution; of P. T. Flawn of the Texas Bureau of Economic Geology and J. L. Calver of the Virginia Division of Mineral Resources, who, respectively, released some of the fossil sketches given in chapter III and the geologic map given as Appendix C; and of the publishers Agfa-Gevaert Inc., W. H. Freeman and Co., McGraw-Hill Book Co., D. Van Nostrand-Reinhold Co., The Ronald Press Co., the Washington *Star,* and John Wiley and Sons, Inc., each of which released diagrams as indicated.

A number of the author's colleagues at V.P.I. have discussed with the author many of the subjects considered in this book. Drs. G. V. Gibbs, C. M. Gilbert, J. M. Hackett, W. D. Lowry, C. I. Rich, R. D. Ross, and C. G. Tillman of V.P.I. read and criticized different sections of the original manuscript. Drs. Gordon C. Grender and Rufus W. Beamer of V.P.I.; Mrs. J. J. Thaxton, Jr., of Liberty High School in Bedford, Virginia; and Kurt R. Dietrich of Blacksburg High School in Blacksburg, Virginia, read and criticized the complete original manuscript. They did this from the viewpoints, respectively, of a college professor who teaches introductory geology to nonmajors, a college professor of education, the chairman of a high school science department, and a high school student.

Sincere thanks are offered for all the aid so graciously given during the preparation of this book.

RICHARD V. DIETRICH

February 7, 1969
Blacksburg, Virginia

Contents

Tables

Figures

He that can draw a charm from rocks, or woods, or weeds, or things that seem all mute, and does it— is wise.

Bryan Waller Procter, "A Haunted Stream"

GEOLOGY is the study of the Earth. Like other broad scientific fields, it consists of a number of branches (table Int. 1). The six main branches are *mineralogy,* the study of minerals; *petrology,* the study of rocks; *paleontology,* the study of fossils; *geomorphology,* the study of land forms; *stratigraphy,* the description of layered rocks; and *structural geology,* the study of deformed rocks. Each of these branches has special subdivisions, most of which also have names— for example, the branch of mineralogy that deals with the crystal structure or atomic makeup of a substance is called crystallography.

TABLE Int. 1. The Geological Sciences

	MINERALOGY	PETROLOGY	PALEONTOLOGY
Materials of Geology	Determinative mineralogy* Crystallography Synthesis studies Pedology	Igneous petrology† Sedimentary petrology‡ Metamorphic petrology Coal petrology Meteorite petrology Phase equilibrium studies	Invertebrate paleontology Vertebrate paleontology Paleobotany Palynology Ichnology Paleoecology‡
	GEOMORPHOLOGY	STRATIGRAPHY	STRUCTURAL GEOLOGY
Geological Features	Descriptive geomorphology Statistical geomorphology	Physical stratigraphy‡ Biostratigraphy	Field mapping Tectonophysics§
	GEOPHYSICS	GEOCHEMISTRY	BIOGEOCHEMISTRY
Interdisciplinary "Geo-sciences"	Geodesy Seismology Geomagnetism Meteorology	Inorganic geochemistry Organic geochemistry Isotopic geochemistry‖	Zoological biogeochemistry Botanical biogeochemistry
	ECONOMIC GEOLOGY	ENVIRONMENTAL GEOLOGY	

Applied Geology	Discovery and delineation# of:
	   Metallic ore deposits
	   Nonmetallic "ore" deposits
	   Petroleum
		Engineering geology
		 Urban and regional planning
		 Waste-disposal studies	

		Ground water geology Resource management	

* Includes such studies of minerals as hand-specimen and optical examination, *x*-ray diffraction, differential thermal analysis, and all kinds of chemical analyses.

† Includes volcanology.

‡ Generally includes sedimentology (studies of sedimentation) and may include oceanography and paleoclimatology.

§ Generally involves geophysics.

‖ Includes isotope-based geochronology.

Includes geophysical and geochemical prospecting.

In addition, geological materials and features are investigated by scientists in interdisciplinary fields such as geophysics, geochemistry, and biogeochemistry.

In this book the subjects that serve as the basis for each of the main branches of geology are treated in the first six chapters and a result of a synthesis of geologic data and an outline of different uses of such data constitute the remaining two chapters.

To view the coverage in a different way: In general, each of the first three chapters deals with geological materials. Chapter I treats minerals, the basic constituents of almost all the earth that can be studied by direct observation. Chapter II is about rocks, the natural aggregates of minerals and natural glass that make up bedrock and may be seen in cliffs, roadcuts, and other kinds of exposures. Chapter III considers fossils, the evidence, generally within rocks, for former life. Although fossils are not geological material in the same sense that minerals and rocks are, they do serve as the basic substance for studies relating to historical geology.

Each of the second three chapters deals with relatively large-scale phenomena that may be designated as geological features. Chapter IV is about the geological features that are most familiar—landforms such as hills and valleys, beaches and sea cliffs. Chapter V deals with layered rocks and some of the things that may be learned from them about conditions that existed during the ancient past. Chapter VI defines some of the frequently used terms of structural geology and describes some rocks that have been deformed.

The last two chapters deal with the synthesis of geological facts and the application of geology to answer Man's questions and to help fulfill his needs and desires. Chapter VII consists of information about some of Virginia's metallic and nonmetallic deposits, her natural fuels and water resources, and the utilization of geological data in engineering and in urban and regional planning. Chapter VIII presents a brief "Geological History of Virginia."

Mineral determinative tables, some information about topographic and geological maps, a generalized geological map of the state, a glossary, supplementary readings, and an index follow the text.

Some readers may wish to examine the geomorphic province map (fig. 4.16, p. 103), the stratigraphic timetable (table 5.1, p. 127), and the geological map (App. C, facing p. 186) before proceeding. Information given on them is referred to in numerous places throughout the text.

Geology and Virginia

Minerals

MINERALS numbering nearly four hundred species have been found to occur in Virginia. Amelia, in central Virginia, is a world-famous mineral locality. The only natural crystals of turquoise ever found come from Virginia. Some of the finest specimens in the world's finest collection—that of the Smithsonian Institution—are from Virginia. This recitation of "mineral facts" about the state could continue—and it will, with elaboration, later in this chapter—but first some historical background and fundamental information about minerals in general should be considered.

Minerals and rocks have whetted man's curiosity for untold centuries. At first, primitive man probably just picked up stones on impulse, looked at them, perhaps used them as weapons or tools, dropped or threw them, and forgot them. Eventually, however, he began to select certain ones to fulfill his different needs and to satisfy his various whims.

His selection processes led to curiosity: Why do some minerals shine or sparkle while others are dull? Why are some red, others blue or yellow, still others purple, green, orange, black, colorless, or white? Why are some hard, others soft? some heavy, others light? What is the significance of all these things?

The questions, of course, led to speculation. Some of the speculation fostered superstitions—for example: a copper band around the left ankle will prevent gout; the swallowing of powdered lapis lazuli will enhance fertility; the carrying of one's birthstone will bring good luck. Other speculations, actually based on good observation, laid the foundation for the science of mineralogy—for example: diamonds will scratch rubies, which will scratch rock crystal (quartz); halite (rock salt) and natural alum have different tastes; gold and silver may be shaped without breaking.

No matter what the basis, man has long had reasons to accumulate several kinds of minerals. Thus began the perpetual cycle consisting of need or desire, search, discovery, utilization, increased need or desire, renewed search and so on. That the search will continue as long as man exists can hardly be doubted. Man's very culture depends upon the minerals he seeks and the products he produces from them.

Perhaps because of its early beginnings, primeval fancy and facts became completely entwined. In any case, not until after the medieval period did mineralogy pass from its infancy. As F. D. Adams said in *The Birth and Development of the Geological Sciences:* "Medieval mineralogy in fact was not a science . . . but a fairy castle, the insubstantial fabric of a dream, often quaint and even beautiful, but destined to crumble away because it had no foundation in reality."

Nearly all historians place the actual birth of the science of mineralogy in 1546 when Georgius Agricola (Georg Bauer) wrote his book *De natura fossilum*. In that book Agricola classified minerals on the basis of their physical properties—color, weight, transparency, luster, taste, odor, shape, and texture. He rather carefully defined those terms and also several others, such as cleavage, hardness, and solubility. Because of this and other works Agricola is sometimes called the "Father of Mineralogy."

Since the sixteenth century mineralogy has continued its growth through additional observation, classification, introduction and utilization of new methods of investigation, and experimental verification, to attain its present "state of the art." Of particular note in this growth were the introduction in 1837 of the still-employed chemical system of mineral classification by the twenty-four-year-old James Dwight Dana, who later became a truly outstanding American scientist; the publication in 1858 of the memoir *On the Microscopical Structure of Crystals* by Henry Clifton Sorby, which introduced the use of optical methods into mineralogy; and the first application of the X-ray to the investigation of crystalline matter in 1912 at the suggestion of Max von Laue. It was x-ray studies which proved beyond doubt that minerals are composed of atoms with a regular, three-dimensional arrangement. (The reader who is interested in the history of the growth of mineralogy and of other geological sciences is referred to the first section of the Supplementary Readings.)

On the basis of our current knowledge, a mineral may be defined as *a natural substance, generally inorganic, with a characteristic internal arrangement of atoms and a chemical composition and physical properties that are either fixed or that vary within a definite range.*

Probably one of the best ways to gain a little insight into the field of mineralogy is to examine each part of this definition.

The *natural* aspect, which merely means occurs in nature, is considered a necessary condition by many mineralogists. They believe that man-made, synthetic minerals should be designated as such. The *generally inorganic* part of the definition excludes most hydrocarbons, even though for years they have constituted the most important "mineral resource" in terms of annual contribution to the world's economy. The requirement of *a characteristic internal arrangement of atoms* not only excludes natural glass and amorphous substances; it is the single most critical part of the whole definition. (The model that is widely employed to aid visualization of the atom depicts a nucleus made up of protons and neutrons around which there are satellitic electrons moving in essentially all directions [fig. 1.1]). The proton, by definition, has an electrical charge of +1; the electron, a charge of −1; the neutron, no charge. Each atom is electrically neutral because

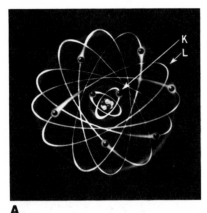

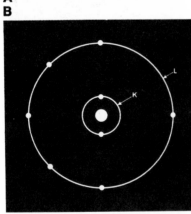

FIG. 1.1. *A.* An atom may be likened to a miniature solar system with a cluster of protons and neutrons forming a nucleus and satellitic electrons revolving, each in its own orbit, around the nucleus. In the oxygen atom shown here the two electrons closest to the nucleus may be considered to be in one shell (*K*), whereas the other six satellitic electrons which are farther from the nucleus may be considered to be in another shell (*L*).
B. The schematic representation often used on paper. (Reprinted, by permission from *The Structure of Matter*, published by Agfa-Gevaert)

the number of satellitic electrons equals the number of protons in its nucleus. Almost all of an atom's mass is concentrated in its nucleus; most of its volume is open space. The atoms of each element have a characteristic number of protons in their nuclei and an equal number of satellitic electrons. (An element, by the way, may be defined as a substance of fixed atomic structure that cannot be separated into substances different from itself by ordinary chemical means.) The number of neutrons in the nuclei may vary, however, and the variants are called isotopes. In any case, the atoms may be considered to be the basic building blocks that make up all substances. They range in diameter from approximately 2 to 6 angstrom units, an angstrom unit being one hundred-millionth of a centimeter (about one 250-millionth of an inch). When atoms are relatively widely spaced and more or less freely moving, they form liquids; when they are closely spaced and more or less fixed with respect to their near neighbors, they constitute a solid. Of the 92 natural elements, 8 (oxygen, silicon, aluminum, iron, calcium, sodium, potassium, and magnesium) are estimated to compose slightly more than 98.5 weight per cent of the earth's crust.

Consistent with the aforementioned natural and inorganic requirements, solids that have characteristic internal arrangements of their constituent atoms comprise minerals. The arrangements, which are three-dimensional arrays such as the one shown in figure 1.2, are called crystal structures. They may consist of atoms of only one element or of combinations of two or more elements. The latter are called compounds. The arrangement of atoms in crystals depends upon such things as the sizes of the atoms and the way they are attached to each other.

The mode of attachment is generally called bonding. There are five fundamental kinds of bonding: ionic, covalent, hydrogen, metallic, and residual. The ionic bond is very common in the mineral kingdom. It depends upon electrostatic attraction between ions, which may be considered to be atoms that have lost or gained electrons. Either a loss or a gain causes an imbalance between the number of protons in the nucleus and the number of satellitic electrons so that the resulting ion has a net electrical charge. An atom that has lost one or more electrons is positively charged and is called a cation; one that has gained one or more electrons is negatively charged and is called an anion. The ionic bond is developed when cations and anions get near enough together to be electrostatically attracted to each other. Typically, the ionic bond is fairly strong. The covalent bond, another very important bond in the mineral kingdom, involves the actual sharing of electrons by two or more atoms. Such sharing often results in the formation of a molecule, which may be defined as the smallest unit that has the properties of the substance. Covalent bonds may range greatly in their strength. Strictly speaking, the bonds within most minerals are not wholly ionic or covalent; rather they are a combination—that is to say, they are partly ionic and partly covalent,

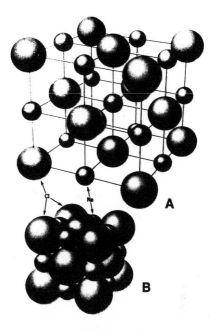

FIG. 1.2.   Crystal structure and cleavage block of halite. *A*. Ions of sodium (small spheres) and of chlorine (large spheres) have been pulled apart in order to show bonds between them. *B*. The ions in their natural positions. *C*. Photograph of cleavage fragment of halite, the cubic shape of which reflects the crystallographic structure. (Diagram reprinted, by permission, from C. R. Longwell, R. F. Flint, and J. E. Sanders, *Physical Geology,* © 1969, by John Wiley and Sons. Photograph courtesy of Smithsonian Institution)

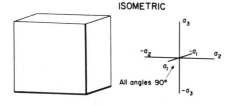

ISOMETRIC

All angles 90°

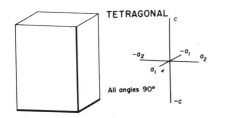

TETRAGONAL

All angles 90°

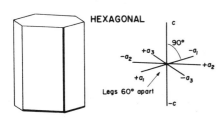

HEXAGONAL

Legs 60° apart

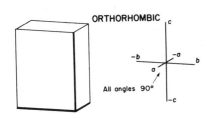

ORTHORHOMBIC

All angles 90°

MONOCLINIC

Larger than 90°

90°

TRICLINIC

NO angles 90°

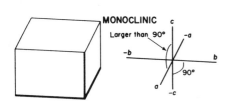

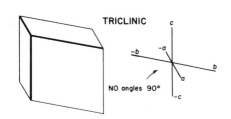

probably in a constant state of shifting from more or less purely ionic to more or less purely covalent (a situation generally called resonance). The metallic bond is important in native metals and in some sulfide minerals. It is commonly considered to be a rather special kind of covalent bond in which the electrons are not localized and thus may move freely from one atom to another. The other bonds are of little significance in mineralogy: the hydrogen bond is electrostatic and important in water, some acids, and a few organic compounds; the residual bond is also electrostatic and pertinent in such things as inert gases and many organic compounds.

There are 230 geometrically possible ways of grouping atoms, ions, and molecules so as to fill space regularly. The 230 groups, called space groups, may be divided into six major categories called crystal systems (fig. 1.3). The faces of each crystal are an outward manifestation of the regular internal arrangement of its constituent atoms. Therefore, each crystal may be placed in its proper crystal system on the basis of its shape (fig. 1.4). Each mineral has its own unique composition and/or crystal structure upon which all its properties depend. But, before consideration of the properties by which minerals are usually identified, one part of the definition of mineral remains to be discussed: *a chemical composition and physical properties that are either fixed or that vary within a definite range.* The proportions of the constituent atoms establish a mineral's chemical composition. For example, if silicon (Si) and oxygen (O) atoms are present in the ratio of 1:2, the composition can be represented by the formula SiO_2, which means that for each silicon atom present there are two oxygen atoms. This is an example of a mineral with a fixed chemical composition. Such a mineral would also have fixed physical properties as long as the crystal structure involving the constituents is set. (This restriction is mentioned because some natural compounds may assume different crystal structures, each with its own physical properties. The phenomenon is called polymorphism, which means "many forms"—that is, many crystal structures—for the same chemical substance.) As noted, however, instead of being fixed, both the chemical composition and the physical properties may vary within a definite

FIG. 1.3. Axes of reference for the six basic crystal systems:

In the isometric (cubic) system, $a_1 = a_2 = a_3$, and all interaxial angles are right angles.

In the tetragonal system, $a_1 = a_2 \neq c$, and all interaxial angles are right angles.

In the hexagonal system, $a_1 = a_2 = a_3 \neq c$, and angles between a axes are 120°, whereas the angle between the c axis and the plane of the a axes is a right angle.

In the orthorhombic system, $a \neq b \neq c \neq a$, and all interaxial angles are right angles.

In the monoclinic system, $a \neq b \neq c \neq a$, and the angle between a and c is not a right angle, whereas the angle between b and the a-c plane is a right angle.

In the triclinic system, $a \neq b \neq c \neq a$, and no interaxial angle is a right angle.
(Modified and reprinted, by permission, from J. Sinkankas, *Mineralogy: A First Course,* © 1966, by Van Nostrand-Reinhold Company, a division of Litton Educational Publishing, Inc., Litton Industries, Princeton, New Jersey)

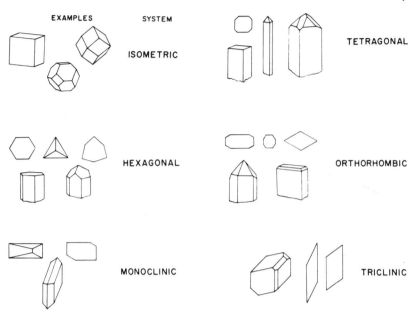

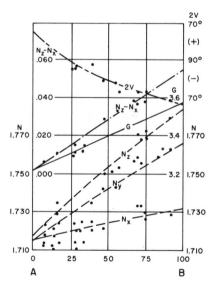

FIG. 1.4. Clues to common crystal shapes of each of the main crystal systems. (Modified and reprinted, by permission, from J. Sinkankas, *Mineralogy: A First Course,* © 1966, by Van Nostrand-Reinhold Company, a division of Litton Educational Publishing, Inc., Litton Industries, Princeton, New Jersey)

range (fig. 1.5). As may be seen, physical properties, such as specific gravity, show regular variation with variation of the chemical composition. Several minerals are of this kind—for example, the olivines range from fayalite (Fe_2SiO_4) to forsterite (Mg_2SiO_4) and the phagioclase feldspars range from albite ($NaAlSi_3O_8$) to anorthite ($CaAlSi_2O_8$).

Each one of the many hundreds of known minerals—including the members of mineral series—may be identified by chemical analysis, microscopic examination, *x*-ray diffraction, differential thermal analysis, or a combination of two or more of these methods. Fortunately, however, most common minerals do not have to be subjected to such complicated investigations for identification. Rather they may be identified from their appearance or by subjecting them to simple tests. The general procedure is to match the properties of the "unknown" with those listed for minerals in determinative tables (see Appendix A). The following properties are usually considered in hand-specimen identification of minerals:

LUSTER is the appearance of a fresh surface of a mineral in ordinary reflected light. In general, minerals have either a metallic or a nonmetallic luster. Minerals with nonmetallic luster may be distinguished from one another by even more precise terms describing their lusters—for example, adamantine (brilliant like a diamond), vitreous (glassy), resinous, pearly, silky, dull, and earthy.

HARDNESS is the resistance of a mineral to abrasion or scratching. Although there are special machines for making quantitative determinations of hardness, the property is usually stated in relative terms, that is, whether the mineral is harder or softer than some other material. For convenience, relative hardness is commonly designated by a number on the scale devised by Mohs. Mohs selected ten

FIG. 1.5. Hypothetical isomorphic series. As an example, *A* could be a sodium-aluminum silicate and *B* its equivalent sodium-iron silicate. *2V* is an optical property; *G* is density; $N_z - N_x$, N_x, N_y, and N_z are properties relating to the velocity of light passing through the substances in diverse directions. (Modified and reprinted, by permission, from A. N. Winchell and Horace Winchell, *Elements of Optical Mineralogy,* 4th ed., part 2, © 1951, by John Wiley and Sons)

relatively common minerals to represent various degrees of hardness. Arranged in order of increasing hardness, these ten minerals are:

1. Talc   6. Orthoclase
2. Gypsum   7. Quartz
3. Calcite   8. Topaz
4. Fluorite   9. Corundum
5. Apatite   10. Diamond

To determine a Mohs hardness value for a mineral, one tries either to scratch fresh surfaces of materials having known hardnesses with a sharp corner of the unknown or to scratch a fresh surface of the unknown with sharp points of materials having known hardnesses. A mineral will scratch materials softer than itself and will be scratched by materials harder than itself, and, of course, minerals or other materials of approximately equal hardness may not scratch each other. For example, a mineral with a hardness of 5½ would scratch apatite but be scratched by orthoclase.

Minerals may be grouped even more readily into three classes of hardness—soft, medium, and hard—by determining whether they are, respectively, softer than the fingernail (H = 2½), harder than the fingernail but softer than a knife blade or a piece of common glass (H ~ 5½), *or* harder than all of these materials. In addition, it may prove helpful to know that copper coins have a hardness on the Mohs scale of slightly more than 3 and most metal files have hardnesses of about 6½.

A few minerals have notably different hardnesses in different directions—for example, kyanite has a hardness of 4 to 5 parallel to the length of its bladelike crystals and of 6 to 7 perpendicular to them. This property should be looked for when examining unknown minerals.

Two additional precautions must be kept in mind: (1) do not mistake the powder of a softer mineral which is left on the surface of a harder material as a scratch, and (2) do not confuse a tearing apart of the grains of an aggregate or the breaking off of small cleavage fragments as a scratch.

COLOR or lack of color is diagnostic for several minerals, but a lack of any diagnostic color, or even a multicolored appearance, may characterize others.

STREAK is the color of the fine powder of a mineral. It is usually determined by scratching or crushing the mineral or by rubbing the mineral on an unglazed porcelain *streak plate*. A mineral may have a streak that differs from its apparent color. The streaks of some minerals are distinctive.

DIAPHANEITY refers to light transmission. Minerals may be transparent (capable of being seen through), translucent (capable of letting light pass through), or opaque (incapable of permitting light to pass through).

A CRYSTAL, as previously noted, is a solid, bounded by plane surfaces, which is the outward manifestation of the regular, periodic arrangement of constituent atoms, ions, or molecules (fig. 1.6). The study of crystals is sometimes valuable in hand-specimen mineral identification because many minerals have crystal forms that are typical. Such forms are termed the mineral's *crystal habit*.

Crystals that appear to consist of two or more parts arranged so that the over-all unit looks like symmetrically united or intergrown crystals are called twin crystals.

Some mineral specimens are made up of many grains with different orientations. Groupings that are relatively common as well as distinctive have been given names: Acicular refers to needle-like groups (fig. 1.7). Plantlike forms are called dendrites (fig. 1.8). Surfaces covered by numerous tiny crystals are called drusy. Crystal groups

FIG. 1.6. Natural crystals: *top*, barite from Glasgow, Virginia (photograph by T. M. Gathright, Jr.); *center*, pyrite; *bottom*, quartz.

FIG. 1.7. Acicular calcite. (Photograph courtesy of Smithsonian Institution)

FIG. 1.8. Dendrites. Treelike growths of manganese oxide are locally common on rock surfaces in western Virginia. (Photograph courtesy of Smithsonian Institution)

may be radiating or concentric or a combination of both (fig. 1.9). Commonly such groups are colloform, that is characterized by external surfaces that are rounded or hemisperical prominences (fig. 1.10). Ellipsoidal or irregularly shaped masses typically surrounding a nucleus are named concretions. Small icicle-shaped forms are termed stalactitic. Pea-sized masses within matrix are called pisolites; buckshot-sized masses of similar shape are termed oölites (fig. 1.11); other descriptive terms such as compact, earthy, columnar, fibrous, platy, and bladed are self-explanatory.

CLEAVAGE refers to the tendency of crystalline substances to break, or split, along certain plane surfaces (figs. 1.12 and 1.13). The positions of the surfaces are controlled by the regular internal arrangement of constituent atoms. Some minerals have no discernible cleavage; some have a single direction, or plane, of cleavage; others have two or more planes of cleavage. Different cleavage surfaces of specific minerals have characteristic angles between them—for exam-

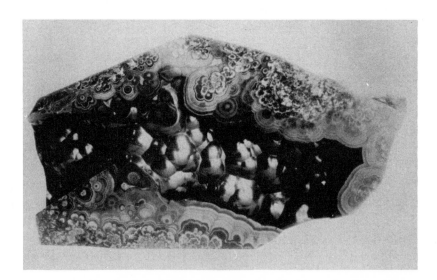

FIG. 1.9. Colloform surfaces, such as those on this malachite specimen, are commonly manifestations of radiating and concentric growths. (Photograph courtesy of Smithsonian Institution)

FIG. 1.10. Colloform psilomelane from Crimora, Virginia—length of specimen approximately 28 cm., or about 11 in. (Photograph courtesy of Smithsonian Institution)

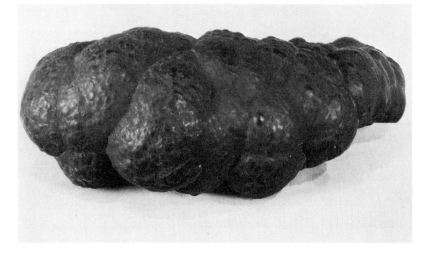

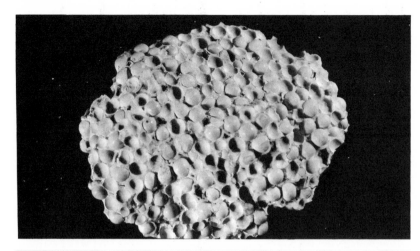

FIG. 1.11. Oölitic calcite. (Photograph courtesy of Smithsonian Institution)

FIG. 1.12. Mica has one direction of cleavage; it cleaves into sheets. (Photograph courtesy of Ward's Natural Science Establishment)

FIG. 1.13. Cacite has three directions of cleavage *not* at right angles to each other. (Photograph courtesy of Ward's Natural Science Establishment)

ple, halite has three directions of cleavage at right angles to each other, whereas calcite has three directions of cleavage not at right angles to each other (compare figs. 1.2 and 1.13). It must be remembered that parallel plane surfaces represent a single cleavage direction.

FRACTURE refers to rough or irregular surfaces along which a mineral breaks when it does not cleave. Different minerals may typically exhibit different fractures designated by such adjectives as conchoidal (smoothly curving like the inside of a clam shell), splintery, rough, smooth, or fibrous (fig. 1.14).

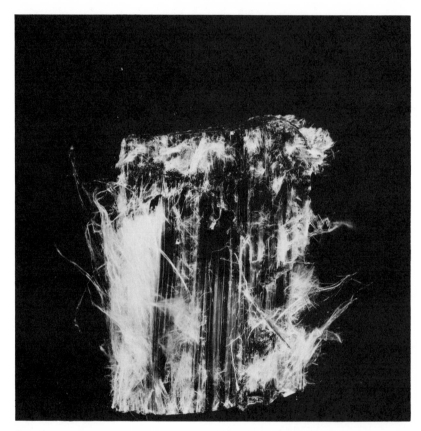

FIG. 1.14. Fibrous asbestos. (Photograph courtesy of Smithsonian Institution)

PARTING is another, rather uncommon type of breakage. It is similar to cleavage in appearance. It may be defined as the tendency to break along composition planes, the planes on which the parts of twinned crystals are united.

SPECIFIC GRAVITY is the ratio of the weight of a certain volume of a substance to the weight of an equal volume of water (at 4° C., strictly speaking). The approximate specific gravity of most specimens can be determined rather simply. One commonly used method consists of weighing the specimen in air and again in water and substituting the proper weights in the appropriate places of this equation:

$$\text{Specific gravity of } x = \frac{\text{weight of } x \text{ in air}}{\text{weight of } x \text{ in air} - \text{weight of } x \text{ in water}}.$$

The main point to recall is that the loss of weight in water is equal to the weight of an equal volume of water (Archimedes's principle). Simply constructed apparatuses for determining specific gravity are described in a number of books, like Sinkankas's *Mineralogy: A First Course*. This property is especially useful in identifying specimens that one does not want to submit to tests that might harm them.

Other properties that may help in the determination of certain minerals are magnetism, relative solubility, taste, feel, odor, fluorescence, phosphorescence, radioactivity, and tenacity. A few minerals such as magnetite are attracted to a magnet. Halite and some of the other "salts" and "alums" are readily soluble, and a few have distinctive tastes. Talc, graphite, and serpentine are unctuous—that is, they feel greasy or soapy. Minerals such as arsenopyrite emit typical odors when broken, scratched, heated, or acted upon by acids. Some varieties of calcite, fluorite, and several other minerals give off distinctive colors under ultraviolet, or "black," light and are said to fluoresce. Some of these minerals continue to glow after the light is extinguished and are termed phosphorescent. Minerals such as uraninite contain radioactive elements that emit charged particles that cause a Geiger counter to click or flash. Because of differences in tenacity, some minerals are malleable and others brittle; some are elastic and others flexible. One or more of these properties may be of great help in the identification of an unknown mineral specimen.

Once a person has gone through the process of successfully identifying a few "unknown" minerals, he is very likely to join the literally millions of persons who make mineral collecting their hobby. Most of these persons proudly call themselves "rockhounds." The next few paragraphs are included especially for those who may want to take up the hobby.

Anyone can become a "rockhound." The hobby is inexpensive because little equipment is needed and many fine collections do not contain a single purchased specimen. Collecting out of doors may give healthful exercise and relaxation. Minerals and rocks stimulate the aesthetic sense: countless specimens possess beauty of form and color unapproached by the works of men. Many collectors have a feeling of adventure while collecting and gain a sense of great accomplishment when they discover some unusual or beautiful specimen. They obtain interesting knowledge about the formation and occurrence of minerals (and rocks and other geological processes as well)—knowledge that increases their understanding of this world of natural wonders. Some collectors have made noteworthy contributions to the geological sciences. A few have made profitable discoveries.

Opportunities for collecting exist in cities and towns as well as in rural areas. Rock exposures, stream beds, beaches, quarries, mine dumps, industrial plant dumps, railroad and road cuts, and other excavations are all potential sources of fine specimens. Collecting is possible within the distance of a hike or a short automobile ride from almost any point in Virginia.

Although the alert collector may be able to gather fine specimens without using any tools, from time to time he may find specimens that cannot be removed from their surroundings without using tools. Most "rockhounds" carry a prospector's pick (or a bricklayer's hammer) and an abundant supply of paper for wrapping specimens. A pocket-knife (preferably magnetized), pocket magnifying glass, portable ultraviolet light, portable Geiger counter, sledge hammer, pickax, trimming hammer, whisk broom or paintbrush, magnet, streak plate (unglazed porcelain tile), shovel, sieve, rake, knapsack, camera, and cold chisel are additional pieces of equipment that often prove useful.

A general collection is usually considered best for beginning collectors. Although a few collectors continue enlarging their overall collection, and some even aspire to having at least one example of each of the nearly 2,000 known minerals, most eventually specialize in some phase of collecting. Several examples could be mentioned. One of the currently popular specialties is the collecting and mounting of micromounts—tiny, perfect crystals that can be seen well only through a microscope. Several other popular specialties involve semiprecious gem materials. The possibilities are numerous, and many collectors change from one phase to another or add a new one from time to time.

A few general rules that collectors should remember are:

1. Permission should always be sought before entering private property.
2. Collecting is prohibited in state and national parks.
3. Specimens should be labeled when collected.
4. Rare or exceptional specimens should be shown to a reputable professional.
5. Crystals should not, in general, be broken away from the surrounding rock.

To elaborate:

Access to many mines, mine dumps, gravel pits, quarries, and other private properties may be restricted. Often owners are concerned not so much about possible damage to their property as about injury to the collectors. In some cases club groups are able to gain admission to areas that are closed to individuals.

In labeling, the exact locality where the specimen is found should be recorded (see fig. 1.15). In addition, it is good practice to note the collector's name and the date. Some collectors paint numbers directly on specimens and keep a catalog of pertinent data.

The reason for showing what appear to be rare or exceptional specimens to a professional is to ascertain whether or not they are important discoveries. It seems quite possible that in the future amateurs will make more of the important discoveries of this kind than will the professionals. This is true because amateurs as a group spend a far greater amount of time searching for minerals.

There are two main reasons why crystals should not be broken away from their surroundings: (1) in the process of removal a crystal may be broken or marred, and (2) most crystals are more interesting and valuable when attached to their naturally associated substances.

This last rule has had rather far-reaching implications. Serious collectors have found it not only much more interesting but very helpful, both in their searching for and in their identification of minerals, to know something about the geological occurrences of minerals. The reason is that many minerals have originated in certain geologic environments and thus typically occur in the particular rocks associated with these environments. This is a consequence of the fact that minerals are formed in accordance with physico-chemical laws and therefore reflect what has happened to a given chemical system under certain conditions of pressure and temperature. (However, unlike the laboratory experiment in which the composition, pressure, and temperature are kept constant or under controlled changes, the natural processes may have had each or any combination of the variables changed or changing.) The branch of mineralogy usually referred to as experimental mineralogy, or as synthesis study, is based on considerations of this kind. In the future such studies will undoubtedly help to explain more and more of the empirical data about mineral occurrences and associations.

The nearly four hundred different minerals thus far found to occur

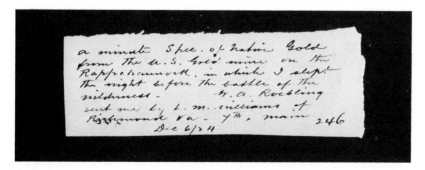

FIG. 1.15. Colonel Washington A. Roebling collected more than 16,000 specimens, at least one sample of all but twelve of the minerals named in the index of the sixth edition of Dana's *System of Mineralogy*. The label shown accompanies a small gold specimen in his collection. (Courtesy of Smithsonian Institution)

within Virginia represent just about all the proved and seriously hypothesized origins for minerals. Some of the mineral descriptions and accounts that follow include selected, relatively widely accepted data relating to origins, occurrences, and associations. The minerals dealt with are relatively common or for some other reason particular noteworthy in Virginia. (Before completing this chapter, some readers may find it helpful to read chapter II, in order to familiarize themselves with rock names. It may also be helpful to look at the maps—figures 4.16, p. 103, and App. C.)

Amphibole is the name given to a family of complex hydrous aluminosilicate minerals that contain magnesium and commonly calcium, iron, or sodium. Included are such minerals as actinolite, hornblende, riebeckite, and tremolite. Although the most common amphiboles are dark green or black, some are white, tan, or other colors. Amphiboles commonly occur as bladed crystals. There are perfect cleavages, parallel to the lengths of the crystals, at about 60° and 120° to each other. Hornblende is relatively common in igneous rocks. Actinolitic amphibole occurs as a major constituent of a number of metamorphic rocks. Rather beautiful crystal groups of actinolite occur sporadically in the Great Gossan Lead sulfide body of Carroll and Grayson counties. The asbestos from Chestnutford, Bedford County, and from the Barton Tract in southwestern Floyd County is a variety of amphibole.

Apophyllite from Centreville, Fairfax County, has gained wide acclaim since its exhibition in the collection of the Smithsonian Institution (fig. 1.16). At the Centreville locality, a quarry, this hydrous potassium, calcium fluosilicate occurs as colorless to white, blocklike crystals with thaumasite and hairlike byssolite on prehnite. These and several other minerals line cavities in a mass of once-molten rock material, now the rock diabase, which dates from the early days of the *Age of the Dinosaurs,* the Triassic Period (see table 5.1, p. 127.). The crystals of apophyllite range from minute to nearly 4 inches along an edge. This occurrence is a fine example of the way the mineral typically occurs—that is, with zeolites, prehnite, and other such minerals in rock cavities. Although the cavities in which these minerals occur are most commonly found within diabase, a few have also been found to be present in pegmatites and other rocks.

Aragonite has the same chemical composition as calcite; the two are polymorphic forms of calcium carbonate ($CaCO_3$). Aragonite and/or calcite cave deposits—designated by such names as anthodites, helictites, drapes, stalactites, stalagmites, and columns—occur in several of the more than twelve hundred caves in western Virginia. Some of the aragonite exhibits deep green fluorescence. Most pearls and the iridescent *mother-of-pearl* layers on seashells are also aragonite. The mineral is typically formed by chemical or biochemical precipitation from relatively low-temperature aqueous solutions. Aragonite effervesces (fizzes) when attacked by cold dilute hydrochloric acid.

Barite is barium sulfate ($BaSO_4$). Its name, derived from the

Greek word for "heavy," is appropriate because barite has an exceptionally high specific gravity for a light colored, nonmetallic mineral. Barite is of widespread occurrence as crystals in cavities (fig. 1.6), massive nodules, and vein fillings throughout Virginia. For several years during the last century Virginia was the chief barite producer in the United States.

Calcite, as noted, has the same chemical composition as but a different crystal structure than aragonite. It also effervesces with cold

FIG. 1.16. Apophyllite. This fine specimen of apophyllite on prehnite, collected at the diabase quarry at Centreville, is in the collections of the Smithsonian Institution. Longest dimension of specimen is approximately 14 cm., or about 5½ in. (Photograph courtesy of Smithsonian Institution)

dilute hydrochloric acid. Calcite is colorless to white when pure, but it may be any color because of the presence of diverse impurities. It has three equally developed perfect cleavages, which cause it to break into rhombohedrons—six-sided solids with diamond-shaped faces (see fig. 1.13). Calcite is the main constituent of two rocks, limestone and most marble. It also serves as the cementing material for many conglomerates, sandstones, and other rocks. Calcite cave deposits have been alluded to in the brief description of aragonite. The rather peculiar "clam geodes" from Chesapeake are lined with calcite crystals. Several fine crystals of calcite have been collected from such

FIG. 1.17. Diverse forms of calcite from Virginia: *A,* helictite, New River Cave, Virginia—× 1. *B,* crystal group from Staunton, Virginia—approximately 30 cm., or about 12 in., across (photograph courtesy of Smithsonian Institution). *C,* arborescent crystal group from Buchanan, Virginia (photograph by G. K. McCauley). *D,* contact twin which exhibits re-entrant angles, from Lone Jack Quarry near Glasgow, Virginia (photograph by G. K. McCauley). (See also figures 1.7 and 1.11.)

A

B C

D

localities as the Lone Jack Quarry near Glasgow, Rockbridge County; the James River Hydrate Company Quarry, near Buchanan; and the Belmont Quarry in Augusta County. Figure 1.17 illustrates several of the different crystal habits of this mineral.

Chlorite is the name given to a group of complex hydrous silicates of aluminum, iron, and magnesium that are rather common in rocks that have undergone metamorphism under relatively low-temperature and low-pressure conditions. Although the common chlorites are green, some are brown, purple, and other colors. They all have one perfect cleavage, but the resulting chlorite flakes, unlike mica flakes, are not elastic—that is, when chlorite flakes are bent, they will not resume their original shape.

Clay is the general name applied to several hydrous aluminum and magnesium silicates that typically occur as particles of very fine size (less than 2 microns, which is a little less than $\frac{1}{10,000}$ inch; see fig. 1.18). Included are minerals like kaolinite, halloysite, illite, paligor-

FIG. 1.18. Electronmicrograph of kaolinite from Cold Spring clay deposit in Augusta County, Virginia (approximately 32,000 ×). (Photograph courtesy of J. J. Comer and T. F. Bates of the Pennsylvania State University)

skite, and montmorillonite. Clay minerals typically have a smooth feel and a musty, claylike odor when damp; they seem dry when touched with the tongue. They are formed chiefly as the result of alteration or weathering of such minerals as the feldspars. Some exceptionally good specimens of fibrous paligorskite have been collected from the Lone Jack Quarry near Glasgow. Clay is an important basic raw material of the ceramic industry, is used as a filler in such things as paper and rubber, and has several other uses. It has been said that in colonial times the Indians fed bentonite, which consists chiefly of montmorillonite, to some of those whom they wished to torture; the victims swelled up, sometimes to the point of bursting their stomachs, because the volume of bentonite so greatly increases when it becomes wet.

Columbite-tantalite series specimens have been collected from pegmatites in the Amelia and Bedford districts. Although the quantities have hardly been of economic value, some of the specimens from the Bedford district are of especially fine quality and have found prominent places in several museums (fig. 1.19).

FIG. 1.19. Columbite-tantalite crystal from Mitchell pegmatite near Bedford, Virginia—longest dimension of crystal approximately 37 mm., or 1½ in. (Photograph by G. K. McCauley)

Copper occurs in the native, pure state and also as a major constituent of many mineral compounds. Native copper occurs in some of the altered basalts of the northern section of Virginia's Blue Ridge Province and its extension into Maryland and southern Pennsylvania. (It is a very peculiar feeling to break a rock containing native copper and have the pieces hang together because an individual grain of the ductile copper is attached to both pieces.) Other copper-bearing minerals that have been found in the Old Dominion are chalcocite (copper sulfide), chalcopyrite (copper-iron sulfide), malachite (hydrous copper carbonate), cuprite (copper oxide), bornite (copper-iron sulfide), covellite (copper sulfide), chrysocolla (hydrous copper silicate), and azurite (hydrous copper carbonate).

Diamond, the hardest known substance, is the only precious gem thus far found in Virginia. Because of its hardness and its brilliance, or fire, the diamond has long been considered the king among gems. Diamonds have been used in betrothal jewelry, such as engagement rings, for many years—probably because legends associate them with purity, innocence, and fidelity. The Dewey diamond, found in 1855 by a man grading one of the streets in Manchester, Chesterfield County, was the largest diamond found in the United States up to 1884. It weighed 23.75 carats in the rough and 11.6875 carats after cutting. The cut stone is a faint greenish white and has a flaw or speck in its interior. It is reported that a "diamond of the first water" was found in 1836 on the Vaucluse Gold Mine Property, Orange County. Another unnamed beautiful "blue white" diamond was reported as found in 1913 near Pounding Mill, Tazewell County. The well-known 34.6-carat "Punch" Jones diamond was reportedly found in Monroe County, West Virginia, which is just northeast of Rich Creek, Giles County, Virginia. Not one of these was found in its rock matrix; instead, each was found in the unconsolidated overburden.

Dolomite, named after the French geologist Dolomieu, differs from calcite in composition only because it contains magnesium as well as calcium, carbon, and oxygen. Its chemical composition is $CaMg(CO_3)_2$. Dolomite is the chief constituent of the rock also commonly called dolomite and of some kinds of marble. Much, if not all, of the dolomite that makes up the rock dolomite is a secondary mineral in that it occupies space previously occupied by either calcite or aragonite. In most cases the change probably took place before the calcite or aragonite mud was consolidated to rock. Well-developed pink and light bluish saddle-shaped groups of dolomite occur in rock cavities lined chiefly with small calcite crystals at the Lone Jack Quarry near Glasgow. Dolomite will not effervesce with cold dilute hydrochloric acid unless the mineral is freshly powdered.

Epidote, a hydrous calcium iron aluminum silicate, occurs in many of the rocks that underlie the Blue Ridge and Piedmont geomorphic provinces of Virginia. Typically it is pistachio green in color, but at a few localities it is nearly white. The green variety is one of the chief constituents of Virginia's best known gemrock, unakite. At a few places this same green variety occurs in large enough masses to be used alone as the raw material for gems. Both cabochons and emerald-cut, faceted stones have been made from such epidote found near Syria in Madison County. Zoisite, also rather common in Virginia, and allanite, a black pitch-appearing radioactive mineral found at various localities within the state, belong to the same family of minerals as epidote. Epidote occurs in metamorphosed rocks (see chapter II) and in veins; zoisite is found chiefly in metamorphic rocks, but it also has a pink variety, thulite, that occurs widely in pegmatitic masses; relatively large masses of allanite occur in pegmatites, and small grains are fairly common as accessory constituents in igneous rocks.

Feldspar is the name given to a large family of minerals that are aluminum silicates of potassium, sodium, or calcium, or a combination of these elements. Of the feldspars, the most common ones in Virginia are the potassium feldspars, orthoclase and microline, and the sodium-calcium plagioclase feldspars, andesine and oligoclase. Noteworthy among the several other feldspars that occur within the Commonwealth are cleavelandite, a platelike type of the sodium plagioclase albite (fig. 1.20); amazonstone, or amazonite, a green

FIG. 1.20. Cleavelandite, a plagioclase feldspar, from Amelia, Virginia—longest dimension approximately 30 cm., or about 12 in. (Photograph courtesy of Smithsonian Institution)

variety of microline; and two different moonstones—one a variety of albite, the other of orthoclase. Amazonstone, so named because it was first noted as carved ornaments worn by primitive tribes of the Amazon River region of South America, occurs in several pegmatites of the Amelia District. White albite moonstone, typically with a pale blue opalescence, also occurs in a few of the pegmatites of the same district. Orthoclase moonstone, quite similar in appearance to the well-known Ceylon moonstone, has been reported from the Harris Mica pegmatite mine in Goochland County. Most feldspars are light colored and have a pearly luster; they have a hardness of 6; they break readily along two cleavages at, or approximately at, right angles to each other. Although 6 is less hard than one might desire for any but costume jewelry and the cleavages make fashioning somewhat hazardous, both the amazonstone and the moonstone are rather popular with amateur lapidaries and jewelry makers. The large feldspar crystals and masses that occur in pegmatite bodies are the most popular with both collectors and those who recover feldspar for economic use. Therefore the specimens from pegmatites are the ones most often found in mineral collections. Actually, however, they make up only a small percentage of all the feldspar that occurs in nature. Feldspars are common in igneous and metamorphic rocks and in some coarse-grained fragmental sediments. Here and there, potassium feldspar lines or fills cavities in rock. A few occurrences have been reported where a rather special kind of the potassium feldspar microline has been found to have formed at low temperatures within unconsolidated overburden.

Galena, lead sulfide, is the most important ore of lead. It is lead gray in color, is very heavy, has a bright metallic luster on fresh surfaces, and cleaves into perfect cubes. Galena occurs in small amounts at several localities within the state, west of the Coastal Plain. It typically occurs in veins with calcite and other sulfides, such as sphalerite. From early colonial times until at least the close of the Civil War galena from Virginia was used locally for the making of bullets. It is now recovered as an accessory of the Austinville zinc ores of southern Wythe County.

Garnet is the general name for a group of minerals that are silicates of calcium, magnesium, iron, manganese, aluminum, and other metallic elements. Garnets in Virginia are typically red or yellow-brown, many-sided, nearly spherical crystals. Red-brown almandine-rich garnets occur in several of the Blue Ridge and Piedmont metamorphic rocks. Gem quality spessartine, which occurs in pegmatites of the Amelia District, is light to deep orange-brown in color and has a brilliant luster. Although it is rarely free from flaws, faceted stones up to one hundred carats have been cut from this Amelia County material and stones of over seven carats are rather common.

Gold has been found in the Virginia Piedmont Province in Appomattox, Buckingham, Charlotte, Culpeper, Fauquier, Fluvanna, Goochland, Halifax, Louisa, Orange, Prince Edward, Spotsylvania, and Stafford counties. It is also known to occur in Blue Ridge areas of Floyd, Grayson, and Montgomery counties. One of the classically shaped nuggets in the Smithsonian Institution's collection came from Orange County. It is about the size of a woman's fist. Small amounts of gold are still being found within the state.

Gypsum is hydrous calcium sulfate, $CaSO_4 \cdot 2H_2O$. Anhydrite, its water-free equivalent, commonly occurs with gypsum. Gypsum is so soft that it can be scratched by a fingernail; anhydrite is harder and cannot be scratched by a fingernail. Both selenite, the clear, coarsely crystalline variety of gypsum, and satin spar, a fibrous gypsum with silky luster, occur in southwestern Virginia. Recently formed twinned gypsum crystals up to 1 inch in length may be found in drill holes and similar cavities within the area. Gypsum is mined and used in the production of plaster of Paris and plasterboard at Plasterco, Washington County.

Halite, sodium chloride, is the mineral name for common table salt. Although most salt is colorless to white or light gray, some of it is reddish, and a little appears bluish. It has three perfect cleavages at right angles to each other—notice, for example, that most grains of table salt are block shaped. It tastes salty, of course. Most of the world's salt deposits were originally formed as the result of the evaporation of sea water. Salt is taken from underground deposits in the Saltville area of Smyth County by introducing warm water into the salt and pumping the resulting brine up through wells. This salt deposit was the chief source of salt for the Confederacy during much of the Civil War. At that time, largely because of the lack of refrigeration, the annual per capita use of salt was nearly 100 pounds.

Hematite is a compound of iron and oxygen. Its name comes from the Greek word for blood. Common hematite is red and earthy. Specularite, sometimes called specular hematite, is a steel gray or black variety with a submetallic luster. Some of the beautifully carved intaglios used in tie pins and cuff links are specular hematite. Both varieties have a red streak. Hematite occurs in thin beds in the Valley and Ridge Province of Virginia, notably in Giles and Lee counties. Specular hematite occurs sporadically along the base of the Blue Ridge, especially in the Buchanan-Roanoke-Thaxton area.

Kyanite is an aluminum silicate that occurs in a few metamorphic rocks and veins in Virginia. It is nearly colorless to sky blue in color and, as already noted, occurs in bladed crystals that have a hardness of about 5 parallel to their lengths and of about 7 across the blades. Kyanite is mined and milled in Prince Edward County for use in the manufacture of high-temperature refractories.

Limonite is the general name given to hydrous iron oxide minerals that cannot be distinguished as to species by mere megascopic examination. Depending on exact composition and structure, limonite may be yellow-brown, dark brown, nearly black, or even multicolored. All types have a typical, yellow-brown streak. Most of the brownish-stained surfaces on rock exposures are limonite. Iron rust is limonite. The major portion of Virginia's former iron industry was based on limonitic ores from the Valley and Ridge Province. A particularly interesting occurrence of limonite in Virginia is as pseudomorphs after pyrite crystals. (A pseudomorph is a crystal form in which the mineral has the form of some mineral other than itself. Pseudomorphs are generally formed as the result of a volume-for-volume replacement of one mineral by another.) Several excellent ones up to 2 inches along an edge have been found at numerous localities on the Piedmont.

Magnetite is an iron oxide. It is dark gray to black, highly magnetic, has a metallic luster, and cannot be scratched by a knife. Octahedral magnetite crystals, which have eight major triangular faces arranged so that they look like two pyramids placed base to base, occur sporadically in some of the metamorphic rocks of Albemarle, Bedford, Carroll, Floyd, Grayson, Greene, and Nelson counties.

Mica is the name given to a group of hydrous alumino-silicate minerals with potassium, sodium, lithium, calcium, and the like. They all split into thin elastic sheets (fig. 1.12). Muscovite is the common light green, buff, or colorless mica sometimes called isinglass; biotite is black mica; phlogopite is brown mica. Each of these micas may be found in the Blue Ridge and Piedmont provinces. Muscovite and biotite are relatively common constituents of several metamorphic rocks. Sheet muscovite has been mined from pegmatites in Henry County near Ridgeway and in Pittsylvania County near Axton (fig. 1.21).

Microlite, a relatively rare mineral in the pegmatites of the Amelia District, is mentioned here because some of it, of a beautiful red to yellow color, has been found to be sufficiently transparent to be prized as gem material.

Niter, also called "potash alum," is a compound of potassium, nitrogen, oxygen, and hydrogen. It is soft and typically white and

FIG. 1.21. Muscovite. Mica from pegmatite mass near Ridgeway, Henry County. (Photograph courtesy of Virginia Division of Mineral Resources)

tastes sort of salty and cooling, although it may pucker the mouth. It occurs as small crystals and crusts on surfaces in some of the Virginia caves. During the Civil War, Virginia niter was used in the production of gunpowder. Several minerals that are hydrous sulfates of different metals taste something like niter—for example, melanterite and pickeringite. Samples thought to be potash alum should therefore be

FIG. 1.22. Marcasite rodlike crystal with parallelepiped-shaped crystal atop it, in a vug from Lone Jack Quarry near Glasgow, Virginia. *Inset, upper right,* shows close-up view of upper end of rod—length of rod in main picture approximately 5 mm., or about ¼ in. (Photographs by G. K. McCauley)

submitted to chemical or other laboratory tests to determine their true identities.

Prehnite is a hydrous calcium alumino-silicate that typically occurs as light green globular masses marked by edges of curved crystals. It commonly occurs with zeolites lining cavities in, for example, basalt. Prehnite is the base upon which the fine apophyllite crystals from Centreville, Fairfax County, grew.

Pyrite, or "fool's gold," is an iron sulfide. It is a brassy yellow, brittle, metallic mineral that is harder than glass. Marcasite, also an iron sulfide, is a similar mineral that is sometimes called "white pyrite." Marcasite is pale yellow to white, tarnishes or decomposes to a white powder upon prolonged exposure to air, and commonly occurs in radiating groups. Mines formerly operated in the northern Piedmont of Virginia have been large producers of pyrite. Marcasite occurs in some of the black shales and is the mineral most people refer to as "sulfur" in coals of the Valley and Ridge and the Cumberland Plateau provinces. Several rather peculiar marcasite crystals, which are rodlike and have parallelepiped-shaped crystals atop the rods, have been found at the Lone Jack Quarry near Glasgow and at the Trego Quarry near Emporia (see fig. 1.22).

Pyroxene is the name of a family of minerals which are complex silicates of magnesium and calcium and which may also contain other metallic elements, particularly iron and manganese. They are typically black or some shade of green, although other colors and white are known. Pyroxenes generally occur as short, column-shaped crystals with two perfect cleavages at about 90 degrees to each other. The most common pyroxenes, augite and pigeonite, are present in several igneous rocks, especially in the basalt and dolerite bodies in the Triassic basins on the Piedmont of Virginia.

Pyrrhotite, often called "magnetic pyrite," is an iron sulfide. It has a reddish bronze color, a metallic luster, and a hardness of about 5. Some, but not all, pyrrhotite is slightly magnetic. The Great Gossan Lead ore body of Carroll and Grayson counties, mainly pyrrhotite, was mined until recently as a source of sulfur.

Quartz has a vitreous luster, a conchoidal fracture, and a hardness greater than that of steel. Six-sided prisms terminated by six faces (two different rhombohedra) are the typical quartz crystals that occur within the state (fig. 1.6). Quartz, which is colorless and transparent when pure, is commonly colored because of the presence of small amounts of impurities. Some of the more common color varieties are amethyst (purple), rose quartz, smoky quartz, and milky quartz. Many varieties occur in the Old Dominion. Doubly terminated, colorless and milky crystals occur at many localities. One of these crystals found in Floyd County weighed about 200 pounds. Varieties from Virginia that have been used for semiprecious gemstones are a greenish, banded quartz, milky chalcedony, colorless quartz with tourmaline inclusions, and cairngorm (a smoky yellow variety), all from the Fairfax Courthouse area; jasper from the Luray area; beautiful deep purple amethyst from Lowesville in Amherst County; quartz containing hairlike crystals of rutile and quartz containing squiggly, wormlike masses of chlorite from southwestern Floyd County; and blue quartz from some of the Blue Ridge gneisses. There is also a fine limpid quartz crystal penetrated by green crystals of actinolite from an "unknown Virginia Locality" in the famous Tiffany Company collection.

Rockbridgeite is interesting, although of relatively limited occurrence, in that it is a mineral named after a Virginia county, Rockbridge County, which in turn was named after a geological feature, Natural Bridge. In addition, this name came about in a somewhat unusual way: when a mineral specimen labeled dufrenite was studied by Dr. Clifford Frondel, a Harvard mineralogist, he found it to be a species distinct from dufrenite; when he named this "new" species, he chose the name *rockbridgeite* because the specimen had a label with the locality given as "near Midvale, Rockbridge Co., Virginia." Typical specimens of the mineral are dark brown colloform masses that exhibit both radial and concentric structures.

Rutile is titanium dioxide. It served as the basis of Virginia's important titanium-oxide production in the Roseland District of Nelson County. Reddish brown to nearly black, highly lustrous, striated prisms (typically long and curved) and knee-shaped twins (fig. 1.23) have been found at several localities within the Blue Ridge and Piedmont provinces. Rutilated quartz—that is, quartz with included hairlike crystals of rutile—has also been found sporadically within the state, for example, in central Floyd County.

Sphalerite (zinc sulfide), which is the most important ore of zinc; *smithsonite* (zinc carbonate); and *hemimorphite* (hydrous zinc silicate) occur at many localities within the Commonwealth. Sphalerite has a resinous or submetallic luster, is softer than a knife but harder than a penny, and is typically yellow-brown, although its color may range from black to white. It is commonly associated with galena and calcite in veins and disseminated-type deposits. Smithsonite, named after James Smithson, founder of the Smithsonian Institution, effervesces with cold hydrochloric acid. It is sometimes called "turkey fat" or "dry bone," which it may resemble. Hemimorphite, or calamine as it is sometimes called, commonly occurs in groups of small radiating white crystals or in colloform masses. These minerals occur at Austinville, Wythe County, and at most other zinc deposits in Virginia.

Staurolite was named from *stauros,* meaning "a cross," because it characteristically occurs in cross-shaped twinned crystals. It is hydrous iron aluminum silicate that occurs in metamorphic rocks at numerous localities in the southern part of the Blue Ridge and western Piedmont provinces of Virginia. It is a gray or reddish brown opaque mineral that is harder than glass. The cross-shaped twins, often called "Virginia fairy stones," have gained nationwide distinction as charms. The staurolite crosses are used in their natural form or are artificially shaped into more nearly perfect cross-shaped charms. They are abundant in some localities, as at Fairy Stone State Park in Patrick County.

Talc is the soft, greasy-feeling mineral of which soapstone is composed. It is a hydrous magnesium silicate. Soapstone makes up relatively small but widespread masses in the Blue Ridge and Piedmont counties of the state.

Topaz has been found as large, essentially colorless crystals in a few of the pegmatites of the Amelia District. Although this topaz does not have one of the yellow hues generally preferred for gems, it has nonetheless found some utilization as a gem material.

Turquoise of a beautiful blue color has been found as crystals on the dumps of the Old Bishop Mine near Lynch Station, Campbell County. Most of the crystals are approximately $\frac{1}{16}$ inch across. This is the only locality in the world from which crystals of turquoise

FIG. 1.23. Twinned rutile from near Galax, Virginia—× 1. (Photograph courtesy of A. J. Stose)

have been reported. Soon after some crystals were collected in the 1940's, it was believed (and very well may have been true) that all of the crystals at the locality had been found and collected. In the early 1960's, however, several more fine specimens were discovered. The apparent anomaly may be explained by the fact that at least some of the specimens found in 1962 had been formed recently; David Leach of Bedford found some turquoise crystals inside the root of a tree which had grown on the mine dump since the original discovery.

Vivianite is a soft, vitreous to pearly, transparent to translucent, colorless to greenish or bluish, hydrous iron phosphate. The lustrous, colorless to greenish blue crystals usually turn pale bluish purple upon exposure. Excellent bladed crystals occur with pyrite and siderite in Carroll County, near Galax. Truly outstanding stellate groups, with individual blades up to 2 inches long and in groups up to nearly 8 inches in greatest dimension, were found in the mid-1960's in a deep cut, now covered, just west of Interstate Route 95 near its underpass beneath Broad Street in downtown Richmond. Specimens collected from this locality have been judged to be some of the finest ever discovered (fig. 1.24).

Wad is the name applied to powdery, clayey forms of hydrous manganese oxide. It is composed of minerals such as pyrolusite,

FIG. 1.24. Vivianite from Richmond, Virginia—greatest dimension approximately 18 cm., or about 7 in. (Photograph courtesy of Smithsonian Institution)

cryptomelane, psilomelane, and manganite. Earthy wad is soft enough to soil fingers; pyrolusite with a hardness of 1 to 2 will mark on paper; manganite has a hardness of 4; cryptomelane and psilomelane, which cannot be distinguished in the field, have a hardness of 6 and typically constitute colloform masses (fig. 1.10). All of these black or dark brown manganese minerals occur together in most of Virginia's numerous manganese deposits. Most of them occur in pockets in clay and are present in nearly all the counties of the Blue Ridge and Piedmont and in all the counties of the Valley and Ridge. The largest Virginia manganese mine was at Crimora, Augusta County; it is still a good locality for collecting minerals.

In Appendix A there are determinative tables that will help identify some of the more common minerals.

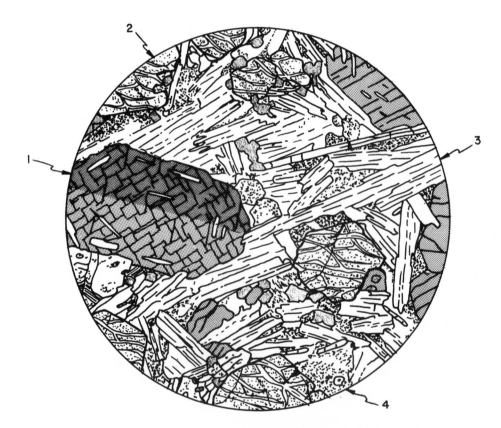

FIG. 2.1. Thin section with minerals represented as follows: *1,* pyroxene; *2,* olivine; *3,* plagioclase feldspar; and *4,* apatite with opaque magnetite inclusions. As an example of the appearance this rock might have in doubly polarized light, each mineral might exhibit these colors: pyroxene, any color, dark gray, or a combination of such colors if differently oriented grains were present; olivine, essentially the same range of possibilities as pyroxene; plagioclase feldspar, black to white with alternate lamellae ranging from black and white to essentially equivalent gray hues; apatite, dark gray to nearly white. A good color reproduction of the olivine appearance is given by P. E. Desautels, *The Mineral Kingdom* (New York, 1968), pp. 166, 167. (Redrawn and reprinted, by permission, from F. H. Hatch, A. K. Wells, and M. K. Wells, *The Petrology of the Igneous Rocks,* 10th ed., © 1949, by Thomas Murby and Company)

Rock to mineral relationships bring several analogies to mind: for examples, rock is to mineral as an exquisite tapestry is to a piece of silk thread; as a forest is to a lonesome pine; or as a spring bouquet is to a daisy. This is true because most rocks are made up of several minerals or mineral grains—that is, most rocks are obviously heterogeneous in composition, in the arrangement of constituent grains, or in both, whereas individual minerals are essentially homogeneous.

The forest-to-tree relationship is especially useful in helping to clarify a number of the diverse aspects of the rock-to-mineral relationship. Although most natural forests contain several species of trees and most rocks contain several minerals, some forests are made up almost wholly of numerous trees of a single species and some rocks are composed almost wholly of many grains of one mineral. Just as the trees of a forest may be of different shapes and sizes, so may the mineral grains of a rock. Although some forests are similar and may be classified together, each is truly unique; the same thing is true of rocks. The analogy becomes especially graphic when one compares the appearance of a mixed deciduous-coniferous forest in all its fall splendor with the appearance of a thin slice of rock as viewed through a polarizing microscope. Anyone who has not been fortunate enough to see a rock slice in this way can get a little idea of the kind of psychedelic effect that may be seen by coloring figure 2.1 as suggested by its legend and by keeping in mind the fact that, if the microscope's stage were rotated, each mineral grain would exhibit at least two different interference colors (the same for identical orientations in opposite quadrants but different in adjacent quadrants) *and* each would also "wink," or black out, four times during each rotation. In addition, in most rocks the different grains "wink" at different positions of rotation.

The following definition is sufficient to include all rocks: *A rock is a natural solid composed of mineral grains, glass, or a combination of these*. Just as with the definition of mineral, this definition warrants some elaboration. The *natural* requirement excludes all man-made materials, such as concrete and slag, which would otherwise fit the definition. The *solid* aspect is highly subjective: a complete gradation exists between unconsolidated fragments and well-consolidated, fragment-bearing rocks. A simple criterion is presented in the observation, "If you need a hammer to break it, it is a rock; if you can break it with a shovel, it is not." The reason for using the designation *mineral grains* instead of merely minerals is the fact, already alluded to, that the heterogeneous quality of some rocks is due to arrangement, involving grains of only one mineral, rather than to composition, requiring the presence of more than one kind of mineral. *Glass* is formed when molten rock material is cooled so rapidly that the atoms do not have time to assume the orderly arrangements characteristic of minerals. A rock composed wholly of glass may appear essentially homogeneous except on a submicroscopic scale. The *combination* of both materials is a necessary part of the definition because a relatively large number of natural solids are made up of both minerals and glass. As will be noted later in this chapter, there are two kinds of igneous and pyroclastic rocks that may be so constituted.

The crust or outer shell of the earth is made up of rocks. Many rock units occupy hundreds of cubic miles. Most geologists classify rocks in three main categories—igneous, sedimentary, and metamorphic—on the basis of their modes of origin (fig. 2.2). Like most

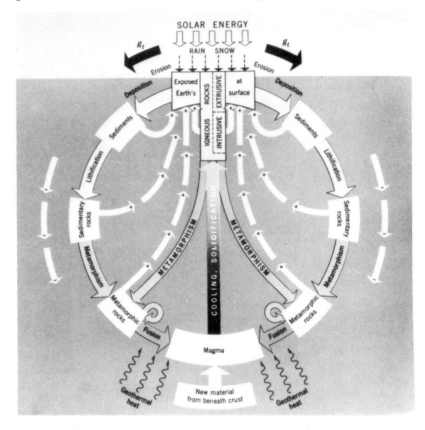

FIG. 2.2 "The rock cycle": The full cycle is shown in each half of the diagram. Rocks and rock-making materials are given in boxes; processes are given in broad arrows; uplift and subsidence are indicated by smaller arrows containing positive and negative signs, respectively. (Reprinted, by permission, from C. R. Longwell, R. F. Flint, and J. E. Sanders, *Physical Geology,* © 1969, by John Wiley and Sons)

classifications of natural substances and phenomena, this tripartite classification is an oversimplification. Some rocks fit better along the boundaries between two of the main categories than within either one. Nonetheless, the classification is of value as long as its somewhat limited application is recognized and kept in mind.

Igneous rocks are formed when molten rock material, called magma, is cooled sufficiently to be solidified. The cooling may be rapid and result in the formation of natural glass or it may take place more slowly thus permitting the crystallization of minerals. Magma may be solidified beneath the surface of the earth, or it may come out onto the surface—in which case it is generally called lava—to be cooled and solidified there. Several kinds of igneous rocks exist because magmas differ in composition and because they cool at different rates.

Sedimentary rocks have two principal modes of origin. They are formed either by cementation of fragments that have been transported and deposited on the surface of the earth *or* by precipitation of substances from natural aqueous solutions on or near the surface of the earth. Most sedimentary rocks have a layered aspect.

Metamorphic rocks are formed by the transformation of pre-existing rocks. They are marked by changes in arrangement of constituents, changes in mineral makeup, changes in over-all composition, or by some combination of these changes. Temperature, pressure, and chemically active fluids promote the changes—usually termed metamorphism—when rocks are subjected to geologic environments notably different from those under which they were originally formed.

Other rocks, most of which combine characteristics of the main classes, include (1) sediments markedly changed by diagenesis, (2) pyroclastics, and (3) migmatites; they may also include (4) pegmatites and (5) the different kinds of coal and related materials. Sediments that have undergone marked diagenic changes fit along the sedimentary-metamorphic classification boundary; pyroclastics are on the igneous-sedimentary boundary; migmatites straddle the metamorphic-igneous boundary. The diverse coals and related materials consist of organic compounds, rather than of minerals or glass, and thus are not even considered by several geologists to be rocks, in the strict sense.

Rocks of each of the three main categories, rocks representative of the boundary types, and coals of several kinds occur in Virginia. With a few exceptions, the different rocks occur in fairly well-defined belts called geomorphic provinces (see chapter IV, especially fig. 4.16). The Coastal Plain is underlain chiefly by unconsolidated sediments and sedimentary rocks. The Piedmont is underlain by igneous and metamorphic rocks except for a few Triassic basins, such as the Midlothian Basin west of Richmond, the Farmville Basin west of Farmville, the Danville Basin east of Chatham, and the southern part of the Potomac Basin in central northern Virginia, which are underlain chiefly by sedimentary rocks but locally by igneous rocks. The

Blue Ridge Province is underlain by igneous, metamorphic, and well-consolidated sedimentary rocks. The Valley and Ridge Province is underlain almost wholly by sedimentary rocks but in a few places by small igneous masses, for example, those that underlie Mole Hill in Rockingham County and Jack Mountain and similar prominences near Monterey, Highland County.

Although some rocks are not easily classified, most do have one or more features that permit determination of their proper category. This is true even with hand-specimen examination. Once this examination is accomplished, fuller examination and consideration of classification schemes will aid in the naming of individual specimens.

IGNEOUS ROCKS, except for glasses, are usually named and classified on the basis of their grain sizes and mineral compositions (table 2.1). Glasses are named on the basis of their chemical compositions.

As the diagram shows, the name of a crystalline igneous rock depends upon the identities and proportional quantities of the constituent minerals and the general grain size of the main minerals. Many petrographers, the specialists who are interested chiefly in describing rocks, consider the component minerals to be of four major kinds: *Specific* minerals are those required by the definition of the given rock. *Varietal* minerals are those generally present and the names of which are used as adjectives in the complete rock designation. *Accessory* minerals are those present in very small amounts and generally not alluded to in the rock's designation. *Alteration* products may or may not occur and, if present, may or may not be referred to in the over-all name; when they are mentioned, the suffix *-ized* is generally used to call attention to the fact that minerals of this kind are believed to have formed as the result of something that happened to the rock after it became solidified from its parent magma. An example may be given: A rock has the following composition:

Mineral	*Volume per cent*
Quartz	18.0
K-feldspar	8.0
Oligoclase (plagioclase feldspar)	45.0
Biotite	10.0
Hornblende	16.0
Apatite	0.4
Zircon	0.3
Others (sphene, magnetite, etc.)	0.3
Chlorite	2.0
	100.0

The specific minerals are quartz and the two feldspars. The varietal minerals are biotite and hornblende. The accessories are apatite,

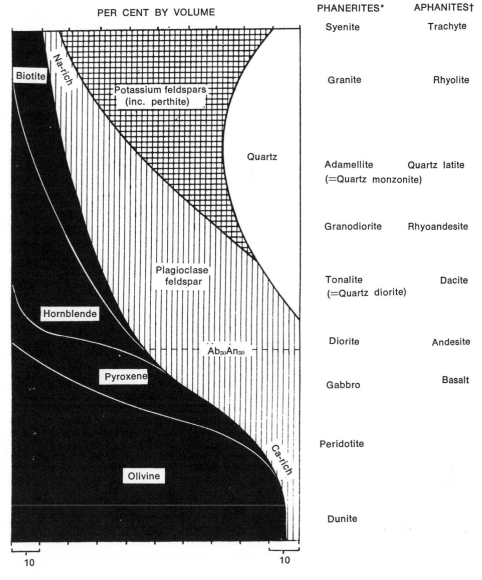

PER CENT BY VOLUME

PHANERITES*　　　APHANITES†

PHANERITES*	APHANITES†
Syenite	Trachyte
Granite	Rhyolite
Adamellite (=Quartz monzonite)	Quartz latite
Granodiorite	Rhyoandesite
Tonalite (=Quartz diorite)	Dacite
Diorite	Andesite
Gabbro	Basalt
Peridotite	
Dunite	

Darkness and specific gravity increase

Biotite

Na-rich

Potassium feldspars (inc. perthite)

Quartz

Plagioclase feldspar

Hornblende

Pyroxene

Ab₅₀An₅₀

Ca-rich

Olivine

10　　　　　　　10

SOURCE: R. V. Dietrich, *Virginia Minerals and Rocks,* Va. Poly. Inst. Bull., Eng. Exp. Sta. Ser. no. 137, 1960; modified and reprinted, by permission, from L. V. Pirsson and Adolph Knopf, *Rocks and Rock Minerals,* © 1947, by John Wiley and Sons.

NOTES: Adjacent rocks listed in the vertical columns grade into one another. Except for peridotite and dunite, for which olivine is the specific mineral, the specific minerals are those which are predominantly white on the diagram and the varietal materials are those indicated by solid black.

Glasses are called obsidian if they have chemical compositions similar to that of granite; they are called tachylyte if their chemistry is similar to that of gabbro and basalt.

* Phanerites are igneous rocks in which the essential minerals are greater than 1 mm. in smallest dimension.

† Aphanites are igneous rocks in which more than 50 per cent of the constituents cannot be distinguished by the unaided eye. Most aphanites contain some visible grains and may be named correctly on the basis of the identities and relative quantities of those grains.

TABLE 2.1. Diagram to Illustrate Relative Proportions of the Chief Mineral Components in Common Igneous Rocks

zircon, sphene, magnetite, and so forth. Alteration is indicated by the chlorite, which did not crystallize from the magma; it is closely associated with the biotite. The rock is, therefore, a biotite hornblende granodiorite that could be described as apatite[etc.]-bearing and as containing biotite that has been partially chloritized.

Grain size is usually dependent upon the speed of cooling. Generally speaking, the more rapid the cooling the smaller the grain size. The cooling rate, of course, depends upon the environment (or environments) in which the magma solidifies. Therefore, the grain size of the resultant rock—considered in conjunction with its composition—offers an important clue as to how and where the rock was formed. The composition must be considered because, for example, under the same general conditions of temperature and pressure a silica-rich magma will cool to glass whereas a magma with a lower silica content may cool to crystalline rock.

As mentioned earlier, magma may solidify beneath, as well as on, the surface of the earth. Igneous rocks and masses formed below the surface are generally termed intrusive, injected, or intracrustal to distinguish them from volcanic rocks and masses, which are usually described as extrusive, ejected, or supracrustal. Strictly speaking, there are probably two main types of igneous masses formed below the surface: those formed from magma that solidified where it originated and those formed from magma that solidified after it moved away from where it originated and was intruded into a different locus within the crust. Masses believed to represent these kinds of phenomena are given such names as bathylith (or "batholith"), laccolith, phacolith, dike, and sill on the basis of their shapes, their relationships to surrounding rocks, and/or the processes by which their parent magma gained the space the masses occupy (fig. 2.3).

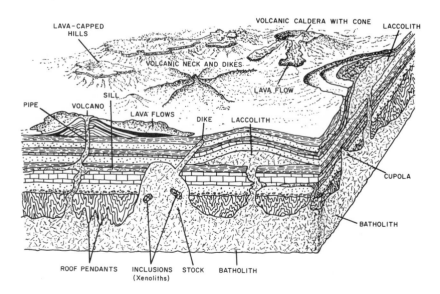

FIG. 2.3. Igneous masses. (Modified and reprinted, by permission, from W. H. Emmons et al., *Geology: Principles and Processes,* © 1969, by McGraw-Hill Book Company)

Large masses which have cooled relatively slowly at rather great depths within the earth's crust generally have their main mineral grains large enough to be distinguished by the naked eye. Such rocks are described as *phaneritic* (fig. 2.4). At the other extreme, rocks which are formed as the result of a quenching or rapid cooling of a

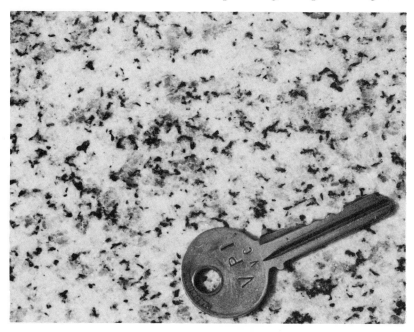

FIG. 2.4. Phanerite—× 1. (Photograph by G. K. McCauley)

magma—for example, in lava flows or in zones directly adjacent to relatively cool surrounding rocks at shallow depths—could be expected to be glassy or to have a grain size so small that they look stony in hand specimens. In those that look stony, the constituents can only be distinguished with the aid of a high-powered microscope; the rocks are called *aphanitic*. Many of the smaller introduced masses and the central portions of some thick lava flows have grain sizes somewhere between those generally termed phaneritic and those termed aphanitic. Specimens with such grain size may be described as *microphaneritic*. In this country, the arbitrary dividing line between phaneritic and microphaneritic is usually set at 1 millimeter and the dividing line between aphanitic and microphaneritic is a matter of whether the grains can or cannot be seen without the aid of a microscope. Although most igneous rocks consist wholly of either glass or crystalline grains, some contain both.

There are two other fairly common grain-size designations used for igneous rocks: *Pegmatitic* describes extremely coarse-grained rocks, some of them containing crystals many feet long. *Porphyritic* describes rocks that contain grains distinctly larger than the vast majority of the constituent grains (fig. 2.5). Some pegmatitic rocks may

FIG. 2.5. Porphyritic dolerite = porphyritic micro-gabbro—×1. (Photograph courtesy of Ward's Natural Science Establishment)

not be of igneous origin and are treated in the "other rocks" section of this chapter.

The distinctly larger grains in porphyries and prophyritic rocks are called *phenocrysts*. The fine-grained matrix which surrounds the phenocrysts is generally called the *groundmass*. The term *porphyry* is applied to rocks made up chiefly of phenocrysts; *porphyritic* is an adjective applied to rocks containing only scattered phenocrysts. The name of the rock whose features match those of the groundmass is prefixed to the word porphyry or is modified by the adjective prophyritic; for example, rhyolite porphyry refers to a porphyry with a rhyolitic groundmass and porphyritic granite designates a porphyritic rock with a granitic groundmass. Many of these rocks may have formed when initial cooling slow enough for formation of the phenocrysts was followed by a later cooling rapid enough to account for the finer grains of the groundmass.

The names of most of the common phanerites and aphanites are given in table 2.1. The names commonly applied to the microphanerites consist of the name of the phanerite prefixed by *micro*—for example, micro-granite. Some microphanerites, however, have been given their own distinctive names. Perhaps the most widely used are diabase and dolerite, the names often applied to the common "trap rock," which is a micro-gabbro.

Micro-gabbro and basalt are commonly filled with holes (gas

cavities) and are then called *vesicular* (fig. 2.6). If the vesicles have been filled with minerals, the rock is called *amygdaloidal*. Obsidian which is filled with holes and thus is frothy and light in weight is called pumice.

Rocks composed of quartz and potassium feldspar that appear intergrown in such a manner that the quartz grains have shapes which on some surfaces are suggestive of cuneiform writing are called *graphic granite* (fig. 2.7). Fine-grained, sugar-textured rocks composed of quartz and both potassium and plagioclase feldspars are called *aplite*. Graphic granite and aplite are commonly associated with granitic pegmatite.

Within the Commonwealth there are occurrences of most of the common igneous rocks and also several of the relatively uncommon

FIG. 2.6. Vesicular basalt. Gas escaping from lava formed the cavities —×.5. (Photograph courtesy of Smithsonian Institution)

FIG. 2.7. Graphic granite, polished surface—×.45. (Photograph courtesy of Smithsonian Institution)

ones such as akerite (hypersthene syenite). Nelsonite, an ilmenite-apatite rock believed by some petrologists to be igneous, was named for Nelson County, Virginia, where it was first found to occur.

The Virginia Piedmont is underlain in part by altered rhyolite, granite, and gabbro. The Triassic basins of the Piedmont contain masses of basalt and micro-gabbro. The Blue Ridge has granodiorite, granite, and several other igneous rocks as part of its bedrock. The Valley and Ridge Province contains sporadic small igneous masses, most of which are porphyritic aphanites.

FIG. 2.8. Layered sedimentary rock. Upper Ordovician Juniata Formation rocks on Walker Mountain, west of Marion. (Photograph by T. M. Gathright, Jr.)

SEDIMENTARY ROCKS, as previously mentioned, are characterized by layering (fig. 2.8). Such layered accumulations are usually termed stratified rocks by geologists. Sedimentary rocks may be classified into two main categories on the basis of their modes of formation: *Fragmental* sedimentary rocks (fig. 2.9) consist chiefly of

FIG. 2.9. Conglomerate—× .9. (Photograph courtesy of Smithsonian Institution)

rock and mineral fragments that have been transported and deposited as the result of gravitational forces or by water, ice, or wind on the surface of the earth. *Nonfragmental* sedimentary rocks (fig. 2.10) consist wholly or chiefly of mineral grains that have been chemically or biochemically precipitated from aqueous solutions on or near the surface of the earth. The terms *(non)detrital* and *(non)clastic* are used by some geologists instead of *(non)fragmental*.

Fragmental rocks are named on the basis of grain size and in some cases on the basis of grain shape and/or mineral composition as well (table 2.2). Most of the nonfragmental sedimentary rocks are named on the basis of their mineral compositions (table 2.3). Relatively

FIG. 2.10. Travertine. Cavers investigate rock formed by chemical precipitation from underground water. (Photograph by Flournoy, Virginia Chamber of Commerce)

TABLE 2.2. Fragments and Fragmental Rocks

Diameter of fragments	Loose aggregates	Consolidated aggregates	Remarks	Fragmental limestones
Greater than 2 mm.	gravel rubble	conglomerate breccia*	rounded fragments angular fragments	calcirudite
1/16 – 2 mm.	sand	sandstone		calcarenite
1/256 – 1/16 mm.	silt	siltstone		calcilutite
Less than 1/256 mm.	clay("mud")	claystone & mudstone shale	if fissile, i.e. if it will split along irregular planes	

* Many "breccias" are not of sedimentary origin.

recently, however, a new classification for the limestones—the sedimentary rocks composed largely of calcite—has been gaining relatively wide acceptance in professional circles. The basic features of this classification are given by Folk (see Supplementary Readings, II).

Many sedimentary rocks have noteworthy mineral contents not directly alluded to in their basic names. A relatively few adjectives suffice to call attention to most of these additional materials. The adjectives and the materials to which each refers are: argillaceous—clay mineral(s); arenaceous—quartz sand; calcareous—calcite and/or

TABLE 2.3. Nonfragmental Rocks

Rock name	Chief mineral constituent
Limestone*	calcite
Dolomite	dolomite
Travertine	calcite or aragonite or both
Gypsum	gypsum
Anhydrite	anhydrite
Rock salt	halite
Chert	submicroscopic quartz
Chalk	calcite or aragonite or both

* Some limestones are fragmental rocks and then are named calcirudite, calcarenite, or calcilutite, as shown in the Fragmental Rocks table.

aragonite; carbonaceous—amorphous carbon and/or some solid organic hydrocarbon(s); and sliceous—silica (SiO_2).

A few relatively common sedimentary rocks that have distinctive compositions or features have been given their own special names. Several of these occur in the Old Dominion and are worthy of note.

Although sandstones may theoretically be made up of any mineral or group of minerals of sand size, most are predominantly quartz; hence the term *sandstone,* unmodified, has generally come to mean quartz sandstone. As a consequence of this, additional names have gained rather wide acceptance for the other relatively common sedimentary rocks made up of sand-sized particles. *Arkose* is a feldspar-rich (greater than 25 per cent) sandstone. *Greywacke* is highly impure sandstone. Green sandstone, or *greensand* as it is more commonly known, is composed largely of grains of glauconite. Zirconiferous sandstone, an example of another method of naming these rocks, is a sandstone containing a notable percentage of zircon grains.

Marl is the name given to impure chalky limestones, porous deposits of travertine, or sandy carbonate sediments that typically contain molluscan shells. *Diatomite* and its impure, partially incoherent equivalent, diatomaceous earth, are powdery siliceous aggregates made up chiefly of shells of microscopic plants. *Bauxite* is a banded or pisolitic rock composed of high-alumina clay minerals. *Phosphorite,* a rock composed of different varieties of apatite and other phosphorus-bearing minerals, is generally heavier and darker in color than limestone, which it closely resembles. *"Sedimentary iron-ore rocks"* are represented in Virginia by limonite-rich and hematite-rich varieties.

The Coastal Plain is underlain chiefly by poorly consolidated sediments consisting of clays, sands, and gravels. Greensand, which underlies relatively large areas, is exposed at many places along the major river valleys in Caroline, Chesterfield, Hanover, Henrico, King William, and Stafford counties. Diatomaceous earth is present at the surface along many of the major rivers north of the James on the Coastal Plain of Virginia; it is especially well exposed near the western border of Richmond. Zirconiferous sandstone occurs near Ashland, Hanover County. Sedimentary rocks of the Piedmont Province are almost restricted to the Triassic basins. Arkosic conglomerates, sandstones, and red shales predominate the bedrock of these basins. Unmetamorphosed sedimentary rocks, most of which are fragmental, occur along the western side of the Blue Ridge Province throughout the Old Dominion and near the crest of the province at several places north of Roanoke. All rocks listed in the sedimentary rock charts are present in the Valley and Ridge Province. Sandstone, siltstone, shale, limestone, and chert may be found in all counties west of the Blue Ridge. Marl, conglomerate, and greywacke occur locally in most counties of the Valley and Ridge. Rock salt, anhydrite, and gypsum are present in Washington and Smyth counties in the area around Saltville. Travertine occurs as "drip stone" in many of Virginia's caves. Phosphorite occurs in the Wassum Valley northwest of Marion, Smyth County. Bauxite is present near Spottswood, Augusta County, and here and there in several of the manganese deposits such as the one at Crimora, also in Augusta County. Hematite "iron-ore rock" occurs in abundance in counties such as Lee and Giles: limonite "iron-ore rock" occurs in relatively large quantities in Alleghany, Bath, Botetourt, Craig, Frederick, Pulaski, Rockbridge, Shenandoah, Smyth, and Wythe counties.

METAMORPHIC ROCKS are, as previously noted, those which have been formed by the transformation of igneous, sedimentary, or even pre-existing metamorphic rocks. Because the changes reflect responses of predominantly solid material to temperature, pressure, and chemical activities, most metamorphism is believed to occur while the rocks are relatively deeply buried.

Metamorphic rocks are commonly classified, on the basis of the arrangement of their constituents, into two main categories: those that have noticeably preferred orientation of their constituents, the *foliated metamorphic rocks,* and those that do not have such an arrangement of constituents, the *nonfoliated metamorphic rocks.* Fo-

FIG. 2.11.　Slate. This panel, from the Arvonia-Buckingham area, exhibits bedding (upper right to lower left) at an angle to the natural splitting surface. (Photograph by Holsinger Studio, Charlottesville, Virginia.)

FIG. 2.12.　Gneiss. It is not known whether this foliation is or is not parallel to premetamorphic layering. (Photograph courtesy of Ward's Natural Science Establishment)

liation may or may not be parallel to pre-existing bedding and other layering (figs. 2.11 and 2.12).

The common foliated metamorphic rocks are described briefly in table 2.4. The pronunciations of their names are as follows: gneiss—nīce; schist—shĭst; phyllite—fĭll'īte; and slate—slāte. These names, except for slate, are often modified by a mineral or rock name to

TABLE 2.4. The Foliated Metamorphic Rocks

Name	Features
Gneiss	imperfect foliation or banding, granular minerals predominate
Schist	well developed, closely spaced foliation, platy minerals appear to predominate
Phyllite	intermediate between schist and slate; glossy luster; commonly corrugated
Slate	homogeneous, fine grained; minerals cannot be distinguished under hand lens; can be split

enhance their descriptive quality. Examples are granitic gneiss, muscovite schist, and graphite-bearing phyllite. They also may be modified by descriptive terms such as *augen,* the German word for eyes, which is used rather frequently to describe gneisses such as the one pictured in figure 2.13. Slates are often modified by color adjectives, for example, red slate. Glacial ice is also considered by some petrologists to be a foliated metamorphic rock. It is of special interest because it affords the opportunity for observing the actual development of foliation.

The commonest rocks of the nonfoliated category are quartzite and marble. Less common ones include mylonite, hornfels, and tactite. It

FIG. 2.13. Augen gneiss from Floyd County, Virginia. The rock is so named because its large grains are eye shaped. (*Augen* is the German word for "eyes.")

is noteworthy that even though these rocks belong to the nonfoliated class each may have a banded or foliated appearance. The point is that although foliation may be present, none is required.

The term *quartzite* has been used in two ways: for silica-cemented sandstones and for metamorphosed sandstones. Therefore, the prudent geologist now uses the term *meta-quartzite* for those formed by metamorphism and ortho-quartzite for those that are sedimentary. Quartzites may be distinguished from sandstones on the basis of the fact that fractures cut indiscriminately across the grains and matrix of a quartzite but around the grains of a sandstone. The fractures in some quartzites are, indeed, conchoidal, just like those in individual quartz grains.

The term *marble* has also been corrupted by dual usage: it has been applied both to any chiefly calcium-carbonate or dolomitic rock that will take a polish and to metamorphosed limestones and dolomites. Metamorphic marble is characterized by interlocking grains. This characteristic, however, is not an exclusive feature that may be used as a criterion of metamorphic origin because the carbonate minerals of some unmetamorphosed limestones and dolomites also are present as interlocking grains. Probably the easiest way to decide whether a marble or a quartzite is metamorphic or not is to determine whether the associated rocks are metamorphic or not.

Mylonite is the name given to dense, fine-grained rocks formed by the crushing and pulverizing of rocks in fault zones (see chapter VI). Coarser-grained rocks that are formed in a generally similar manner are called fault breccia or fault gouge. Some mylonites are so fine grained that they have the appearance of glass under the microscope as well as in hand specimens. These ultramylonites, or "pseudotachylytes," may be identified as such on the basis of x-ray studies that show they are composed of crystalline materials rather than of glass.

Hornfels is the name given to rocks that have been metamorphosed in response to high temperatures near intruding magma. They commonly have a hornlike appearance. In contrast, tactites, which also occur near intrusives, reflect an introduction of material, probably in the gaseous state, from magma. The term *skarn* refers to limestones that have both had materials introduced into them and undergone high-temperature metamorphism near the borders of igneous masses. Metasomatism is the term generally applied to the whole group of processes that involve essentially simultaneous chemical introduction and removal of certain rock constituents during metamorphism. Metasomatic processes may cause changes in both the chemical and mineral compositions of the affected rocks.

Other metamorphic rocks also occur in Virginia. Soapstone, or steatite as it is sometimes called, is a massive metamorphic rock composed mainly of talc. Greenstone is a greenish gray or green, commonly foliated rock composed chiefly of chlorite and green amphibole. Amphibolite is the name given to gneissic or schistose rocks composed largely of some amphibole and feldspar. (The reason they are not called amphibole gneiss or schist is that traditionally geologists have required that quartz be a major component of gneisses and schists.) Granulite is a nonfoliated granular metamorphic rock. Epidosite is a metamorphic rock consisting predominantly of the mineral epidote.

Metamorphic rocks are often mapped on the basis of the occur-

rence of certain "key" constituent minerals. Such minerals are thought
to be good indicators of the intensity of the temperature-pressure
conditions under which the rocks were metamorphosed. This intensity
is generally referred to as metamorphic grade. The conditions are
inferred on the basis of the minerals present; for example, kyanite is
believed typically to signify conditions of high pressure; sillimanite,
conditions of high temperature; and chlorite, conditions of low temperature and pressure. Empirical field relationship data, laboratory
investigations, and theoretical considerations have established guidelines and certain restrictions for such hypotheses.

Metamorphic rocks underlie large areas of the Piedmont and Blue
Ridge provinces of Virginia. Gneisses, schists, phyllites and amphib-
olites of diverse grades, and mylonites are common in both provinces. Rocks of each of these types have been derived from both
sedimentary and igneous rocks. Metamorphic marble occurs locally in
the western Piedmont. Soapstone is quarried near Alberene, Albemarle County, and Schuyler, Nelson County, and has been reported
from several other areas. Slate is produced in the Arvonia District of
Buckingham and Fluvanna counties and has also been quarried at
Esmont in Albermarle County and in Fauquier and Culpeper counties
near Warrenton. Greenstone, which occurs sporadically throughout
the provinces, is quarried in Lynchburg. Unakite, an epidotized granitic rock, occurs in several places, notably near Vesuvius Station,
Rockbridge County, and just west of Airpoint, Roanoke County.
Made up chiefly of salmon-colored to flesh-colored feldspar, smoky
quartz, and green epidote, it is a well-known gemrock.

OTHER ROCKS is the designation used in this book for rocks that
do not fit well into any of the three main categories. Examples are
pyroclastic rocks, migmatites, some pegmatites, and rocks formed
chiefly as the result of diagenesis.

Although dolomite is usually classified as a nonfragmental sedimentary rock, most of such dolomite of rocks was probably not
precipitated directly from seawater but was formed instead as the
result of chemical activities which resulted in its replacing pre-
existing calcitic and/or aragonitic sediment. Much of this kind of replacement appears to have occurred before the calcium carbonate
sediment was consolidated into rock and thus is referred to as diagenesis instead of metamorphism. To elaborate, diagenesis is the name
given to processes that take place in sediments after their deposition
but before, and commonly contributing to, their conversion to solid
rock. Some chert appears to have been formed in the same general
way. Rocks whose chief characteristics were formed by diagenesis
fit better along the boundary between sedimentary and metamorphic
rocks than in either major class.

Pyroclastic rocks are consolidated igneous fragments which were
extruded explosively from ancient volcanoes and deposited, like sediment, by settling either on land or in water. Some geologists prefer to
call these rocks igneous; others, sedimentary. Perhaps the best sugges-

tion—reportedly made by C. K. Wentworth, an American sedimentary petrologist, who spent much of his professional life observing volcanic activity in Hawaii—is that they are igneous on the way up and sedimentary on the way down.

Pyroclastic rocks are usually classified on the basis of the size of their constituent fragments, in the same general way that fragmental sedimentary rocks are. Tuffs are rocks composed of fragments less than 4mm. in diameter; ash is the name given to the unconsolidated equivalent. Volcanic breccia and agglomerate are the names given to pyroclastic rocks composed chiefly of angular and rounded fragments, respectively, that are larger than 4mm. in size; lapilli is the unconsolidated equivalent. Fragments greater than 4mm. across that were liquid when ejected are called volcanic bombs, most of which have characteristic shapes. According to the nature of the fragments, pyroclastic rocks are generally described as vitric (glass), crystal (mineral), lithic (rock), or mixed. Bentonite is the name given to pyroclastic rocks that have been altered to montmorillonite-rich clays that swell upon the addition of water.

Pyroclastics occur in the Mount Rogers section of Grayson County, where there was volcanic activity about 800 million years ago. Thin bentonite beds occur at numerous horizons in the sedimentary rock sequences of western Virginia.

Migmatites are "mixed rocks" made up of intimate intermixtures of metamorphic *and* igneous or igneous-appearing components. They typically occur in contact zones surrounding igneous masses but are not restricted to those loci. An outstanding example of a migmatite constitutes the cenotaph on the V.P.I. War Memorial Chapel in Blacksburg, Virginia (fig. 2.14). Migmatites occur naturally at a few localities in the Blue Ridge and Piedmont areas.

Pegmatites are, for the most part, composed predominantly of quartz and feldspar. In fact, the unmodified word *pegmatite* almost always refers to pegmatitic rock of this composition. Crystals up to several feet long have been found in pegmatite bodies. A few pegmatite masses contain relatively rare and often valuable minerals such as beryl. Several minerals have been found to occur only in pegmatites. As already mentioned, pegmatites have long been considered by many geologists to have been formed from magmas and thus to be igneous rocks; according to other geologists, however, certain features of pegmatites support better the idea that they were formed from gases and/or hot aqueous solutions. If the latter alternative is correct for even some pegmatites, those so formed do not fit well into any of the three major rock classes. In any case, it is clear that some mineral veins have been formed as the result of deposition from such fluids; thus, this kind of "other rock" category exists no matter what the true origin(s) of pegmatites.

As noted previously, *solid natural hydrocarbons* are of organic origin and are therefore not considered to be rocks by some geologists. Nearly all of them are so intimately associated with rocks, however, that it seems quite legitimate to treat them in this chapter.

FIG. 2.14. Migmatite. This migmatite, which is more than 3.5 billion years old, constitutes the cenotaph on the Virginia Polytechnic Institute's World War II Memorial. (Photograph by C. D. Putnam)

Peat, which resembles compressed tobacco, is composed of only slightly modified plant materials. It represents the first stage in the change of vegetable matter into coal. Lignite, the next member of the gradational series between peat and anthracite, is a dull brown or brownish black earthy "coal." Bituminous coal is a brittle brownish or gray-black coking coal that typically is banded (fig. 2.15). Anthracite, a vitreous black coal with conchoidal fracture, is the "hard coal" that is generally thought to have been formed by subjecting lower-rank coals to the great pressures associated with major rock-folding processes. Semianthracite is the name commonly applied to bitumi-

FIG. 2.15. Pocahontas bituminous coal. (Photograph by G. K. McCauley)

nous-grade coal that will not coke. Natural coke, which is similar to, although typically more compact than, artificial coke, is produced when hot magmas inject coking coal. In the series from peat to anthracite a gradual loss of moisture and volatile material and a gradual gain in fixed carbon percentage occur. Ranks of coal are based upon these factors.

Peat is found in the Great Dismal Swamp of southeastern Virginia. Lignite occurs as small masses in unconsolidated materials here and there along the western flank of the Blue Ridge, for example, in Smyth County, and also within the Valley and Ridge Province. Lignite and bituminous coals occur in the Triassic Midlothian and Farmville basins of the Piedmont. Bituminous coal is the basis of the coal industry of southwestern Virginia and adjacent states. Semianthracite occurs locally in Augusta, Bland, Botetourt, Craig, Montgomery, Pulaski, Roanoke, Rockingham, and Wythe counties. Natural coke occurs in the Triassic basins of the Piedmont where hot basaltic magmas injected and coked some of the coal.

Fluid natural hydrocarbons are certainly not rocks under any extant definition. Nevertheless, they also are so intimately associated with rocks and constitute so important a "mineral resource" that they too warrant brief treatment here.

Natural gas is the name generally applied to any mixture of gaseous hydrocarbons found in nature. Petroleum, more commonly called oil, is the term generally applied to natural liquid hydrocarbons. Probably nearly all natural gas and petroleum originate from organic material.

Natural gas is chiefly methane, although numerous other gases are common coconstituents. All the diverse petroleums are composed of compounds of carbon and hydrogen with minor amounts of oxygen and nitrogen and at least trace amounts of other elements such as sulphur. Petroleums are classified as paraffin-base, asphalt-base (= naphthene-base), or mixed-base, depending upon the character of the residue they leave upon distillation removal of their light fractions. Typically paraffin-base oils are lighter in color and weight and are less viscous than asphalt-base oils. Most fluid, natural hydrocarbons burn readily.

Natural gas has been found in the Early Grove Field of Scott County and in the Bergton Field of Rockingham County. Oil occurs in rocks that are nearly 500 million years old in the Rose Hill Field of Lee County.

Petrology, the study of rocks, probably has the broadest base of any of the branches of the geological sciences. The petrologist must use the basic tools and data of the other branches of geology and of the other basic sciences in his attempts to determine a rock's origin and its subsequent history. In addition, he often may have the satisfaction of knowing that the results of his investigations are basic to other geological considerations and studies, both theoretical and practical in nature.

What does a petrologist actually do? He records facts in the field and in the laboratory; he synthesizes the facts; he considers multiple hypotheses in the light of his individual facts, his syntheses, and other pertinent data; and he suggests possible conclusions, which may even involve predictions. To do well, the petrologist needs to be very observant, logical, and highly imaginative (although in a disciplined way) and to have acquired a good background in the basic sciences.

Rocks, the subjects of petrologists' investigations, are end products rather than elementary building blocks. The mode of thinking of the petrologist must therefore be different from that of most other scientists. He must spend most of his time inferring causes from results rather than predicting results on the basis of causes. As Raymond Siever said in *American Scientist* in 1968, it is "as if someone who wanted to find out what was going on in an elementary chemistry laboratory would go to the laboratory when no one was in it, analyze what he found in the sink and analyze what he found in the sewer leading from the laboratory [and,] noting how the laboratory is equipped, . . . make some deductions as to the experiments that were performed and guess what the starting reagents might have been." In addition, the rocks the petrologist studies are often the results of processes that have involved an interaction among more variables (including one or more that were changing) in larger systems and for longer periods of time than can possibly be dealt with in the laboratory.

Thus, there is, in a sense, no such thing as an amateur petrologist. But, this does not mean that there is no role for the layman who is interested in rocks rather than in, for example, minerals. Quite the contrary! Rocks may be collected along with, or instead of, minerals. Many persons have found that the names, appearances, and histories of rocks are extremely interesting and that rocks therefore make fine conversation pieces. In a few cases, interested laymen have discovered peculiar rocks and have called them to the attention of a professional petrologist, who, in turn, has found the rocks to be of great value in his research. A few of the most versatile and imaginative sculptors and lapidaries have found that rocks offer greater challenges to their skills and give them more satisfying end products than any other material (fig. 2.16).

FIG. 2.16. Ancient dragon carving. Dark gray dragon is limestone; nearly white background is calcite of a vein that transects the rock chosen for the carving; maximum dimension about 20 cm. (Photograph courtesy of Smithsonian Institution)

F OSSILS permit us to know that hundreds of millions of years ago there were coral reefs in western Virginia, that scorpionlike creatures up to six feet long once inhabited swamps in southwestern Virginia, that dinosaurs formerly roamed the Piedmont, that eastern Virginia was at one time a luxuriant rain forest, and that other similarly fascinating things happened during Virginia's prehistoric past.

What exactly are these fossils that provide such interesting information? Until about 150 years ago the term *fossil* (from the Latin word *fossilis* — "something dug up") was used in a very broad sense. Even earth scientists used it to refer to such things as minerals, for example, as well as to what are now called fossils. Currently, a generally acceptable definition is that *a fossil is a life form or evidence of life recorded in rock.*

To examine the different aspects of this definition: *Life form* covers any complete or distinguishable part of an animal or a plant. *Evidence for life* is generally considered to refer to such things as tracks, burrows, coprolites (petrified excrement), and calculi (gallstones, kidney stones, and so forth). A few scientists, however, also include artificial structures (artifacts) produced by prehistoric man. *In rock* serves mainly to emphasize the antiquity of fossils and the requirement of natural preservation.

There are many methods whereby an organism may be preserved as a fossil. Nonetheless, when the requirements for preservation are considered fully, it becomes apparent that a very large percentage of all past life never became part of the fossil record. Many animals and plants have undoubtedly lived and died in environments never recorded in rocks; many more, especially those which were soft-bodied, never became fossils because they decayed or were destroyed as the result of weathering and/or the scavenging of animals before entombment. Furthermore, many of the fossils that have existed are no longer available because the rock in which they were formed no longer exists (it has been exposed, weathered, and eroded away). In addition, a very large part of the now existent rock record and its included fossils are buried and thus practically inaccessible. Although these considerations make the prospects for the paleontologist, the scientist who studies fossils, seem rather dismal, actually the opposite is more nearly true. Paleontology has gained a highly esteemed place in both biology and geology, and its most interesting and challenging studies, everyone agrees, are in the future.

For preservation as a fossil, the life form or evidence for life must be entombed before decay or destruction. As a consequence burial must be relatively rapid. The possession of hard parts by the organism is also a great asset, although not an absolute requirement, for fossilization. The embedding material has usually been one of the common sediments, such as sand or mud, but has also included lava, volcanic ash, tar, conifer resin, permafrost gravel (mud and gravel which have been frozen), and even glacial ice. It has been within the last four of these materials that some soft as well as hard parts of plants and animals have been preserved at a few localities. Once embedded, the organic material may persist, it may have its volatile constituents distilled off leaving chiefly carbon films, it may be replaced by mineral matter (petrified), or it may be permineralized. Minerals that have been found to compose fossils include calcite, quartz (both macrocrystalline and microcrystalline), pyrite, hematite, and several less common minerals such as vivianite. During fossilization, the original material is sometimes removed, leaving a cavity, or mold, with the shape of the original life form. This mold may become filled with "new" material, which is then termed a cast. Either a mold or a cast of this kind is considered to be a fossil. Once formed, a fossil may be extremely persistent and recognizable even after metamorphism. Also, of course, it may undergo repeated replacement.

It is clear that, in origin, fossils are biological as well as geological. In naming fossils it therefore is standard procedure to use the same binomial system of nomenclature that biologists use. The two-name method of designating plants and animals now used internationally was introduced in the 1750s by the Swedish naturalist Karl von Linné (also known as Carolus Linnaeus). The value of the method is quite apparent when one considers that to date unique names have been given to approximately 1.5 million animals and nearly 400 thousand plants.

The dual name consists of genus and species designations. When written, both names are italicized and the generic name is capitalized and precedes the species name, which is not capitalized (e.g., *Homo sapiens*). In some cases, the last name of one or more persons is given after the species name; this indicates that the species was originally described (authored) by the named person(s). If the author's name is enclosed in parentheses, it means that the species was originally described under a genus other than the one listed. If the genus name plus *sp.* is given, it indicates that the genus, but not the species, of the specimen was identified. The names must be in a Latin or Latinate form, but their derivation may be quite diverse—descriptive (e.g., *oblongus*), geographic (e.g., *virginianus*), patronymic (e.g., *darwini*), mythological (e.g., *pandora*), and so on. The species name alone is not sufficient because more than one genus may include species with the same name (just as persons with different last names may have the same first name).

The complete biological classification scheme is based on kinship and similarities of anatomical features. Three examples—one for a vertebrate, one for an invertebrate, and one for a plant—are given in table 3.1. Resemblances among differently named members of each hierarchy increase from top to bottom. Conversely, each category is only one of those included in the category above it. A diagram of the scheme would be similar to that of a tree with its trunk called a

TABLE 3.1. Biological Classification

	A VERTEBRATE	AN INVERTEBRATE	A PLANT
Kingdom	Animalia	Animalia	Plantae Embryophyta (subkingdom)
Phylum	Chordata	Mollusca	Tracheophyta Pteropsida (subphylum)
Class	Mammalia	Pelecypoda	Angiospermae Dicotyledoneae (subclass)
Order	Primates	Eulamellibranchia	Atiales
Family	Hominidae	Ostreidae	Cornaceae
Genus	*Homo*	*Ostrea*	*Cornus*
Species* (Common name)	H. *sapiens* (man)	O. *virginica* (the common, edible, East Coast oyster)	C. *florida* (dogwood)

* As noted in the text, species names alone are meaningless in that species of different genera may be given identical names.

phylum; its main branches, classes; its smaller branches (in descending order of size), orders, families, and genera; and the twigs, species.

To elaborate on this classification scheme, let us examine the first example in the table:

The Kingdom Animalia is generally considered to include all life except plants.

The Phylum Chordata includes all animals with gill pouches, nerve cord, and notochords.

The Subphylum Vertebrata (not given in the table) requires the presence of a backbone.

The Class Mammalia adds such requirements as warm blood, mammary glands, and hair.

The Order Primates includes only animals with a superior nervous system, an opposing thumb-finger relationship, and nails on digits.

The Suborder, or superfamily, Anthropoidea includes apes, man, and monkeys.

The Family Hominidae includes man's close relatives, who have bipedal posture, nonopposable big toes, legs longer than arms, no tail, and certain other characteristics.

The Genus *Homo*[1] includes manlike anthropoids.

[1] With man, generic and specific definitions may be biologically and/or anthropologically based. Biological criteria depend on sizes and shapes of anatomical features; anthropological, on such things as tool making and sociability parameters, which measure intangible characteristics such as intelligence.

The Species *sapiens* (of *Homo*) is modern man (as compared with, for example, *H. neanderthalensis,* one of the prehistoric men.)

The different races—australoid, caucasoid, mongoloid, and negroid—would be subspecies.

Species are kept distinct in that their members are able to breed only with others of their kind and thereby produce offspring which have that same capability. For the extinct "species" known only in the fossil record, morphological appearances, along with geographic and/or stratigraphic distribution, behavioral characteritics, and the like, are used in lieu of the knowledge that such breeding potentials obtained.

Just as there are subphyla, superfamilies, etc., as mentioned previously, there are sub- and super- and even infra- categories for other hierarchies—for example, subgenera, superclasses, and infraorders.

The nomenclature used for conodonts (a group of fossils of unproved kinship), ichnofossils (fossil trails, tracks, and burrows), and sporomorphae (fossil forms that have appearances suggesting that they were spores or pollen) is of the same binomial form. This application of the binomial name, however, is different: the form is not known to have species status and also is not necessarily known to belong to, or be directly attributable to, any given phylum, class, or the like.

The animal phyla known to be well represented in the fossil record are listed in table 3.2. Similarly represented plant phyla are given in table 3.3. Some phyla of each kingdom are represented only poorly or apparently not at all in the fossil record. Descriptions follow for a few of the animals that are particularly well represented in the fossil record or that are, for some other reason, of special interest to the geologist.

Although the biological classification of animals is based more on the functional qualities of anatomical elements than upon morphology of hard parts, the following descriptions are based chiefly on hard parts because they are best represented in the fossil record. Because occurrences in Virginia and ranges of representatives of the phyla and classes are tabulated (table 3.4) and treated briefly in the last part of this chapter, only a few statements about these aspects are given in the following descriptions. The reader is referred to the geologic timetable (table 5.1, p. 127) for an explanation of the time designations.

PROTOZOA—This phylum includes all single-celled animals. Some of these that secrete or construct skeletons (called tests) are preserved as fossils. Foraminifers secrete chambered tests: some composed of calcium carbonate, some of chitin (nearly the same material as fingernails and hair), and others of silica. A few incorporate sand grains in their skeletons. Most of the tests are extremely small, but a few have become as large as a fifty-cent piece. The commonest fossil

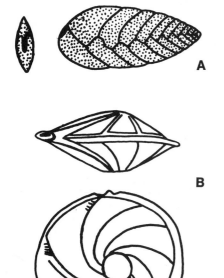

foraminifers in Virginia look like miniature snail shells (fig. 3.1B). Radiolarians, all of which are microscopic, secrete rather elaborate silica skeletons, which look like spherical lattice works with protruding spines (fig. 3.1D).

There seems to be little doubt that protozoans existed in Precambrian time, although no undisputed fossils of this antiquity are known. Foraminifers, probably the most widely employed microfossils in geological studies, are abundant in Tertiary sediments of the Coastal Plain.

TABLE 3.2. Animals Well Represented in the Fossil Record

Phylum Subphylum	Class Subclass	Common names and/or description
Protozoa	Sarcodina	foraminifera, radiolaria
Porifera		sponges
Coelenterata	Hydrozoa	hydroids, *stromatoporoids*,*
	Anthozoa	sea anemones, *tetracorals*, hexa-corals, *tabulate corals*
Brachiopoda		brachiopods
Bryozoa (or Ectoprocta)		"moss corals"
Echinodermata	Stelleroidea	starfish, brittle stars
	Echinoidea	sea urchins, sand dollars
	Crinoidea	sea lilies
	Blastoidea	*blastoids (or "sea buds")*
	Cystoidea	*cystoids*
Mollusca	Pelecypoda (or Lamellibranchiata)	clams, oysters, scallops
	Gastropoda	snails, conchs, etc.
	Cephalopoda	squids, nautiloids, *ammonoids*, *belemnoids*
Annelida		earthworms, etc. (segmented worms)
Arthropoda	*Trilobita*	*trilobites*
	Crustacea	lobsters, barnacles, crabs, ostracodes
	Arachnoidea	
	Arachnida	spiders, ticks, scorpions
	Merostomata	*eurypterids*, king (or horseshoe) crabs
	Insecta	insects
Chordata Vertebrata	Pisces	fishes
	Amphibia	salamanders, frogs, toads, *stegocephalians*
	Reptilia	crocodiles, lizards, turtles, *dinosaurs*, *ichthyosaurs*, *plesiosaurs*, *mosasaurs*, *pterodactyls*
	Aves	birds
	Mammalia	horses, cattle, elephants, whales, men, kangaroos, bats, cats, rats, etc.
Hemichordata	Graptolithina	*graptolites*†
Unknown	Unknown	conodonts

* Names of extinct creatures are italicized.

† Regarded as coelenterata by some paleontologists.

FIG. 3.1. Protozoa. Both fossil and living foraminifers (*A, B, C*) occur in Virginia. Fossil forms are especially common in the Tertiary rocks of the Coastal Plain. The figured forms are: *A, Bolivina,* × 40; *B, Robulus,* × 20; *C, Globigirina,* × 80; *D, Headoridium,* × 75. Reprinted, by permission, from R. C. Moore, C. G. Lalicker, and A. G. Fischer, *Invertebrate Fossils,* © 1952, by McGraw-Hill Book Company)

PORIFERA—Nearly all sponges lack or have very few hard parts; hence this phylum is not well represented in the fossil record (fig. 3.2). The only fossil representative of the sponge that is at all common is the spicule. Several of these constitute the framework that

TABLE 3.3. Plants Well Represented in the Fossil Record

Phylum	Class	Common names and/or description
I. SUBKINGDOM THALLOPHYTA		
Cyanophyta		Blue-green algae (Cryptozoons?)
Chlorophyta		Green algae
Euglenophyta		Euglenoids
Charophyta		Charophytes
Phaeophyta		Brown algae
Rhodophyta		Red algae
Chrysophyta		Golden-brown algae, diatoms
Pyrrophyta		Cryptomonads, dinoflagellates
Myxomycophyta		Slime molds
Eumycophyta		True fungi
	Phycomycetes	Algaelike fungi
	Ascomycetes	Sac fungi
	Basidiomycetes	Club fungi
	Deuteromycetes	Fungi imperfecti
Schizomycophyta		Bacteria
II. SUBKINGDOM EMBRYOPHYTA		
Bryophyta		
	Hepaticae	Liverworts
	Musci	Mosses
Tracheophyta		Vascular plants
Subphyla-		
Psilopsida		
Lycopsida		Club mosses, *Sigillaria*,* *Lepidodendron*
Sphenopsida		"Horsetails," *Calamites*
Pteropsida		
	Filicineae	True ferns
	Gymnospermae	Ginkgos, seed ferns, conifers, *Cordaites*
	Angiospermae	Flowering plants, palms, grasses

* Italicized names are for extinct plants.

A

B

C

D

FIG. 3.2. Porifera. Fossil sponges, like present-day ones, are irregular in form. They are locally common, though generally rare. Spicules (*D*), the only at-all-common remains, are frequently found as insoluble microfossil residues from, e.g., calcareous shales. The above forms are: *A*, Two types of Late Paleozoic sponges, × .65; *B*, *Girtycoelia,* × .85; *C*, *Astraeospongia meniscus* (Roermer), × 1; *D*, sponge spicules, greatly enlarged. (Pictures courtesy of Smithsonian Institution; diagram reprinted, by permission, from W. H. Matthews III, *Texas Fossils,* 1960, published by Bureau of Economic Geology, the University of Texas)

A
B

FIG. 3.3. Coelenterata. Corals are abundant in certain formations of the Paleozoic (Ordovician and younger) and the Tertiary in Virginia. *Above, A* (*Heliophyllum halli* (Dana) × .65) is a solitary "horn" coral; *B* (*Favosites*, × .25) and *C* are colonial corals. *C* is of Miocene age and was collected from the famous Rice Pit at Hampton, Virginia. (Photographs courtesy of Smithsonian Institution)

supports the main soft cellular masses of some sponges. Spicules are typically microscopic and may be of many diverse shapes even in the same individual. Questionable sponge spicules have been found in Precambrian rocks; definite sponge remains occur in Cambrian and later rocks.

Archaeocyathids, which are locally common in early and middle Cambrian rocks (for example, near Austinville), were formerly placed in this phylum but are now regarded by many paleontologists as belonging to the new phylum Archaeocyatha.

COELENTERATA—Coral is the name given to skeletons of anthozoan polyps. All corals exhibit radiating septa (partitions). Both solitary and colonial corals are known from ancient fossils as well as in present-day seas. Common forms look like honeycombs, horns, fans, and brains (fig. 3.3). Almost the only hydrozoan of any real importance in any but relatively recent rocks is the stromotoporoid of Paleozoic and Mesozoic time. The various corals have had quite different histories so far as first appearance, development, and extinction. For example, whereas the chain corals were of importance only in the Silurian period and became extinct in the Devonian, the hexa-corals did not emerge until about the Triassic but now are the chief reef builders. Many corals are more plantlike than animallike in appearance.

Graptolites, which are relatively common fossils in some ancient rocks, are considered by some paleontologists to belong to the Hydrozoa class of this phylum. Relatively recent thorough work seems, however, to indicate that they are invertebrate chordates. They are described under that heading in this book.

BRACHIOPODA—Brachiopods are bivalved, that is to say, they have two shells (fig. 3.4). Most brachiopods are ½ to 2 inches along their greatest dimensions. In the articulate class of brachiopods, the two shells are hinged, with the hinge area having a tooth-and-socket relationship and ranging from a very narrow beaklike point to a relatively long straight line (fig. 3.5). In the inarticulate class, there is no hinge, although there is a beak. The two shells of most brachiopods differ rather markedly from each other. The pair may represent any of several diverse appearances ranging from one convex and the

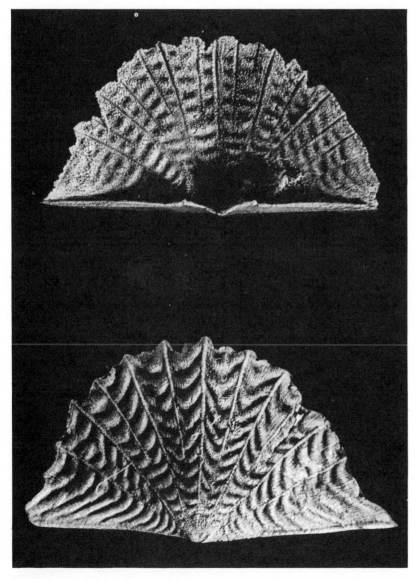

FIG. 3.4. Brachiopod. This beautifully preserved brachiopod (× 6.5) came from the Ordovician Edinburg Formation about 5.9 miles east of Harrisonburg. Its name is *Ptychoglyptus virginiensis* Willard. (Photograph courtesy of Smithsonian Institution)

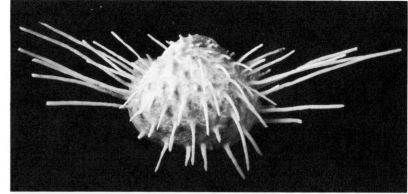

FIG. 3.5. Brachiopoda. There was a great diversity of form in Paleozoic brachiopoda: *A, Echinauris,* × .6; *B, Rafinesquina ponderosa* Ulrich, × .8; *C, Mucrospirifer arkonensis* (S. & G.), × .9; *D,* a mucrospirifer with silicified internal structures exposed × 2.7. (Photographs courtesy of Smithsonian Institution)

other concave to both convex. Each valve exhibits bilateral symmetry — that is to say, it may be bisected, the equivalent halves being mirror images of each other. This symmetry reflects the fact that the valves are ventral and dorsal (bottom and top) to the animal rather than right and left, as is true of clams. The shells of live brachiopods, commonly called lampshells, are composed of chitin, calcium phosphate, or calcium carbonate. Brachiopod fossils may also be composed of silica, probably because of replacement of their original shell material. The live animal is attached to the bottom by a stalklike pedicle, which emerges from between the shells of the inarticulate brachiopods but from a hole in the ventral valve of the articulate types. Although there are now only a few living members of this phylum, throughout much of geologic time brachiopods were very common "shellfish." Articulate brachiopods were well developed in Cambrian time and reached a maximum in the Silurian. One inarticulate brachiopod, *Lingula,* has retained its simple form for at least 550 million years. Brachiopods are currently rather uncommon except at a few localities.

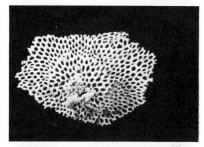

BRYOZOA — This phylum consists of "moss corals," which are attached to rocks and seaweeds on a rather widespread basis. The skeletons are either chitiniferous or calcareous. Individual bryozoans, which are about the size of a dot on one of the *i*'s on this page, are always colonial. Some colonies have reached reeflike dimensions. The colonial skeletons are typically of lacy appearance and may additionally be mosslike, branching, or leaflike (fig. 3.6). Although they may superficially resemble corals, bryozoan colonial skeletons contain distinctive internal structures and they lack the radial septa of corals.

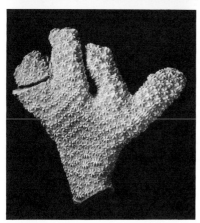

FIG. 3.6. Bryozoa. Some typical Paleozoic bryozoan colonies: left slab × 2; others × 1. (Photographs courtesy of Smithsonian Institution)

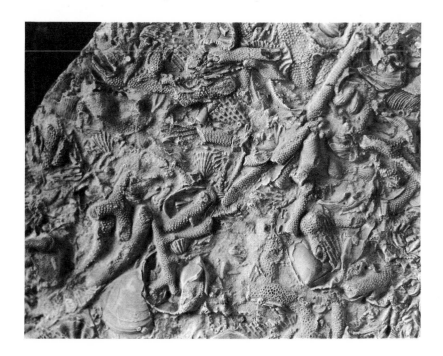

These animals, which first appeared in the fossil record in the Ordovician period and still exist in abundance, had a rather bizarre representative during the Mississippian—the genus *Archimedes,* which was so named because it resembles the well-known Archimedes screw.

ECHINODERMATA—Each of the five Echinoderm classes listed in table 3.2 are represented in the fossil record (fig. 3.7). Two of them, the blastoids and cystoids, are known only from that record. The stelleroids (starfish, etc.) and the echinoids (sea urchins, sand

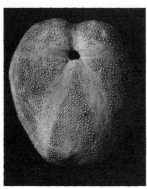

A.1 **A.2** **A.3**

B

FIG. 3.7. Echinodermata

A. Echinoids. Fossils of free-moving echinoids are relatively widely distributed in Cretaceous and Tertiary formations. The pictured forms lack spines, which are common in washed residues of Cretaceous and Tertiary rocks. They are: *1, Epiaster whitei* (Clark) × 1; *2, Stereocidaris hudspethensis* Cooke × .5; *3, Encope tamiamiensis* Mansfield × .5. (Photographs courtesy of Smithsonian Institution)

B. Blastoids. "Sea buds" without their stems and hold-fasts, like the one shown, are fairly common in Mississippian rocks of the Appalachians of the Virginias. This one is *Pentremites pyriformis* Say × 1. (Photograph courtesy of Smithsonian Institution)

C. Crinoids. "Sea lilies" have been fairly common here and there in seas since early Paleozoic time. Columnals are the commonly found part. On *3,* the arms of the crinoid are hanging down thereby exposing a long anal sac. The arrow points to columnals of stem. (Diagrams *1* and *2* reprinted, by permission, from W. H. Matthews III, *Texas Fossils* 1960, published by Bureau of Economic Geology, the University of Texas; photograph *3* is courtesy of Smithsonian Institution)

D. Stelleroids. Starfish and brittle (or serpent) stars are rare in the fossil record. This fine specimen (*Devonaster eucharis* (Hall), × .9) is from a Devonian formation exposed in the Colgate University Quarry in central New York. (Photograph courtesy of Smithsonian Institution)

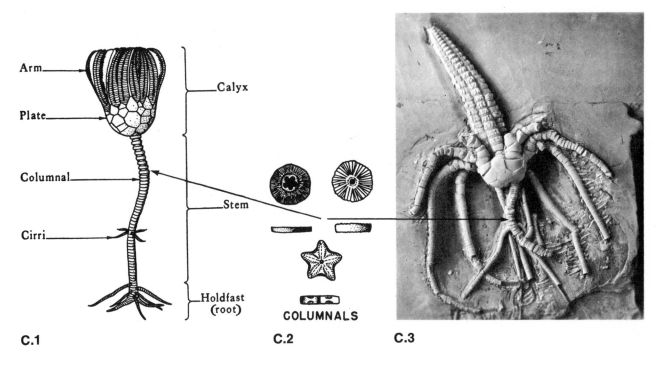

Arm — Calyx

Plate —

Columnal —

Stem

Cirri —

Holdfast (root)

C.1

COLUMNALS

C.2

C.3

D

dollars, etc.) are mobile. In contrast, most of the crinoids ("sea lilies"), blastoids ("sea buds"), and cystoids are (or were) fastened to the bottom. Starfish are rare in the fossil record. Echinoderms are commonly represented by circular or polygonal calcareous plates, a fraction of an inch across, and less commonly by their complete bun-shaped skeletons or by spines. Crinoids often grow in groups and look like undersea flower beds. Segments of crinoid stems, which are called columnals and resemble small washers, are common fossils; crinoid heads, called calyces, are rather rare; arms that branch out from the calyces have been preserved in some cases. Blastoid heads, which resemble flower buds with fivefold symmetry, are fairly common locally. Cystoids, a few of which probably did not have stems, had calyces without symmetry; most recognized cystoid remains consist of unsymmetrical ovoid heads. Primitive cystoids inhabited early Ordovician seas; the last cystoids apparently lived in Devonian time. Blastoids appear to have been extinct in all but one small asylum area by the end of the Pennsylvanian Period and wholly extinct at the end of the Paleozoic Era. Crinoids appear to have reached their climax in Mississippian time but still exist.

MOLLUSCA—This phylum is said to have more than 100,000 living species (fig. 3.8). It includes pelecypods (clams, oysters, and scallops), gastropods (snails, etc.), and cephalopods (squids, nautiloids, the extinct ammonoids and belemnoids, etc.). The pelecypods are bivalved like brachiopods but, unlike the brachiopods, have shells that are right and left (rather than bottom and top). The two shells of a clam are mirror images of each other; the two shells of an oyster may differ from each other, but neither has symmetry like that of the individual brachiopod valves; the two shells of a scallop may nearly but not quite match and the individual shells may at first appear to have symmetry, but not one has. Each gastropod has a single shell which is typically coiled like a screw (not on one plane). As noted, the class Cephalopoda includes such different-appearing creatures as the pearly nautilus, the squid, and the octopus. Fossils of members of the nautiloid and ammonoid orders are fairly common. Representatives of each of these classes may be straight or coiled. The coiling is typically like a clock spring (in one plane). A characteristic feature of cephalopods is the presence of septa (partitions) within the shells. The septa in the nautiloids are relatively simple in shape, whereas those within the ammonoids are commonly rather complex. Cambrian

FIG. 3.8. Mollusca

  A. Pelecypods. These are typical of the Paleozoic and, as is evident, not unlike some living forms: *1, Orthonota undulata* (Conrad), × .8: *2, Cimitaria corrugata* (Conrad), × .7. (Photographs courtesy of Smithsonian Institution)

  B. Gastropods. A typical Paleozoic snail, *Worthenia tabulata* (Conrad), × 1. (Photograph courtesy of Smithsonian Institution)

  C. Cephalopods. Two Paleozoic and one Mesozoic cephalopod: *1,* a nautiloid, *Foordiceras gregarium* Miller, × 1; *2,* an ammonoid, *Imitoceral rotatorius* (Dekon.), × 1; *3,* an ammonoid, *Scaphites preventricosus* Cobban, × 1. (Photographs courtesy of Smithsonian Institution)

A.1

A.2

B

C.1

C.2

C.3

A

snails were among the earliest mollusks. Cephalopods are known to be as ancient as Late Cambrian. Pelecypods appeared in the Ordovician Period. Straight cephalopods were apparently rather common inhabitants of the Ordovician seascape. Ammonoids first appeared in the Devonian, were very abundant in the Triassic, but became extinct in the Cretaceous. Belemnoids, another extinct cephalopod group, are chambered, cigar-shaped cephalopods, which lived from Mississippian through Early Tertiary time. They are of the same class as squids and cuttlefish.

ANNELIDA—This phylum includes segmented worms like the common earthworm. Despite the fact that these animals are composed almost wholly of soft parts, they are apparently represented in

B.1   B.2

FIG. 3.9.   Arthropoda

A. Eurypterid. A Silurian "sea scorpion" (*Eurypterus* [*locustris* ?] Harlan, × .25)

B. Trilobites: 1, a lower Cambrian trilobite; *2,* a rather common Ordovician trilobite; *3,* a group of Devonian trilobites (*1, Paedumias yorkensis* R. & H. × .55; *2, Cryptolithus tesselatus* (Green) × 2; *3, Pacops rana* Green × .5)

C. Barnacles. Present-day barnacles have attached themselves to a Cretaceous oyster, which was washed out of its original, containing strata.

D. Insects. 1, a caddis fly in amber (fossilized fir gum); *2,* a flying ant in volcanic ash (both × 1).

E. Ostracodes. These small arthropods occur in rocks from Cambrian to Recent age and are represented by living forms. There are both marine and fresh-water ostracodes. The fossils are abundant in Paleozoic and Tertiary rocks of the Old Dominion. The main picture is *Zygobolbina cleora* (× 1.2). The diagrams are: *top, Hollinella* Coryell (× 30); *upper middle, Ceratopsis* Ulrich (× 30); *lower middle and bottom, Hollinella* Coryell (× 35). (Photographs courtesy of Smithsonian Institution, except *C,* by G. K. McCauley; diagrams in *E* reprinted, by permission, from R. C. Moore, C. G. Lalicker, and A. G. Fischer, *Invertebrate Fossils,* © 1952, by McGraw-Hill Book Company)

B.3

the fossil record. Tracks, tubes, and burrows are relatively common. Numerous small tooth jaws (scolecodonts) found in rocks of all ages since about 600 million years ago have also been attributed to marine polychaete worms. (Nearly all scolecodonts have a glossy black appearance, whereas conodonts, which they superficially resemble, may be of several different compositions and appearances.) Annelids may have existed in Precambrian time. Several features, like the early Cambrian *Scolithus* tubes that are relatively common in quartzite beds along the western Blue Ridge front, have been attributed to worms, although not without question.

ARTHROPODA—All of the diverse members of this phylum have segmented bodies and jointed legs (fig. 3.9). Many of their anatomi-

D.1

D.2

C

E

cal parts are composed of the horny material chitin. Members of the phylum that are relatively well known as living forms and as fossils are: crustaceans—barnacles, ostracodes, crabs, lobsters, and shrimps; arachnids—scorpions and spiders; merostomates—king, or horseshoe, crabs; and insects—the true insects. Chiefly terrestrial forms, such as most insects, are generally fossilized only under unusual conditions, for example, in conifer resin (now amber) or volcanic ash. Members of two extinct families, the trilobites (class Trilobita) and the euryp-terids (subclass Merostomata), are especially important in the fossil record but are now extinct. The trilobites were so named because each has three longitudinal lobes. Of the segments, the heads and tails are commoner as fossils than are the midsections (thoraxes). Most trilobites were 1 to 3 inches long, although a few were much longer. The eurypterids looked like large scorpions. They grew to nearly 10 feet long. Nearly everyone is familiar enough with the general appear-ances of animals of these groups to recognize them or even some of their dismembered parts. The trilobites appear to have dominated the Cambrian shallow marine environment. They climaxed in the Ordovi-cian Period, declined noticeably in the Devonian, and were extinct by the end of the Permian. Eurypterids, the large scorpionlike animals, which were locally common during the Silurian and Mississippian periods, were also extinct by the end of the Paleozoic Era. Insects are known to have existed since Devonian time. The crustaceans in general gained most of their modern aspects by late Jurassic time.

CHORDATA—Although there are four subphyla of chordates, for practical purposes the phylum may be divided into two groups: the invertebrate chordates and the vertebrate chordates. As mentioned, graptolites may belong to the Hydrozoa class of the Coelenterata phylum instead of to the invertebrate chordates (Hemichordata class). In any case, they are now extinct. Many apparently floated in marine waters. Typical specimens are flattened carbon films that look like coping-saw blades with teeth on one or both sides (fig. 3.10).

FIG. 3.10. Graptolites are common in some Paleozoic shales. (Photograph courtesy of Smithsonian Institution)

FIG. 3.11. Collecting large vertebrate fossils
  A. Preliminary stage in the excavation of a porpoise skull in the Miocene Calvert Formation at Wakefield, Washington's birthplace, in Westmoreland County.
  B. Applying plaster bandages and wood reinforcements to a block of matrix that contains the skull of a fossil whale in the Miocene Calvert Formation at the Stratford Cliffs, Westmoreland County. (Photographs courtesy of Smithsonian Institution)

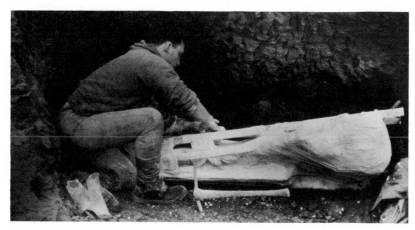

Most of these occur on bedding planes in carbonaceous and/or calcareous shales of Ordovician and Silurian age.

The vertebrates include the five classes listed in table 3.2: the fishes, the amphibians, the reptiles, the birds, and the mammals. Vertebrate fossils, most of which are bones or teeth, are rather rare as compared to invertebrate fossils. Most would be recognized by almost anyone as parts of vertebrates and many as to the group of the animal. The collecting methods and a reconstruction of an extinct vertebrate are shown in figures 3.11 and 3.12.

The first vertebrate fossils are of Ordovician age. The first known land vertebrates are of the Devonian. Early reptiles appeared in the Mississippian. The first birds of the known record date from the

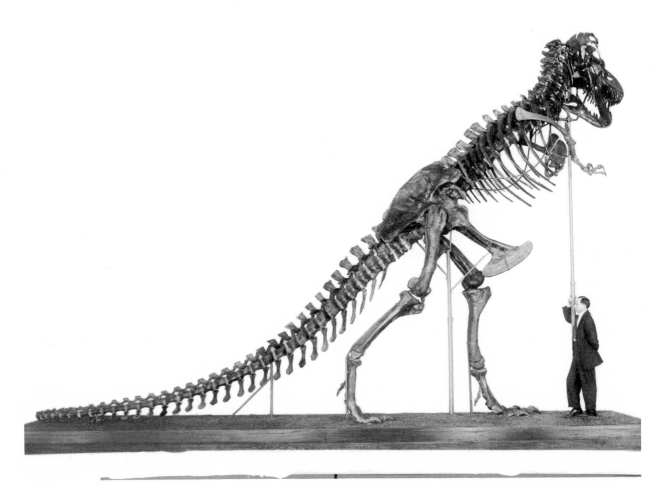

FIG. 3.12.   Vertebrata. Skeletal remains of dinosaurs have been found in Mesozoic rocks of the eastern United States. Numerous tracks have been found preserved in Triassic shales in northern Virginia. The pictured skeleton is *Tyrannosaurus rex*. (Courtesy of American Museum of Natural History)

Jurassic. Dinosaurs lived in the Mesozoic Era. Man did not appear until very recently.

CONODONTS—Each of these microscopic, toothlike fossils appears to be only a small part of some animal. The actual kinship between a given conodont and any animal has not been established. Different paleontologists and biologists have suggested variously that they belonged to cephalopods, crustaceans, fish, gastropods, and worms. The typical conodont is a tiny toothlike object (fig. 3.13) composed

FIG. 3.13. Conodonts — each greatly magnified. (Reprinted, by permission, from W. H. Matthews III, *Texas Fossils*, 1960, published by the Bureau of Economic Geology, the University of Texas)

wholly or chiefly of brown calcium phosphate. One of the problems in trying to establish their kinship is that conodonts have not been found in rocks of more recent age than Triassic.

INCERTAE SEDIS—Several fossils, such as the just-mentioned conodonts, are often referred to as of *uncertain category* in geological reports. These are the forms which are obviously fossils but have no currently known biological affinities above some certain category (for example, it may not be known to what group or phylum the form belongs). Some of these fossils are relatively common in the Old Dominion (fig. 3.14).

ICHNOFOSSILS—Fossil trails, tracks, and burrows are often referred to as ichnofossils (fig. 3.15). Some may be attributed to certain kinds of animals—for example, trilobites, snails, or worms. Others may not be so identified. Several of both kinds may be related to a certain activity, such as simple crawling, foraging, or tunneling for shelter. All may be of value to investigations of ancient environments. Those in folded and/or faulted strata may serve as valuable geopetal indicators (see chapter VI).

Major groups of the plant kingdom are listed in table 3.3. Some of the plant phyla (sometimes referred to as divisions) are poorly or not at all represented in the fossil record. Although plant fossils are

FIG. 3.14. *Incertae sedis: A, Tentaculites* have been considered by some paleontologists to be planktonic mollusks but now are generally not referred to any phylum because their true biological affinities are unknown, × 1.3. *B* and *C, Scolithus* tubes, which are common in some of the lower Cambrian sandstones of the western Blue Ridge of Virginia, may represent ancient worm borings. (Photographs: *A,* courtesy of Smithsonian Institution; *B* and *C* courtesy of W. D. Lowry)

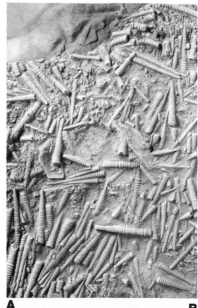

A

B

C

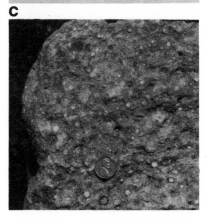

generally not so good as invertebrate fossils for determining the ages of their including strata, they are often better than other kinds of fossils so far as indicating former climatic conditions. Those that are known to be well represented or of particular interest to the geologist warrant brief descriptions here.

THALLOPHYTA—Plants of this subkingdom lack leaves, roots, and stems. They also have no vascular tissue and produce no embryos. Plants of the algae group possess chlorophyll, whereas those of the fungi group do not. The algae group includes plants generally called seaweeds as well as the common algae and diatoms. The fungi group

A   B

FIG. 3.15. Ichnofossils: *A*, trail of unidentified animal; *B*, trilobite track. Each black and white space on scale is 1 cm. long. (Photographs courtesy of G. C. Grender)

includes bacteria as well as molds, mushrooms, and other kinds of fungous growth. Lichens are a combination of algae and fungi.

Fossil algae (fig. 3.16) have been identified in rocks of all major subdivisions of the geologic time scale, including the Precambrian (table 5.1, p. 127). In fact, some algae with all modern aspects have existed since Precambrian time. The fossils are commonly carbonaceous films or calcareous.

Diatoms are minute, one-celled aquatic plants of this group which have the appearance of concentric hemispheric plates, microscopic stemlike forms with radiating tubular branches, and other forms. They are known to have existed since the Cretaceous Period. They are well represented in the fossil record because they produce siliceous skeletons. Accumulations of these organisms are called diatomaceous ooze; the rock equivalent is called diatomite or diatomaceous earth.

Fossil fungi are rare, although members of the group have apparently existed since at least Middle Devonian time. The chief evidence for fungi in the fossil record consists of damage effects which appear to represent activities of fungi on animals which have become preserved as fossils.

EMBRYOPHYTA—Plants of this subkingdom (fig. 3.17) are more complex than the thallophytes. Most embryophytes are terrestrial; nearly all contain vascular tissues; all form embryos. There are two main phyla, the Bryophyta and the Tracheophyta.

The bryophytes are simple plants without roots. The liverworts and mosses are included. Members of this phylum date from at least the

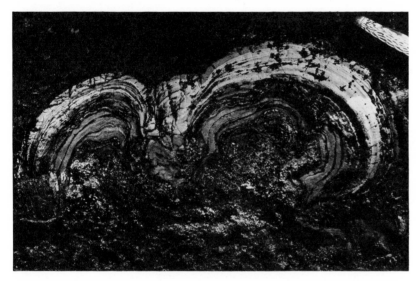

FIG. 3.16. Algal structures in Upper Cambrian Conococheague Formation, near Staunton; pocket knife in upper right gives scale. (Photograph courtesy of Virginia Division of Mineral Resources, T. M. Gathright, Jr., photographer)

Mississipian Period. They are, however, rare in the fossil record.

The phylum Tracheophyta includes four subphyla (or subdivisions). Although most parts of the plants of this phylum are so delicate that they are typically only partially preserved and, therefore, often difficult to identify, each subphylum is known to be well represented in the fossil record. Psilopsida, the primitive, rootless, and leafless plants, is the least known. Representatives appear to range from the Silurian to the present with few present-day species. Lycopsida, the club mosses, is represented by such well-known plants as the scale trees *Lepidodendron* and *Sigillaria,* which grew to be 100 feet high and 3 feet in diameter at their bases within the Misissippian and Pennsylvanian swamps that became the major coal fields of North America. Sphenopsida, which includes present-day scouring rushes and "horsetails," has jointed stems and, in some species, leaf whorls at the joints. Both the stems and the leaf whorls of the Mississippian-Pennsylvanian *Calamites* are relatively common fossils. Pteropsida

A

B

FIG. 3.17. Land plant fossils: *A*, Tertiary leaf impression in volcanic ash; *B*, Recent leaf impression in calcareous tufa from Steele's Tavern; *C*, Carboniferous frond impression from Bluefield District; *D*, Carboniferous tree trunk exhibiting leaf scars from southwestern Virginia coal fields. (Photograph *A* courtesy of Smithsonian Institution; *B* and *D*, G. K. McCauley; *C*, Norfolk and Western Railway.)

C   **D**

includes a very large percentage of the world's living plants. Each has leaves, stems, true roots, and vascular tissues. There are three classes within this subphylum: Filicineae includes the true ferns, which are known to have existed since the Devonian; Gymnospermae includes the conifers, cycads, ginkgos, and seed ferns and is also known from the Devonian to the present; Angiospermae includes the flowering and fruiting plants and grasses. The class Angiospermae includes the subclasses Dicotyledoneae and Monocotyledoneae. The former is characterized by leaves with networklike veining. Two good examples are the maple tree and vegetables like the beet. Monocotyledoneae is characterized by leaves that have parallel veins. A couple of good examples are corn and the common grasses. The angiosperms, of which the oldest undisputed fossils are of Cretaceous age, have dominated the world's total flora since Cretaceous time. They make up some 70 per cent of the approximately 375,000 known living plants.

SPOROMORPHAE—Fossil pollen grains and spores have been studied for about fifty years. They have recently been used rather widely to elucidate archeological as well as geological history, especially that relating to fairly recent events. Palynology is the name which was given in 1943 to investigations of both living and fossil representatives of these microscopic organisms. Fortunately pollen grains and spores have distinctive features that sometimes lend themselves to correlation with at least the general kind of plants that produced them. As has long been known, these tiny organisms have an essential role in plant reproduction. Because most plants respond rather rapidly to marked climatic changes, palynological studies are of particular value to investigations relating to ancient climate.

Strictly speaking, the term *fossil* should be restricted in its application to life forms or evidences for life preserved in rock. Nonetheless, for a long time the word has also found convenient use as an adjective to aid distinction between ancient and present-day inorganic features —for example, "fossil" ripple marks versus ripple marks (unmodified). Most paleontologists, however, consider such usage to be a corruption of the term even though the features designated by the word have often been of great value in paleoecology, the study of ancient environments.

Another kind of "fossil," the pseudofossil, warrants brief consideration. Some of these false fossils—features in rock that resemble but are *not* fossils—have deceived many people, especially beginning collectors. The commonest of these are concretions (septeria in particular), cone-in-cone structures, dendrites, slickensides, and stylolites (fig. 3.18). Once familiar with these features, one finds it relatively simple to distinguish them from true fossils. The differences, however, defy brief description; the best approach is to take any questionable specimen to a professional paleontologist for evaluation.

About 2,400 years ago, Herodotus was shown fossil sea shells in

FIG. 3.18. Pseudofossils: *upper left,* cone-in-cone; *other four in upper row,* concretions; *lower left,* septerian concretion; *center,* erosion form; *middle* and *right of bottom row,* concretions; *right center,* barite "roses." (Photograph by G. K. McCauley)

the Libyan desert and quite correctly suggested that they were there because the Mediterranean Sea had once covered that region. Nearly all the other early references to fossils, however, connected them with fanciful or mystical ideas. Even Aristotle appears to have believed that fossils grew within the rocks in which they occur. With a few exceptions, this kind of misconception prevailed until the Renaissance. By the middle 1400's, however, the organic origin of such remains became rather widely accepted. Nonetheless, it was not until the late 1700's that paleontology as a science really began to emerge. Paleontology now consists of several branches. Included are:

Invertebrate paleontology, the study of invertebrate fossils
Vertebrate paleontology, the study of vertebrate fossils
Paleobotany, the study of plant fossils
Micropaleontology, the study of fossils of micro-organisms.
Palynology, the study of spores and pollen
Ichnology, the study of fossil trails, tracks, and burrows
Paleoecology, the study of the relations of ancient animals to their environments

Most modern paleontologists specialize even further. For example, some invertebrate paleontologists restrict their investigations to members of only one phylum, class, or order or, more rarely, to a single family, a genus, or a few genera.

In addition, there are two rather different approaches; the extremes may be described as biologically oriented and geologically oriented. The biological approach has as its aim the answering of questions relating to morphology, function, taxonomy (classification), evolution, or some combination of these. Biologically oriented investigations are extremely interesting and often aid in clarifying geological as well as biological problems. The geological approach has as its chief aim the determination of the distribution of organisms in space and/or in time and thus the reconstruction of geological history.

Until a few years ago the entire geological time scale from the beginning of Paleozoic time was based almost wholly on fossils. Isotopic age determinations (see chapter VI) now supplement this work. Most subdivisions of the geologic calendar, however, are still distinguished mainly on the basis of fossils. Fossils are therefore used to correlate strata of one area with those of other areas. This kind of information can be extremely important in working out a geological history and, consequently, in exploring for natural resources, such as petroleum, that occur in stratified rocks. The study of fossils may also be very enlightening in geological investigations because they commonly reflect the environment under which the animals lived, died, and/or were entombed. With exceptions of course, marine forms are found in marine sediments, terrestial forms are found in terrestrial deposits, and so forth. Often, however, fossils yield even more detailed information. For example, fossil coral reefs—if formed under conditions similar to those required for present-day reefs—indicate clean, warm, marine water shallow enough for the penetration of light.

Such inferences are dependent upon one of the main "laws" of geology, the Principle of Uniformitarianism. This principle, stated briefly, is that "the present is the key to the past," which in essence means that interpretations involving the past may be based on what can be observed today.

Invertebrate fossils are generally used more than either vertebrate or plant fossils by the geologically oriented paleontologist. The main reason is that invertebrates are more abundant, especially in the marine sedimentary rocks which constitute a very large percentage of the known stratigraphic record.

Certain kinds of fossils have been shown to be especially well suited for certain purposes. Plant fossils, as stated earlier, may be particularly useful in paleoclimatic determinations. For example, plant fossils revealed that the Coastal Plain of Virginia was a luxuriant rain forest during part of the Cretaceous period. Microfossils are generally most valuable when one has only small drilling samples to study; in fact, they are the only fossils that are likely to be complete after a drill bit has chewed the rock it encountered into small pieces.

For correlation, animals that had wide geographic ranges but very restricted time ranges (that is, those which appeared on the scene, became widespread, and either changed or became extinct rapidly) are best. Fossils of such animals are generally called *index fossils*.

Nearly everyone has seen a fossil of some sort: the replaced skeleton of an ancient shellfish, a dinosaur footprint, a shark's tooth, a piece of petrified wood, or the like. Each year more and more "rockhounds" are beginning to collect fossils along with, or even instead of, minerals and rocks. They find fossil collecting to be a most interesting and stimulating avocation. Some of these collectors also make worthwhile contributions to paleontology.

A few bits of information and words of advice may be useful to those who are interested in pursuing this hobby. Just as for mineral and rock collecting, a relatively few pieces of equipment are needed. Generally a prospector's pick, or brickmason's hammer, a chisel or two, a hand lens, paper for wrapping, and labels will suffice. Several other pieces of equipment, such as a paintbrush, suede brush, old dental tools, needles, tweezers, and a sledge or even a shovel, may also be of use. A boat and a ladder are desirable if a collector wishes to work along the bluffs of the coastal area. Final preparation of a fossil specimen is often done in the laboratory or workroom. Here chemicals and even a binocular microscope may be of great aid.

Most fossils occur in layered sedimentary rocks. In Virginia this means that most collecting will be restricted to the Coastal Plain, Valley and Ridge, and Plateau geomorphic provinces and to the Triassic basins on the Piedmont (fig. 4.16, p. 103). All natural and man-made exposures—outcrops, railroad and highway cuts, excavations, and quarries—are worth a look. Weathered exposures are most likely to yield good specimens. A few guidelines to follow are:

1. *Be sure to get permission before entering private or government properties.*

2. *Try to obtain whole animals.*—It is especially important with the arthropods and vertebrates, if only a single part is found at first, to hunt for more parts because a skull, backbone, tooth, or some other particular part or parts may be necessary for identification.

3. *Be sure to label each specimen.*—Include on the label not only the location of the exposure but also a description of the rock unit from which the specimen is taken. The objective is to record the locality so that anyone may find it.

In addition, if other fossils are present in the same or different rock units at the locality but for some reason or other cannot be or are not collected, photograph or sketch them. This may be valuable information because a group of associated fossils usually affords much more information about, for example, environmental conditions than any single fossil does. Such associations are called *faunas* (if animals), *floras* (if plants), and *biotas* (if both animals and plants).

Undoubtedly the best advice that can be offered to anyone interested in collecting fossils is that a professional paleontologist or a well-trained and experienced amateur should be contacted for suggestions on how to start and how to proceed. Correct field and laboratory methods will be invaluable. In addition, the professional may be willing to give directions to good localities for collecting and even to suggest activities that may be of value to the science as well as of general interest. The "old hand" will be especially needed when the collector starts to classify his fossils and to place them in their proper category within the lower hierarchies. Professional paleontologists are usually associated with geology departments of colleges, universities, museums, and certain mineral industries and with state and federal geological survey offices.

Table 3.4 briefly summarizes fossil occurrences in Virginia. There are almost innumerable fossil localities in the Coastal Plain region of the state. Within the almost flat-lying sediments of this province there are representatives of all animal and plant phyla that have hard parts capable of being fossilized. Outstanding examples of both invertebrate and vertebrate fossils from these sediments were reported as early as 1835. Yet even with continual hunting and collecting since that time, extremely fine specimens are still being found rather frequently. As late as 1960 an almost complete whale fossil—with a skull "about twice as long as that of the largest whale previously found in the East Coast Miocene"—was discovered by an amateur collector. (As was proper, it was recovered by experts from the Smithsonian Institution.) Although large pectens, oysters, and sharks' teeth are the most commonly collected fossils, numerous kinds of vertebrate remains, generally considered more exotic, are not rare. These include remains of crocodiles, fish, porpoises, sea turtles, skates, and walruses. For those who are interested in microfossils, diatoms, foraminifers, ostracodes, and sporomorphae are locally abundant. And, as already mentioned, fossil spores and pollen from these sediments constitute the evidence for a luxuriant rain forest in the region during Cretaceous time.

Numerous fossil localities also occur in the Valley and Ridge and the Cumberland Plateau provinces of the Commonwealth. Rocks of these provinces span Paleozoic time with the exception of the last period, the Permian. Fine fossil representatives of nearly all the phyla have been collected from these rocks. Exceptionally fine archaeocyathids, numerous articulate brachiopods, cystoids, blastoids, crinoids, many different mollusks (including both straight and coiled cephalopods), trilobites, ostracodes, eurypterids, graptolites, conodonts, and ancient plants have been found. Some of the corals and their associated algae and other animals constituted local reefs. The large scorpionlike eurypterids referred to earlier have been found in shales associated with Mississippian coal beds in Coal Bank Hollow near Blacksburg. In addition, unconsolidated deposits on top of bedrock and cave deposits within limestone and dolomitic rocks of these provinces have yielded interesting faunas and sporomorphae. Perhaps the most famous of these are the vertebrate fossils found in the deposits around the ancient brackish, or salty, marshes of the Saltville area. These deposits have yielded mastodon tusks up to eleven feet long and other less spectacular bones and teeth of bisons, caribou, horses, woolly mammoths, extinct muskoxen, and ground sloths. In addition, fossil pollen and spores have been found in these deposits. Different sporomorphae have also been collected from lignite deposits that occur sporadically within colluvium along the western foot of the Blue Ridge. These have been determined to be of Late Cretaceous and/or Early Tertiary age.

Even though dinosaur tracks are not uncommon in red shales of the Triassic basins on the Piedmont, only a few good localities for other fossils have been found in these rocks. In Virginia only the Clover Hill (Winterpock) locality in the Midlothian Basin and a couple of lesser horizons within the Farmville Basin are noteworthy. Numerous plants, saurian teeth, fish scales and partial skeletons, and worm burrows have been described from these areas.

Although there are only two good, well-authenticated fossil localities in the metamorphic rocks of the Piedmont and Blue Ridge provinces, collectors should always be on the lookout for fossils in these rocks. A discovery in these rocks could be of extremely great geological importance. The one rock unit that has yielded rather outstanding metamorphosed fossils is the Arvonia slate (fig. 3.19). The fossils include bryozoans, brachiopods, trilobites, and echinoderms. They indicate the rock to be of Late Ordovician age.

Table 3.4 gives a general idea of the distribution of different major

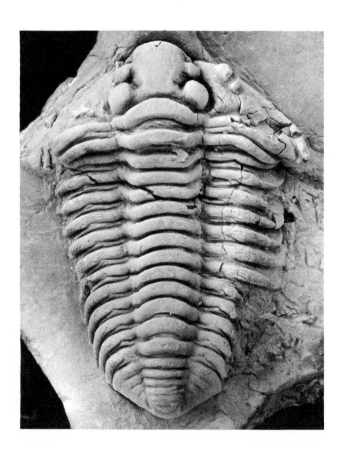 

FIG. 3.19. Undistorted and distorted trilobites. The two trilobites, although different species, belong to the same family; in other words, the two trilobites would have resembled each other when alive. The distorted one on right is a nearly flat surface of Ordovician Arvonia Slate; the distortion appears to have resulted from folding and/or metamorphism of the enclosing rock (see also fig. 3.20). (Photographs by C. G. Tillman)

groups of organisms within rocks in Virginia. Those who become truly interested in fossils will soon learn that such generalizations— even if used in conjunction with geologic maps—are of little real value. The real need is for each person to keep abreast of the professional literature pertinent to his interest(s) and to maintain contact with professional paleontologists and with other amateurs whose interests are like his own. One of the best words of advice to the beginning collector is that he should always remember that one of the best ways to gain acceptance within the "inner circles" is to search actively and discover localities on his own so that he may contribute as well as receive information of interest to the group.

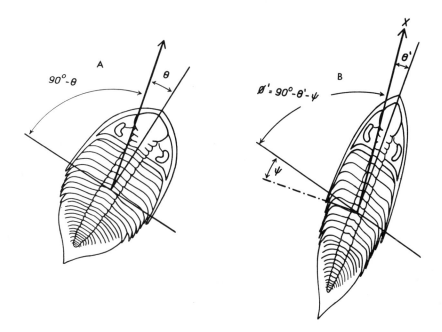

FIG. 3.20. Diagram of fossil distortion. Notice that the distortion shown in the righthand diagram is opposite in sense to that indicated by the orientation of the trilobite in figure 3.19. These two diagrams indicate a kind of analysis that may be made of distorted fossils. Such analyses often offer valuable clues in structural investigations. (Modified and reprinted, by permission, from J. G. Ramsay, *Folding and Fracturing of Rocks,* © 1967, by McGraw-Hill Book Company)

TABLE 3.4. Ranges and Reported Occurrences of Common Fossil Groups in Virginia

PHYLUM OR SUBKINGDOM	ANIMAL OR PLANT	RANGE*	REPORTED OCCURRENCES IN VIRGINIA									
			Coastal Plain			Basins	Plateau		Valley and Ridge			
			Quaternary†	Tertiary	Cretaceous	Triassic	Pennsylvanian	Mississippian	Devonian	Silurian	Ordovician	Cambrian
Protozoa:	foraminifers	Cambrian–‡	X	X	X		X	X	X	X	X	
	radiolarians	Cambrian–	X	X					X			
Porifera:	sponges (spicules)	(?)Precambrian, Cambrian–	X	X	X		X	X	X	X	X	X
	(?)archaeocyathids	Early-Middle Cambrian										X
Coelenterata:	stromatoporoids	Cambrian–Cretaceous					X	X	X	X	X	
	tetra-corals	Ordovician–Permian						X	X	X	X	
	octa-corals	Triassic–	X	X								
	tabulate corals	Ordovician–Permian					X	X	X	X	X	
Brachiopoda:	articulate	Cambrian–	X	X			X	X	X	X	X	X
	inarticulate	Cambrian–	X	X			X	X	X	X	X	X
Bryozoa		Ordovician–	X	X	X		X	X	X	X	X	
Echinodermata:	stelleroids	Ordovician–		X								
	echinoids	Ordovician–	X	X	X			X				
	crinoids	Ordovician–					X	X	X	X	X	
	blastoids	Silurian–Permian						X	X			
	cystoids	Ordovician–Devonian							X	X	X	
Mollusca:	pelecypods	Ordovician–	X	X	X		X	X	X	X	X	
	gastropods	Cambrian–	X	X	X		X	X	X	X	X	X
	cephalopods	Cambrian–	X	X	X		X	X	X	X	X	
	nautiloids	Cambrian–	X	X	X		X	X	X	X	X	
	ammonoids	Devonian-Cretaceous			X		X	X	X	X		
Annelida		(?)Precambrian, Cambrian–		X		X						?
Arthropoda:	trilobites	Cambrian–Permian						X	X	X	X	X
	ostracodes	Cambrian–	X	X	X		X	X	X	X	X	
	crabs	Triassic–	X	X								
	arachnids	Silurian–						X				
	eurypterids	Ordovician–Permian							X	X		
	insects	Devonian–	X									
Chordata:	graptolites	Cambrian–Mississippian						X	X	X	X	X
	fishes	Ordovician–	X	X		X			X	X		
	amphibians	Devonian–	X	X								
	reptiles	Pennsylvanian–	X	X								
	dinosaurs et al.	Triassic-Cretaceous				X						
	birds	Jurassic–	X	X								
	mammals	Triassic–	X	X	X							
Incertae sedis:	conodonts	Cambrian-Triassic						X	X	X	X	

TABLE 3.4 (cont.)

PHYLUM OR SUBKINGDOM	ANIMAL OR PLANT	RANGE*	REPORTED OCCURRENCES IN VIRGINIA									
			Coastal Plain			Basins	Plateau		Valley and Ridge			
			Quaternary†	Tertiary	Cretaceous	Triassic	Pennsylvania	Mississippian	Devonian	Silurian	Ordovician	Cambrian
Thallophyta:	algae	Precambrian–						X	X	X	X	X
	diatoms	Cretaceous–	X	X	X							
Embryophyta:	lycopsids	Devonian–	X			X	X	X	X			
	sphenopsids	Devonian–	X			X	X	X	X			
	pteropsids	Silurian–	X	X		X	X	X				
	angiosperms	Cretaceous–	X	X	X							
Sporomorphae		(?)Precambrian, Silurian–	X	X			X	X				

* No definitely Precambrian fossils have been reported from Virginia. It seems likely that several of the blanks in this chart will be filled as paleontological investigations are continued within the state. The Permian and Jurassic periods are not known to be represented by sedimentary rocks in the Old Dominion; hence they are not included in the chart. Tertiary includes the (Paleocene), Eocene, (Oligocene), Miocene, and Pliocene; the two in parenthesis are not known definitely to be represented in Virginia, although the Aquia Formation may be wholly or in part Paleocene. Quaternary includes Pleistocene and Recent.

† Several fossils of Quaternary age have also been found within some of the caves and marsh deposits in western Virginia.

‡ A long dash after the name of a period means that the range extends to the present. The reader's attention is drawn to the geologic time scale (table 5.1, p. 127).

FIG. 4.1. Natural Bridge. (Photograph by Flournoy, Virginia Chamber of Commerce)

LANDFORMS serve as the basis of all the questions posed in the
Preface—for example, "How was Natural Bridge formed?" This
calls attention to the fact that landforms are the geologic features
which are the most familiar to most people. The branch of geology
that deals with all such questions—What is that landform? How was it
formed? Why is it where it is?—is called geomorphology. Geomorphology[1] may be defined therefore as the description and study of
landforms and the processes that are responsible for their evolutions
and thus for their appearances.

To describe a geomorphic feature, good observational powers are
the primary requisite. One does not even need to acquire a technical
jargon. To decipher the geomorphic history of an area, however, a
thorough knowledge of the processes that act upon materials at or
near the surface of the earth is needed. In many cases a combination
of good observations and insight permits significant interpretations,
predictions, and even recommendations if they appear to be
warranted.

Geomorphic processes fall into two major classes: *degradation*
(tearing down) and *aggradation* (building up). Degradation, often
called erosion, involves both the breaking up (weathering) and the
moving (transportation) of material. Weathering may be chiefly
chemical or chiefly physical; transport may be the result of gravitational forces alone or of these forces plus running water, wave action,
groundwater, wind, or glacial ice motion either singly or in combination. Aggradation involves the deposition or accumulation of material
and thus may be looked upon as an end product of transportation.

Anyone who has seen a tarnished fork, a rusty nail, or a crack in a
sidewalk over a tree root has witnessed a result of weathering.
Weathering includes all the physical and chemical processes which
serve to decay or break up rocks and rock materials that are exposed
to atmospheric effects (figs. 4.2–5).

Chemical weathering, also termed *decomposition,* involves such
activities as solution, oxidation, hydration, and carbonation. Some of

---

[1] Physiography, the term that is sometimes used practically as a synonymous
term, has a broader coverage. It includes geomorphology, climatology, certain
aspects of oceanography, and other branches of natural science.

FIG. 4.2.   Spheroidal weathering. Exposure along Blue Ridge Parkway in south-western Floyd County. As shown on diagram, weathering may convert rectangular blocks into rounded forms. (Diagram reprinted, by permission, from A. N. Strahler, *Introduction to Physical Geography,* 2d ed., © 1965, by John Wiley and Sons)

FIG. 4.3.   Residual boulders. Near the top of Sharp Top of the Peaks of Otter. (Photograph by P. Flournoy, Virginia Chamber of Commerce; drawing reprinted, by permission, from A. N. Strahler, *Introduction to Physical Geography,* 2d ed., © 1965, by John Wiley and Sons)

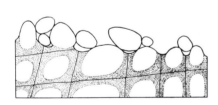

FIG. 4.4. Physical weathering. Angular exposure formed as the result of chiefly physical weathering near the top of the Blue Ridge in Nelson County, Virginia. (Photograph courtesy of Norfolk and Western Railway)

FIG. 4.5. Physical weathering. Growth of plant roots in cracks often promotes or enhances weathering. (Photograph by H. C. Porter)

the reactions may be represented by chemical equations. Commonly cited examples are:

$$\text{(1)} \quad \underset{\text{(water)}}{H_2O} \quad + \quad \underset{\substack{\text{(carbon} \\ \text{dioxide)}}}{CO_2} \quad \rightarrow \quad \underset{\substack{\text{(carbonic} \\ \text{acid)}}}{H_2CO_3}$$

$$\text{(1a)} \quad \underset{\substack{\text{(carbonic} \\ \text{acid)}}}{H_2CO_3} \quad + \quad \underset{\substack{\text{(calcite or} \\ \text{limestone)}}}{CaCO_3} \quad \rightarrow \quad \underset{\substack{\text{(calcium bicarbonate,} \\ \text{which is water soluble)}}}{Ca(HCO_3)_2}$$

$$\text{(2)} \quad \underset{\text{(K-feldspar)}}{2KAlSi_3O_8} \quad + \quad \underset{\text{(water)}}{2H_2O} \quad + \quad \underset{\substack{\text{(carbon} \\ \text{dioxide)}}}{CO_2} \quad \rightarrow$$

$$\underset{\substack{\text{(a clay} \\ \text{mineral)}}}{H_4Al_2Si_2O_9} \quad + \quad \underset{\text{(silica)}}{4SiO_2} \quad + \quad \underset{\substack{\text{(potassium carbonate,} \\ \text{which is water soluble)}}}{K_2CO_3}$$

Chemical weathering tends to prepare materials for ready transport (1a, 2, and others) and/or to produce products that are more stable than the original substances under the extant temperature, pressure, and chemical (especially moisture) conditions (2 and others). Most of the chemical reactions involved in weathering require the presence of water, the "universal solvent," and are enhanced, as are nearly all chemical reactions, by relatively warm conditions. The formation of soil is one of the many important consequences of chemical weathering.

Physical (or *mechanical*) *weathering,* also termed *disintegration,* involves the loosening and breaking up of large fragments into smaller ones without changing the compositions of the original substances. Some of the common causes are frost wedging, plant growth, and the activities of animals. Frost wedging, which sometimes causes the breaking up of rock materials, occurs when water within cracks and pore spaces of rocks or rock materials freezes. (Water expands approximately 10 per cent when it freezes.) Growing plant roots may also loosen or break up rocks and rock materials. Animals may disrupt unconsolidated rock debris by burrowing or trampling. Step-like features formed by trampling are rather common on hillsides in pastures (fig. 4.6). The work of earthworms as burrowers is prodigious. In areas where exposed rocks are made up of mineral components which react differently to heating and cooling, temperature changes alone may cause disintegration if the changes are of sufficient magnitude and fairly abrupt.

Chemical and physical weathering processes frequently act together. For example, chemical activities may be hastened by increasing the absolute surface—the total external surface area—of attack. In the laboratory, this effect is achieved by grinding up a few large pieces into many smaller ones; in nature, disintegration causes the diminution of grains. Conversely, chemical decay rather frequently facilitates physical loosening and breakage.

Nonetheless, in many places the over-all characteristics of landscapes and other manifestations of weathering strongly support an interpretation that either physical or chemical weathering has been predominant. In general, warm humid regions are characterized by rounded rock exposures and topography and other evidences of chemical weathering (fig. 4.3), whereas cold dry areas more commonly have angular rock outcrops and topography and other features usually attributed to physical weathering (fig. 4.4).

The nature of the rock is another important control of the features that develop. This control, however, is not absolute; it is dependent upon climate. That is to say, one rock might be more resistant than another in a cold and dry region but less resistant than the same rock in a warm and humid area. It is therefore necessary to have data relating to climatic and other conditions in order to consider fully the relative resistances of diverse rocks.

Roadcuts afford the commonest and most easily accessible exposures where the results of any but extremely superficial weathering effects may be examined. In Virginia's roadcuts there are good examples of such diverse features as spheroidal weathering (fig. 4.2),

FIG. 4.6. Terraced slope. These "terraces" in northeastern Floyd County, Virginia, were formed as a result of trampling by cattle plus soil creep.

poorly-to-well-developed soil profiles, and thick saprolites (figs. 4.7 and 4.8). Saprolite is the name given to unconsolidated, near-surface material in which certain structures of the parent rock are still easily recognized.

Domelike exposures, such as Striped Rock, which is located just north of Independence in Grayson County, have been interpreted by

FIG. 4.7. Shallow soil. Essentially A-C-D (see Table 4.1), developed on Martinsburg Shale in western Virginia. (Photograph by H. C. Porter)

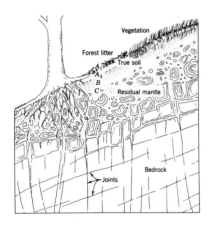

FIG. 4.8. Deep soil and saprolite developed on granitic gneiss in the Piedmont of Virginia. The light zone near the surface is A; the thick zone in which rock structure can still be recognized is an excellent example of saprolite. (Photograph by H. C. Porter; sketch reprinted, by permission, from A. N. Strahler, *Introduction to Physical Geography,* 2d ed., © 1965, by John Wiley and Sons)

many geologists as exfoliation domes formed chiefly as the result of chemical weathering. There are, however, alternative interpretations. For example, the present surface may represent the original top of the igneous mass, or the surface may have developed as the weight of overlying rocks was removed and fracture surfaces were formed in response to accompanying releases in pressure. This is a fine example of the numerous geological problems yet to be solved.

The formation of soil, as already mentioned, is probably the single most important result of weathering so far as man is concerned. Man is dependent upon soil for his very existence. The three main kinds of unconsolidated rock materials in Virginia are *residuum*—material formed essentially where it now is; *colluvium*—material that has moved down slope under the influence of gravity; and *alluvium*—stream-deposited material. Soils have been developed from each of these kinds of unconsolidated rock material. Colluvial soils occur on many slopes in the Blue Ridge and the Valley and Ridge provinces. Residual soils, most of which are thin, are found on the tops and upper slopes of many of the ridges and mountains. Thicker, well-developed residual soils are present in the Piedmont and Coastal Plain provinces. Alluvial soils are located along several streams and rivers and sporadically elsewhere within each of the geomorphic provinces of the state. Table 4.1 is a schematic soil profile. Under Virginia's

TABLE 4.1. Hypothetical Soil Profile with All Principal Horizons

A_{00}	Loose leaves and organic debris, largely undecomposed	
A_0	Organic debris, matted or partially decomposed	
A_1	Mineral matter mixed with high content of organic matter; dark colored	A
A_2	Horizon that has undergone maximum removal of materials as a result of solution or suspension transport in water; light colored; typical in Podzolic soils but slight to no development in Chernozemic soil.	
A_3	Transitional to B but more like A than B; may be absent	
B_1	Transitional to A but more like B than A; may be absent	
B_2	Horizon of maximum accumulation of clay minerals and/or iron and organic matter, maximum development of blocky or prismatic structure, or both	B*
B_3	Transitional to C	
C	Weathered parent material; may contain layers of accumulated calcium carbonate (C_{ca}) or calcium sulfate (C_{cs}); may be absent	C
D	Any stratum beneath the soil—for example, hard rock	D

SOURCE: Modified from diagram in U.S. Department of Agriculture, *Soil: The 1957 Yearbook of Agriculture* (Washington, D.C., 1957).
NOTE: No one profile would contain all the indicated horizons, but each profile has two or more of them.
* May include "G," gley or glei, which is a horizon consisting of more or less sticky and compact soil materials which are gray or bluish gray in color and typically structureless; it is poorly drained and apparently developed under the influence of excess moisture.

current climate most of the soluble materials, such as carbonates, have been leached from the soil. As indicated in the table: In many places there is a thin layer of organic litter, decayed plant materials and the like ("duff"), on top of A. The A horizon has lost much of its clay fraction and iron as well as its carbonates. The B horizon is a zone of accumulation of material moved in suspension in ground water from A. The C horizon is transitional with the underlying bedrock, D. If the B horizon becomes hard and impermeable, it is commonly called "hardpan." Where there is a very thick saprolite, there may be a zoning below B which from the fresh rock surface-ward consists of weathered rock, structured saprolite, and massive or essentially structureless saprolite.

The main result of weathering, however, is not soil formation. It is the preparation of rock materials for transport, either physical or chemical, from higher to lower elevations. A loosened rock fragment may drop directly, bounce along, or even slide to the bottom of a cliff or a fairly steep hill. An undercut stream or wavecut bank may slump or slough off. Unconsolidated rock debris, often called mantle, may creep very slowly down a fairly gentle slope. Gravity is the chief agent responsible for each of these processes. *Mass wasting* is the term generally applied to these phenomena, and colluvium is the designation given the material so moved.

Much more material is moved as the result of mass wasting than of any other kind of natural transport. All that is necessary for mass wasting is material to be moved and a slope down which the material may move. The tendency, of course, is to decrease the differences in relief. In general, the steeper the slope, the faster the movement.

Whereas talus slopes, slumps, and landslides (fig. 4.9) are quite

FIG. 4.9. Landslide. Along highway near Claypool Hill in Tazewell County. (Photograph by H. C. Porter)

obvious, the results of creep may not be. Unconsolidated material which has been moved by creep may, in fact, closely resemble residuum. In some places, however, creep has resulted in such features as leaning fence posts and trees with bent trunks.

Mass wasting can be a major cause of loss of soil. Several methods have been formulated to check such movements. Fortunately, one of the commonest causes of mass wasting may be dealt with rather easily. The general rule is not to remove natural growth from relatively steep slopes. If the rule has already been broken, damage may often be alleviated by planting something that will help anchor the remaining mantle. The preparation for such planting should generally involve contour plowing.

Unfettered mass wasting is usually kept on the move through the action of one of the other natural transportation agents. For example, streams commonly transport materials away after they have moved downslope, thus making room for material farther upslope to continue its downslope movement, and so on ad infinitum.

Mass wasting grades into running water activity through a process usually called mudflow. Mudflows, as the name would suggest, are pasty mixtures of unconsolidated material and water that flow downslope in response to gravity. Essentially all gradations between flowage of dry mantle and of sediment-laden streams occur.

About a third of all of the water that falls on the land as rain or snow becomes directly involved in the activities of *running water* (figs. 4.10 and 4.11). These activities may include hydraulic action,

FIG. 4.10. Stream action. New River Gorge in Giles County is a good example of stream erosion. (Photograph by T. M. Gathright, Jr.)

FIG. 4.11. Stream deposit. Little Stony Creek near Pembroke in Giles County sometimes carries large fragments during flood stage; very small amounts of water flow mainly below the surface, within the stream deposits, during dry periods. (Photograph by T. M. Gathright, Jr.)

cavitation, abrasion, solution, transport, and deposition. *Hydraulic action* is the designation given to force inherent in the water itself. In general, this action is of little consequence. The effect is sometimes increased, however, when air bubbles are included in the water; the activity is then termed *cavitation. Abrasion* is the wearing away of, for example, a stream channel as the result of impacts on the materials of the channel by fragments carried in the water. The concomitant breaking and wearing of the fragments themselves is called *attrition. Solution* is relatively unimportant in nearly all cases. It is mostly a subsurface groundwater phenomenon, although the solutions formed by groundwater activities may become part of surface runoff. Transportation occurs by *traction* (pushing or rolling along the bottom), *saltation* (hopping), or *suspension* (floating within the water). Abrasion and attrition occur, of course, as a result of fragment transport. Deposition by streams has seldom been of great enough extent to be recognized in the geologic record. Deltaic deposits, which consist of stream-transported materials, are described briefly in chapter V.

Several of the activities of running water have been analyzed mathematically; a few have even been resolved into equations or "laws." For example, it has been shown that the effective diameter of a fragment that running water is able to move is directly proportional to the square of the velocity of the water. (Thus, for example, by merely trebling the velocity, a fragment with a nine-times-larger effective diameter may be transported.) This accounts for the fact that most streams carry much larger fragments in their relatively steep gradient headwaters than in their relatively flatter downstream portions and also during flood stages as compared with "normal" flow. Other activities of running water, although apparently less susceptible to such definition, have been closely investigated, particularly those of practical significance. For example, the Mississippi drainage system has been replicated at the U.S. Waterways Experiment Station at Vicksburg, Mississippi, so that effects of such things as local heavy precipitation and flood control dams may be studied and their results predicted.

One of the major principles relating to stream erosion, the base-level concept, was first proclaimed by the American geologist Major John Wesley Powell, who is probably best known as the first navigator of the Grand Canyon. This concept recognizes the general principle that a stream cannot deepen its channel below sea level ("ultimate" baselevel) or locally below some downstream control surface like a falls or a lake ("local" or "temporary" baselevel).

Several other aspects of and results dependent upon running-water activities are of interest to the geomorphologist. It suffices here to pose a few questions that may serve as "food for thought" for the reader: What would the long and cross profiles of most of Virginia's streams look like at different places along their courses? How might one control slope wash or runoff in order to impede gullying or other soil erosion? Why do some stream systems within the Commonwealth have rectilinear patterns while others have highly irregular patterns? Why do some parts of some of the state's streams have meandering courses? Why are the alluvial deposits where streams come out of the Blue Ridge to flow on the adjacent lower regions made up chiefly of rather large fragments? Why do these streams almost always have water in their headwater reaches, whereas they are often dry in the deposit areas?

During the time it has taken to read this account about some of the activities of running water, more than three and one-half million pounds of sediment were added to the Gulf of Mexico by the Mississippi River. Within the next month more than 130 million pounds of rock material will be carried from the United States into the Gulf and the Atlantic and Pacific oceans. Many of these materials will undergo further transport within the oceans. These activities will modify the shapes of the oceanic basins and their coastal features.

The ceaseless pounding of waves (fig. 4.12) on the seashore undoubtedly impressed men long before the famous encounter of King Canute and it will doubtless continue to impress future generations. Further observation will serve mainly to emphasize the continuity, magnitude, and kinds of wave actions and how these actions move material, help shape coastlines, and do various other things. Geological considerations of the seas are not, however, restricted to investigations of wave action. They also include such things as bottom topog-

FIG. 4.12. Wave activity is ceaseless. (Photograph courtesy of Norfolk and Western Railway)

raphy, chemistry of sea water, marine biology, and current and tidal activities. Research relating to subjects such as these belongs to the realm of oceanography. (For more about diverse aspects of this fascinating and rapidly expanding field of study the reader's attention is directed to some of the books and articles listed in the Supplementary Readings.)

From the geological viewpoint, the erosional roles of the sea are largely overshadowed by its role as a basin of deposition. Ocean basins are the loci of ultimate deposition for essentially all rock material that becomes exposed, weathered, and eroded at the earth's surface.

Activities of the oceans and their resulting features are usually designated by the adjective *marine*. In fact, the marine and nonmarine realms are the two major subdivisions so far as many geological considerations are concerned. Only a few of the numerous marine activities and features are worthy of note here.

The coast of Virginia is best described as a low plain, with bluffs here and there along the shore. The northern part of the Eastern Shore has an offshore bar that extends from southeastern Delaware across all of Maryland's coast into Virginia. The southern coastal area of the state similarly has an offshore bar that extends southward through Kitty Hawk, North Carolina, to beyond Cape Hatteras. The area between is made up of Accomack Peninsula with its fringe of small, disconnected offshore bars and shoreward swampy lagoons and the water connection between the open sea and Chesapeake Bay. It is especially enlightening to compare and contrast the features of this coastline with those of the coast of California, Oregon, and Washington. There, beaches are essentially restricted to bay areas between headlands that are undergoing rather rapid erosion.

Although the offshore bars along the coast of the Mid-Atlantic states may reflect simply deposition by breakers, it seems likely that at least some of them also reflect in some manner the counterclockwise eddies of the Gulf Stream that moves in a general southwest to northeast direction along this section of the coast.

Wave forms have depth below as well as height above the general level of the water. Breakers start to form wherever a wave form reaches water too shallow to contain its total dimensions. Initially, the wave form merely steepens but finally it curls over and "breaks." In doing this, a turbulence is set up, and materials of the bottom within the area of the break are usually suspended and carried shoreward. Under certain conditions the materials are deposited to form a bar just shoreward from the general breaker line.

Marine erosion involves the same processes as stream erosion—namely, hydraulic action (including cavitation), abrasion (including attrition of fragments), solution, transport, and deposition. Solution is a relatively insignificant process almost everywhere. Wave action and tidal and other currents all carry on the other activities. (Undertow, by the way, is merely the downslope, generally seaward flow of water back into the basin.) Just as floods increase stream activity, storms increase marine activities. Also, just as streams tend to level the land, the ocean tends to straighten its coastline. Both activities work toward the wearing away of continents.

Perhaps one of the most interesting aspects of shoreline processes so far as Virginia is concerned is that several features within a few miles of the present coastline indicate that formerly there were lower (emergence) and higher (submergence) sea levels than that of the present day. The estuaries of the Potomac, Rappahannock, York, and James rivers, which are stream valleys that have been flooded by the sea, attest to the lower sea level in former times. The presence of several marine erosional and depositional forms on land attests to former times of higher sea levels. Two especially well-defined sets of such features are related to the Surry and the Suffolk scarps. The Surry Scarp is farther inland and appears to be more ancient than the Suffolk Scarp. Each of the scarps, which appear to reflect a relatively long period of formation, is nearly parallel to the present coast. They very likely were formed during times when higher sea levels existed all over the world, probably when less water was tied up in glacial ice than is at present.

Man is able to impede marine erosion just as he can most other types of natural destruction. Generally, he does so by constructing groins or breakwaters to divert certain waves and currents. Dredging has also been effective in some instances. The main hazard in these efforts is that it is easy to overlook some of the possibly bad side effects of artificial controls.

Lakes are like oceans in that they too are basins of water into which sediment is carried and deposited. Large lakes, in particular, may witness several of the same general activities as the oceans and thus may exhibit similar features. The activities and the features of lakes are often described as *lacustrine*.

Lakes are formed whenever, wherever, and however a stream is dammed. They are short-lived, geologically speaking, in that they start to fill up with sediment as soon as they are formed, and the filling, if uninterrupted, persists until the lakes no longer exist. In this suicidal process, swamp formation is a common, relatively late-stage event.

Although there are several thousand lakes in the United States, nearly all are located within glaciated areas. In Virginia the only present-day natural lake is Mountain Lake in Giles County. Lake Drummond in the Dismal Swamp, although once a natural lake, is now almost wholly artificial. Numerous artificial lakes or impoundments, however, have been developed within the state and many more are scheduled. The life expectancies of the impoundments, which may range from a few years to centuries, are important considerations for the power companies and water-supply boards which are financing the construction of the dams. Predictions are based on knowledge gained through the study of previously formed lakes, both man-made and natural.

Eolian (aeolian) is the descriptive term usually applied to natural wind activities and features. The transportation activities of the wind are important only in dry areas which are more or less devoid of vegetation (fig. 4.13). Even in these places the wind generally merely

FIG. 4.13. Windblown sand. Near coast of eastern Virginia. (Photograph by Kanode, Norfolk and Western Railway)

shifts small fragments from one place to another (and perhaps back again). Therefore, even in a desert, for example, one good rain every several years may be a more important erosion agent, in the long run, than all the daily wind activities.

Careful studies have shown how the direction and velocity of the wind and the amount of material available for movement control both the creation and the maintenance of various dune forms. Knowledge of these factors is a basic requirement for those who find it necessary or advisable to try to control wind activities. Such control is often desired because transportation by wind may have rather far-reaching effects. The great loss of top soil from the Dust Bowl of the central United States during the 1930's serves as a tragic example. The conditions that caused the great loss of top soil were created when the soils were exposed by cultivation and then dried by a drought. Exposed and dry, they were easily taken up by the wind and blown away. Establishment of a vegetation cover atop bare areas is the only sure method of preventing such catastrophes.

Glacial activities differ from stream activities mainly because the higher viscosity of ice permits it to carry much larger fragments than water can. Furthermore, this higher viscosity precludes the sorting of the fragments carried by the ice. An additional difference depends upon the fact that glacial ice cannot dissolve anything.

Most geologists agree that Virginia has not undergone glaciation within Pleistocene or Recent times. There are, however, a few features at relatively high elevations within the Old Dominion which may have been formed in response to Pleistocene (Ice Age) periglacial or subglacial conditions, that is, the conditions that exist near areas undergoing active glaciation. One cannot help but wonder what beauty might have been added to Virginia's Blue Ridge and some of her other western ridges if they had "suffered" glaciation, particularly mountain glaciation.

Subsurface water, commonly called *groundwater,* is different from the other natural transportation agents in that it carries essentially all of its load in chemical solution. Most groundwater is able to dissolve certain rock materials because it is a weak acid or base. Upon dissolving the materials, the water generally carries them away, in solution, to be redeposited elsewhere. Sometimes groundwater solutions rejoin runoff water. Water with a few dissolved materials is termed *soft;* water with a dissolved mineral matter content of more than about 250 parts per million is commonly described as *hard*.

The numerous caves and associated sinkholes and natural bridges in western Virginia are fine examples of the great amount of material that may, under certain conditions, be dissolved and transported away as the result of groundwater activities. Stalactites and other cave growths are evidence for the opposite process, deposition by precipi-

FIG. 4.14. New River Cave. Cave deposits in a chamber of one of the several hundred noncommercial caves in western Virginia. (Photograph by J. W. Murray)

tation from the solutions (fig. 4.14). The mineral springs of western Virginia also reflect chemical activities of groundwater. On the other hand, most of the hardness of the water pumped from wells on the Coastal Plain of Virginia has little, if anything, to do with these activities. It is, instead, a reflection of sea-water incursion from the Atlantic Ocean.

The study of groundwater is a geologic endeavor of steadily growing importance. The reason is that man is becoming more and more dependent upon the availability of relatively pure water for several significant uses (see chapter VII).

All weathering, transportation, and associated activities cause landscapes to undergo continual change. The face of the earth reflects the complexity of the changes that have occurred and that will continue to occur. The aim of the geomorphologist is to gain an understanding of landforms and their evolution. This understanding may become the basis of attempts to modify future geomorphic evolution.

Fortunately, man has been interested in landforms for such a long time that a vast amount of literature on the subject is available. This literature ranges from the almost wholly descriptive to the highly interpretive. Interpretations range from the sound to the widely speculative. Some hypotheses have been resolved mathematically.

G. K. Gilbert, a famous American geologist, introduced the concept that landforms tend to evolve systematically. The Swiss geologist L. Rutimeyer and the American scientist T. C. Chamberlain extrapolated these ideas to a concept that has been called the "concept of topographic age." Chamberlain, in fact, described different topographic features as exhibiting youth, maturity, or old age. W. M. Davis, another American geologist, elaborated on these age ideas and more than anyone else popularized the concept now widely known as the "concept of the geomorphic cycle." Although this concept has value, especially in giving the beginning student a good overview of the subject, Davis's use probably overemphasized its applicability. A very simple example of one of the innumerable possible geomorphic cycles is presented in figure 4.15.

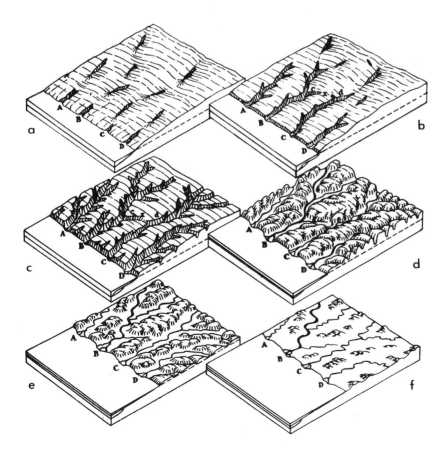

FIG. 4.15. Ideal geomorphic cycle promoted by mass wasting and stream activity under a humid-temperate climate on homogeneous rocks: *a*, initial stage, showing gullies developing at points where the runoff is concentrated; *b*, early youth, showing headward growth of young valleys; *c*, later youth, showing reduction of the initial surface to irregular ridges; *d*, early maturity, showing dissection of interstream areas into slopes and development of straths; *e*, later maturity, showing decrease in relief, reduction of slopes, and widening of valleys; *f*, old age, showing development of peneplane with monadnocks. (Reprinted, by permission, from C. R. Longwell, A. Knopf, and R. F. Flint, *Outlines of Physical Geology*, 2d ed., © 1941, by John Wiley and Sons)

Several things must be kept in mind with regard to a geomorphic cycle. Although it is a time concept, no absolute period is implied, only the amount of work already accomplished versus the amount to be accomplished in order to complete the cycle if that cycle is allowed to go on uninterruptedly to completion. No one area exhibits, or has been observed to go through, all of the stages of a cycle. It takes too long. Therefore, reconstruction of the stages of the cycles has been based on observations at several places or only deduced. The landforms of an area depend not only on the stage within the pertinent cycle but also upon the climate, the composition and structure of the underlying rocks, the elevation of the area above sea level (the ultimate baselevel), the distance of the area from the sea, and the identity and relative importance of the active processes. Thus, each cycle must be based on all of these variables if it is to serve any useful purpose. In addition, the fact must never be overlooked that any given geomorphic cycle may be interrupted at any stage as the result of such things as uplift, volcanic activity, and/or climatic changes, including those that may result in world-wide sea-level changes. Several areas have undoubtedly undergone multicyclic evolution because of such interruptions.

Nonetheless, once familiar with the cycle concept and its vagaries, one may find it extremely valuable for reference as well as for certain other considerations. The statement "The area has the appearance of maturity," for example, may give a reader a general concept about an area that otherwise might require thousands of words of description. It must be emphasized, however, that such a statement should not be construed to imply that there is evidence that the area passed through a stage of youth in its development. The area may, in fact, never have had a youthful character. The cycle concept may also be useful in suggesting things to look for when one is attempting to reconstruct a geomorphic history.

Any region with an over-all similarity of landforms may be called a geomorphic province. Virginia includes parts of five such provinces. From east to west, these are the Coastal Plain, the Piedmont, the Blue Ridge, the Valley and Ridge, and the Cumberland Plateau (fig. 4.16). Like the other twenty-odd geomorphic provinces of the coterminous United States of America, each of these provinces is fairly distinct. The distinctive characteristics relate to bedrock, topography, soil, and vegetation or to some combination of such features.

The *Coastal Plain* of Virginia is a generally oceanward-sloping surface of very low topographic relief with a maximum elevation of about 300 feet above mean sea level. The plain continues generally to the east beneath the Atlantic Ocean to form the continental shelf, which extends some 200 miles or less off shore to where the water is 80 to 100 fathoms deep. Although the land portion of the Coastal Plain extends only from Cape Cod on the northeast, the over-all province actually extends from Newfoundland to Florida and thence around the Gulf of Mexico.

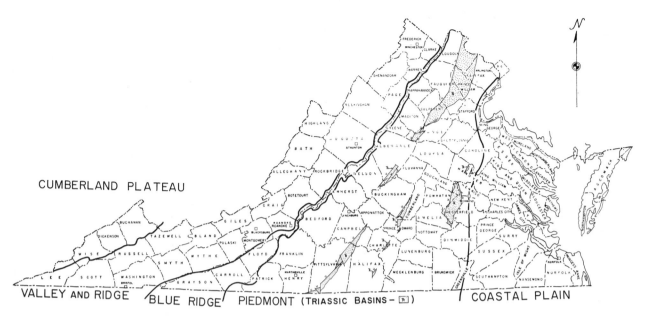

CUMBERLAND PLATEAU

VALLEY AND RIDGE   BLUE RIDGE   PIEDMONT (TRIASSIC BASINS - ▣)   COASTAL PLAIN

FIG. 4.16.   Geomorphic provinces of Virginia.

The bedrock of the Coastal Plain is made up of partially consolidated sedimentary rocks that dip generally to the east at slightly steeper angles than the slope of the over-all surface. The rocks consist of Cretaceous, Eocene, and Miocene marine sands (some of which contain fairly large percentages of glauconite), gravels, clays (a few of which are lignitic), shell marls, and diatomaceous sediments. In places the rocks are overlain by Pleistocene, Recent, and possibly Pliocene sand and gravel veneers, some of which constitute marine terraces formed when the level of the ocean was higher.

As already mentioned, the onshore part of the Coastal Plain exhibits characteristics of both emergence and submergence, such as shell beds on land and drowned valleys, respectively. The surface is slightly dissected in that the general slope of the surface is steeper than the gradients of the streams that cross it. There are local swamps, of which the Great Dismal Swamp is the largest. The coastline is cut deeply by branching bays and estuaries. Because of the resulting appearance it has been referred to somewhat poetically as a "fringe of peninsulas." Here and there, bluffs up to 100 feet high border the the estuaries. Fine natural harbors, sandy beaches, and barrier beaches are common.

Most of the streams north of, and including, the James River and a few to the south are tidal as far west as the Fall Line. The line was so named because it marks the zone where each stream has a rapids or falls as it flows from the relatively harder metamorphic rocks of the Piedmont onto the softer sedimentary rocks of the Coastal Plain. Examples are the "Great Falls" of the Potomac River, which is less than three miles upstream from the District of Columbia; the Rappahannock falls of between 40 and 50 feet, within two miles of Fredericksburg; and the James falls of about 85 feet, within three miles of the center of Richmond. Although the line is not so apparent away from the stream valleys, it is generally considered by geomorphologists to mark the western edge of the Coastal Plain Province. Geologically, the boundary essentially coincides with the western edge of the wedge of Cretaceous-Tertiary sedimentary formations.

The geomorphic province directly west of the Coastal Plain is called the Piedmont. The term *piedmont* appears to have been first applied to an actual area in what is now northwestern Italy. It has since been used for several areas in its more or less literal sense, that is, to indicate position at or near the foot of a mountain or mountain range.

In the United States the term appears to have been first applied, in the literal sense, to an area northeast of Roanoke, Virginia. It is unclear how this application became extended to designate the whole broad area between southern New York and central Alabama that is now called the Piedmont Province. It suffices to say that the name has been so extended and that it is now widely applied in this broader sense by both professional geologists and laymen. Therefore, even though this usage is recognized as a corruption of the original word, it seems futile even to advocate a change.

The *Piedmont Province* within Virginia has a rolling landscape (fig. 4.17) – a surface of gentle slopes where valley bottoms, valley sides, hillsides, and hilltops all merge without any well-defined break in slope. There are, however, a few exceptional features such as *monadnocks* (isolated mountains like Willis Mountain in Buckingham County) and streams with relatively steep-walled valley sides. Nonetheless, the over-all character of the province is that of a well-defined old-age-erosion surface, commonly called a *peneplane*. In Virginia the province is about 30 miles wide just south of the Maryland border and about 160 miles wide at the North Carolina line. The

FIG. 4.17. Rolling landscape typical of the Virginia Piedmont near Warrenton. (Photograph courtesy of P. Flournoy, Virginia Chamber of Commerce)

main surface, excluding monadnocks, slopes generally toward the east from an elevation of 1,000 to 1,350 feet above mean sealevel to the Fall Line, which is about 300 feet above mean sealevel throughout the Old Dominion.

The Piedmont is underlain chiefly by Precambrian and Paleozoic metamorphic and igneous rocks, but it also has relatively large areas underlain by Triassic sedimentary rocks and sporadic basaltic sills and dikes. Although the trends of the metamorphic rock units and their foliations are rather diverse because of complex structures, there is a general northeast-southwest regional trend. In contrast, most of the Triassic rocks are structurally uncomplicated and most have relatively low dips.

Prolonged weathering, much of which has apparently taken place under relatively humid temperature conditions, is indicated by soils and saprolites containing such minerals as gibbsite and by weathering profiles which are at least 150 feet deep in some places. Because much of the area is covered by relatively deep soil, the topographic grain (trend of surface features) does not reflect the rock trends except where there are prominences with little or no soil cover. The major streams also show little apparent control by the trends in the underlying bedrock. In fact, they flow generally southeastwardly, across the regional trend. Nonetheless, certain segments of each of the major streams and several of the tributaries do reflect the underlying geology remarkably well. A fine example is the James River between Lynchburg and Scottsville, where it flows northeastwardly for nearly 45 miles within a belt underlain by relatively soft marble.

The mode of origin for the general old-age surface and for the drainage pattern of the Piedmont has long been a subject of great interest to geomorphologists (see Thompson reference in Supplementary Readings).

As one approaches the adjacent province to the west, the Blue Ridge, the main surface of the Piedmont is more and more interrupted by an increase in the number, height, and over-all dimensions of mountains and ridges (fig. 4.18). Nonetheless, in many places the main old-age surface of the Piedmont extends uninterruptedly to the base of the Blue Ridge and in a few places is recognizable even between spurs of the Blue Ridge Escarpment.

The *Blue Ridge Province* is a long, narrow area that extends from south-central Pennsylvania through Maryland, Virginia, and western North Carolina to northwestern Georgia. Within Virginia the province consists of two rather distinct parts: one northeast of the Roanoke River, the southernmost stream that breaches the Blue Ridge, and the other southwest of the river.

Northeast of the Roanoke River the province is an irregular mountain chain, which ranges from a single ridge less than two miles wide (fig. 4.19) to a complex group of closely spaced ridges with an over-all width of ten to fourteen miles. The area is relatively rugged, has many rock exposures but also several slopes covered with rubble

FIG. 4.18. Peaks of Otter with Bedford, Virginia, in the foreground. These peaks are near the western edge of the Piedmont. (Photograph courtesy of Norfolk and Western Railway)

or talus, and supports a sporadic growth of scrub fir and other trees and bushes. Although the general character is one of irregularity, neighboring summits are commonly about the same elevation. Summit elevations range from about 1,200 feet near the Potomac River to nearly 4,100 feet just southeast of Luray. Southwestward from Luray there is another, although less marked, general decrease in elevation of the "crest" toward Roanoke.

Southwest of the Roanoke River, the Blue Ridge Province is a dissected mature erosion surface, commonly termed upland, that ranges up to nearly seventy miles in width. This part of the province is marked by a gradual increase in breadth and a general increase in summit levels southwestward from the Roanoke River and northeastward from northeastern Georgia to a culmination in the Smoky Mountains of western North Carolina. On the upland there are forty-six peaks and forty-one miles of divide above 6,000 feet as well as numerous peaks and three hundred more miles of divide above 5,000 feet. In Virginia the hilltops of the main upland surface range from 2,300 to 3,200 feet in elevation and neighboring peaks have roughly the same elevations. The elevation of the main surface is greater near the North Carolina–Virginia state line than northeast of

FIG. 4.19. Blue Ridge. Looking north from the southwestern side of Sharp Top of the Peaks of Otter. (Photograph courtesy of National Park Service)

it. Monadnock mountains and ridges, such as Buffalo Mountain and Willis Ridge in Floyd County, are as much as 1,000 feet above the surrounding hilltops. Mount Rogers, which at 5,719 feet is Virginia's highest elevation, is on this upland.

Rejuvenation of streams that drain the upland is actively taking place today. It may reflect relatively recent uplift or the removal or downcutting of a local baselevel control downstream from the province, or perhaps even a combination of such processes.

The bedrock of the Blue Ridge differs rather markedly from place to place. Along the western margin throughout Virginia, there are relatively resistant, late Precambrian and early Cambrian clastic sedimentary rocks. East of these late Precambrian volcanics occur in some places (for example, northeast of Waynesboro and southwest of Speedwell) with several diverse Precambrian and Paleozoic metamorphic and intrusive igneous rocks in other places.

In the area northeast of the Roanoke River the general topographic grain reflects the trends of the bedrock units rather faithfully. In the upland part of the province to the southwest the interrelationships are more like those on the Piedmont, that is, where the unconsolidated overburden is relatively thick, there is little if any direct correlation between rock structure and topography whereas in places where the soil is thin or essentially absent, most trends of the rock units and their foliation are expressed topographically.

The differences between the two parts of the province are mainly dependent upon their different drainage histories. The ridges northeast of the Roanoke River are drained wholly by steep-gradient portions of streams of Atlantic Ocean drainage, that is, either by tributaries of streams that flow directly to the ocean or by tributaries to the segments of the three Atlantic slope rivers of Virginia that have cut gorges through the Blue Ridge (the Potomac at Harpers Ferry, the James west of Lynchburg, and the Roanoke east of Roanoke) to drain the western side of the province. On the other hand, south of the Roanoke River nearly all of the upland is drained by low-gradient reaches of streams of the Gulf of Mexico drainage basin (in Virginia mainly by the New River and its tributaries but also in a small part by tributaries of the Holston River).

As noted, the Blue Ridge–Piedmont boundary north of the Roanoke River ranges from sharp to rather gradational. The boundary southwest of the Roanoke is more easily defined because the upland has an east-facing escarpment (fig. 4.20). The only real problems in

FIG. 4.20. Part of the Blue Ridge Escarpment located about 22 miles southwest of Roanoke, Virginia, and 22 miles southeast of Blacksburg, Virginia. Note the sprawling spurs. (Aerial photo with scale of approximately 1:20,000 and bottom to east. Courtesy of U.S. Department of Agriculture, Soil Conservation Service)

establishing the boundary for this southern section involve outlying masses like Cahas Knob in Franklin County, which certainly was part of the main upland until relatively recently, and areas like the Meadows of Dan, which are on the upland but are now drained by tributaries of direct Atlantic master streams. Quite arbitrarily the outliers have been assigned to the Piedmont Province, whereas the Meadows of Dan is generally considered to be part of the upland.

It is thus evident that the eastern escarpment of the upland is one side of an asymmetric divide. And, even for exceptional areas such as the Meadows of Dan, the escarpment certainly was the divide until rather recently. Asymmetric divides of this type are usually shifting toward the area drained by the lower-gradient streams. This divide is no exception. Piracies of low-gradient streams on the upland side of the divide by steep-gradient streams of the escarpment have been relatively common in the past, and others appear to be imminent. The headwater portion of the Dan River that drains the Pinnacles and Meadows of Dan is a fine example. Both geomorphic and biological evidence support the hypothesis that this part of the Dan was part of the New River system until it was captured by a headwater tributary of the Dan River that eroded its valley back into the escarpment to the junction of piracy. (For more information about this relationship see the writer's paper cited in the Readings.)

The western boundary of the Blue Ridge Province is geologic as well as geomorphic. The Late Precambrian–Early Cambrian clastic sequence, which consists chiefly of conglomerates, sandstones, siltstones, and orthoquartzites, holds up relatively steep ridges, which are commonly covered with rubble and talus deposits; directly west of these, younger Cambrian shales and dolomites underlie a broad area of low relief which serves as fair to excellent farmland. Here and there, these areas, just as those along the eastern foot of the Blue Ridge, are veneered by alluvial gravels deposited where the gradients of the streams change rather abruptly from relatively high to relatively low. The base of the steep ridges is rather generally considered to mark the boundary between the Blue Ridge Province and the Valley and Ridge Province to the west.

The *Valley and Ridge Province,* as the name suggests, consists to a large extent of fairly well-defined valleys and intervening ridges (figs. 4.21 and 4.22). In Virginia this province, like the Blue Ridge, is naturally divisible into two areas: a northern one drained by direct Atlantic Basin streams and a southern one drained by Gulf of Mexico Basin streams. The Atlantic drainage part is made up of the Great Valley on the east and a series of subparallel, narrower valleys and ridges in the west. (The Great Valley includes the Shenandoah Valley which is so well known in song and history.) The Gulf of Mexico Basin part also has a relatively broad, nearly ridgeless area near its eastern boundary and several narrower valleys and ridges to the west. Its valley floors, however, are more than 1,000 feet higher than the major valleys within the northern subdivision of this province.

The rocks which underlie the Valley and Ridge Province range in

FIG. 4.21. Panoramic view of the Valley and Ridge. Note the three linear ridges near the horizon. (Photograph courtesy of Norfolk and Western Railway)

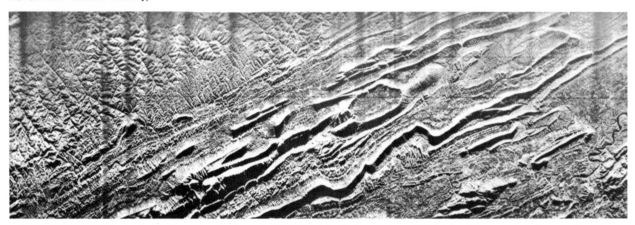

FIG. 4.22. Valley and Ridge. Southwestern Virginia from the air; oval-shaped area near center is Burke's Garden. (U.S. Air Force radar photograph furnished by the U.S. Army Engineer Topographic Laboratories, TOPOCOM)

age from about Middle Cambrian through Early Mississippian. The structural designation often applied to the province is the "Folded Appalachians." Most of the rock units trend northeast-southwest. Southeastward dipping thrust faults and asymmetric folds (see chapter VI) overturned to the northwest are common in southeastern belts. More open folds are common in the central and northwestern belts (fig. 6.14, p. 142). Most ridges are "held up" by Silurian sandstones; a few are underlain by Mississippian conglomerate. Most valleys, including the Great Valley and its counterpart in southern Virginia, are underlain by less-resistant shales and carbonate rocks. Relatively small igneous intrusive masses of post-Early Mississippian age occur sporadically within the province near Harrisonburg, Monterey, and Staunton; a few of these masses "hold up" discordant topographic features.

Only a few master streams cut across the trends of the rock units in the Valley and Ridge area. Most of the streams flow either within the main valleys, or down the valley sides, nearly perpendicular to the valley trends. This gives an over-all rectilinear drainage pattern often referred to as trellis drainage.

The boundary between the Valley and Ridge Province and the Cumberland Plateau to the west is geologic as well as topographic. Folded rocks give way to essentially flat-lying strata and consequently the linear ridges give way to highly irregularly shaped hills and valleys.

Cumberland Plateau is the name generally applied to the southern part of the composite Appalachian Plateaux Province. In Virginia this province is nearly restricted to the southwestern counties of Buchanan, Dickenson, and Wise. The area is a highly dissected plateau. As the word plateau indicates, the bedrock is relatively flat-lying sedimentary rocks, here of Mississippian and Pennsylvania age. In places, the dissection of the plateau is of such nature that the area has the appearance of mountains. Indeed, adjacent West Virginia, which is almost wholly within this province, has the nickname the Mountain State. The Virginia portion of the plateau is drained by streams of the Tennessee River system of the Gulf of Mexico Basin. The over-all drainage pattern may be characterized as highly irregular, tending toward dendritic.

Virginia's rich and varied geomorphic history has endowed her with several well-known scenic features. Millions of people have visited the Old Dominion's Blue Ridge, the numerous developed and undeveloped caves, Natural Bridge, the Breaks of the Cumberland, Natural Chimneys, and Mountain Lake. Less known but equally interesting are some of Virginia's falls and cascades, Natural Tunnel, the Pinnacles of Dan, and the sweeping meanders of the Shenandoah River.

The Blue Ridge Mountains of Virginia, long celebrated in song and folklore, are part of the already described Blue Ridge Province. The Skyline Drive–Blue Ridge Parkway, a scenic highway which is maintained by the National Park Service and which connects the Shenandoah National Park of Virginia and the Great Smoky Mountains National Park of North Carolina and Tennessee, gives ready access to many magnificent views and features of the Blue Ridge.

More than 1,250 caves are known in Virginia. With a couple of exceptions, all occur west of the Blue Ridge. Nearly all of them show evidence of at least two stages in their formation: the solution, or excavation, stage and the precipitation, or cave formation-forming, stage. The commercial caverns of Virginia—Battlefield-Crystal, Dixie, Endless, Grand, Luray, Massanutten, Melrose, Shenandoah, Skyline, and Virginia caverns—have been developed so that their remarkable features may be easily and safely seen. The features include stalactites, stalagmites, columns, draperies, flowstone formations, helictites, subterranean streams and pools, and "bottomless" pits. The undeveloped caves are visited yearly by hundreds of amateur cavers, or spelunkers.

Natural Bridge, one of the most famous geological features in the world, is located in southern Rockbridge County, about six miles northeast of Buchanan (fig. 4.1). It is said of the bridge, which was mentioned in a written account as early as 1742, that "Indians worshipped it, George Washington surveyed it, Thomas Jefferson owned it, and its visitors' register constitutes a Who's Who of American History." In precolonial days animals and Indians utilized this natural span to cross Cedar Creek, which flows beneath the bridge about two miles upstream from where it flows into the James River. Today U.S. Route 11, one of the main northeast-southwest highways through western Virginia goes over Cedar Creek on this natural span. Approximate dimensions of the bridge are: height of lower surface of the arch above the creek, 160 feet; width of span, 150 feet; thickness of rock of span, 37–50 feet; and intrados of arch, 150 feet. The rock that forms the bridge is a dolomite-bearing limestone of upper Cambrian age. Although there is some disagreement concerning its origin, most geologists who are best acquainted with the bridge and with the surrounding area favor the idea that most of a cave roof collapsed to leave only the part which is now the bridge.

Natural Tunnel is a similar feature, probably also of similar origin, located near Clinchport in Scott County. It has the following approximate average dimensions: length, 900 feet; width, 130 feet; height, 75 feet above creek level (Stock Creek of the Clinch River system); and thickness of arch, 200 feet. There is one large, nearly circular dome in the roof. The lower approach to the tunnel is through a deep gorge. Trains have utilized Natural Tunnel ever since a line was constructed through it in the late 1800's.

The Breaks of the Cumberland (variously called the Breaks of Sandy and the Grand Canyon of the South or of Kentucky) lie in a state-park area (official name Breaks Interstate Park) in northern Dickenson County and western Buchanan County, Virginia, and adjoining Kentucky. Within the park, Russell Fork River, a tributary of the Levisa Fork of the Big Sandy River system, has cut a gorge nearly five miles long in the Cumberland Plateau. The gorge is almost 1,000 feet deep in places and contains many remarkable erosional features referred to by such names as "The Palisades," "The Towers," and "The Chimneys."

The "Pinnacles of Dan" make up a somewhat similar area just southeast of the Blue Ridge Parkway in central western Patrick County. They owe their origin to deep cutting by a portion of the Dan River, which formerly was part of the New River system on top of the Blue Ridge Upland. The original meandering stream pattern has been preserved as the river has cut down through the rock.

The Natural Chimneys, also referred to as the "Cyclopean Towers" and the "Towers of Solon," are located about fifteen miles north of Staunton and one mile north of Mount Solon, in Augusta County (fig.

4.23). These "chimneys" are erosional remnants that rise nearly perpendicularly from the floodplain of North River. Weathering along numerous nearly vertical joints in a flat-lying impure limestone formation has resulted in the separation of the chimneys from the main

FÍG. 4.23. Natural Chimneys. Near Mt. Solon. (Photograph by Flournoy, Virginia Chamber of Commerce)

rock outcrops. Apparently North River removed the debris that fell when the chimneys were formed. Somewhat similar remnants may also be viewed in a beautiful setting along New River near Eggleston.

Perhaps one of the most interesting bits of scenery in the whole state is Mountain Lake, "The Silver Gem of the Alleghanies." This lake is located in Giles County, about twenty miles northwest of Blacksburg, Montgomery County. Its elevation (3,874 feet, nearly 1,000 feet above most of the surrounding ridgetops and more than 2,000 feet above New River, which is less than six miles from the lake) plus its size (about two-thirds mile long and nearly one-fifth mile wide) makes it outstanding among nonglacial lakes. Many modes of formation have been suggested for Mountain Lake: the lake fills a solution sink; the lake represents a stream that has been dammed by talus or slide-rock; the lake fills a glacial cirque; the lake fills a depression formed by some type of volcanic activity; or the lake fills a meteoric impact crater. Folding of the bedrock within the area has added complications to the formulation and acceptance of some of these hypotheses. The true origin has not yet been definitely established. Most data, both geologic and historical, appear to fit best a combination of hypotheses whereby the lake occupies a depression that was formed originally as the result of erosion and solution, probably controlled by the structural setting, but with part of the

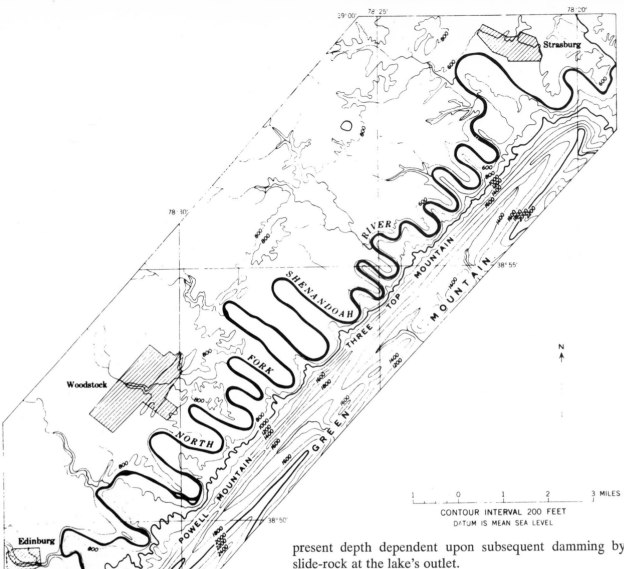

Strasburg

Woodstock

Edinburg

Base from U S Geological Survey topographic
map of the Strasburg quadrangle

N

1   0   1   2   3 MILES

CONTOUR INTERVAL 200 FEET
DATUM IS MEAN SEA LEVEL

FIG. 4.24. Meanders of the North
Fork of Shenandoah River (see text).
(Diagram from J. T. Hack, Professional
Paper 354A, 1959, U.S. Geological
Survey)

present depth dependent upon subsequent damming by talus and
slide-rock at the lake's outlet.

Both the North and South forks of the Shenandoah River exhibit
some of the finest meanders known anywhere in the world. The
best-developed ones are on the North Fork between Edinburg and
Strasburg, where the meandering course of the river is nearly fifty
miles long although the straight line distance is only about fifteen
miles (fig. 4.24). These meanders may be viewed from a few locations along the Forest Service road over Green Mountain east of
Woodstock as well as from the air.

Several rather picturesque falls and cascades occur in the Blue
Ridge and the Valley and Ridge provinces of Virginia (fig. 4.25). A
few are especially noteworthy. More water probably flows over the
cascades on Little Stony Creek in Giles County than over any other of
the 50-foot or higher falls in the state. Crabtree Falls, on the South
Fork of the Tye River near Montebello in western Nelson County,
and Twin Falls, where a pirated stream of the Blue Ridge Upland now
empties into Bottom Creek in southern Montgomery County, are the
highest. Each of these falls consists of both cascades and free drops.
They have over-all falls of approximately 500 and 400 feet, respectively. Falling Springs in Augusta County, which has been known

FIG. 4.25. Waterfalls near outlet of Mountain Lake in Giles County. (Photograph courtesy of Norfolk and Western Railway)

since its description by Thomas Jefferson, involves a drop of about 125 feet in the Jackson River of the James River Basin. Balcony Falls on the James River just downstream from Glasgow, although perhaps the best-known falls in the state, is hardly a falls at all with a drop of only a few feet.

There are innumerable other scenic rocks within the Commonwealth. Many impressive scenes await the interested visitor.

FIG. 5.1. Stratified rock. Imboden coal has been mined from lower part of this exposure, near Norton in Wise County. Note the differences in the thicknesses of the layers. (Photograph by T. M. Gathright, Jr.)

LAYERING is a common feature in sedimentary rocks (fig. 5.1). It is present because of differences in grain size, composition, arrangement of fragments, or some combination of such characteristics. The differences reflect changes that occurred during deposition.

The layers are usually called beds, or strata. The layering is usually referred to as stratification. The branch of geology that deals with these features is called stratigraphy and the professional who specializes in stratigraphy is called a stratigrapher.

Although stratigraphy literally refers only to the description of strata, most geologists consider that it includes interpretation and correlation as well. The aim of the stratigrapher is therefore to gain a knowledge of the earth's history as it is recorded in sedimentary rocks.

In his attempts to find answers to the pertinent questions—What happened? How did it happen? Where did it happen? When did it happen?—the stratigrapher has had to become somewhat of a "jack of all trades," to help himself to others' data, or to do both. Consequently he must be well acquainted with, if not proficient at, the tasks of the field geologist, the sedimentary petrographer, and the sedimentationist. In addition, he often needs paleontological skill; he may need knowledge of structural geology; and he may even find use for familiarity with certain geomorphic principles, activities, and/or features. As a result, the stratigrapher is today's professional who most closely resembles the layman's conception of the geologist.

The basic assumption of the stratigrapher is that a sedimentary rock reflects the environment in which its constituents were deposited. In some cases it may even reflect conditions that existed in the area from which the constituents were derived. The stratigrapher's task therefore becomes the deciphering of the history recorded in sedimentary rocks. He interprets the rocks he sees today in terms of what happened in the past. Thus this branch of geology, although based on description, is to a large extent an endeavor in quite the opposite direction: it relies very heavily on the making of inferences from observations. It is much like medical diagnosis in which the doctor has the current condition of a patient as the main fact upon which to reconstruct a medical history.

The previously alluded-to Principle of Uniformitarianism has long served as the main tenet upon which stratigraphic interpretations have been based. The principle was introduced in 1785 by the

Scottish naturalist James Hutton, "The Father of Geology." It was first given a wide audience in 1833 when the English geologist Sir Charles Lyell, in his book *Principles of Geology,* elaborated on the principle and its use as a basis for the inductive method in geological interpretation.

As previously stated, this principle says that "the present is the key to the past." This means that if one carefully and thoroughly observes and understands processes that are active today and if he keeps in mind universal physical and chemical laws, he will have a good basis upon which to interpret features of rocks that reflect geologic history. It does not mean or even imply, as some people have mistakenly stated, that everything that happened in the past is happening today or that everything that is happening today happened in the past.

It is readily apparent that one of the primary requirements of a stratigrapher is an understanding of as many of the interdependent aspects of present-day sedimentation as possible. Unfortunately, this requirement is all too often overlooked. Old mistakes based on judgment rather than on knowledge are perpetuated, and new errors continue to be introduced—generally by those stratigraphers who fail to avail themselves of the numerous opportunities that now exist for them to study present-day sedimentation processes and the resulting features.

The two fundamental processes responsible for sedimentation involve either physical deposition of fragments or chemical (including biochemical) precipitation of materials from solutions. The two major environments of sedimentation are marine, the environment of the sea, and nonmarine, the environment of the land.

Both nonmarine and marine sedimentation may take place in diverse realms. On land, deposition occurs in lakes, streams, swamps, and even on dry land; in the ocean, deposition occurs in the deep sea, or abyssal zone, on the continental slope, or bathyal zone, and on the continental shelf, or neritic zone (fig. 5.2). There is also a zone, not strictly marine or nonmarine, commonly referred to as the strand,

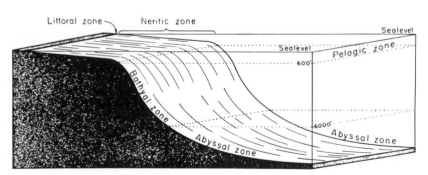

FIG. 5.2. Block diagram showing depth zones of the ocean. (Reprinted, by permission, from C. O. Dunbar and J. Rodgers, *Principles of Stratigraphy,* © 1963, by John Wiley and Sons)

shore, or littoral zone. It consists of the area between the levels of the lowest and highest tides and thus is alternatingly marine and nonmarine.

A large percentage of sedimentary rocks represent marine or mixed environments. For this and other reasons it seems fitting to consider some of the major features of a hypothetical marine delta to show the kind of background knowledge a stratigrapher needs as a basis for both his investigative procedures and his interpretations.

Where streams enter lakes, oceans, or other bodies of relatively still water, their currents are slowed, and thus their physical loads tend to be deposited. If the amount of sediment is large enough and the area of deposition is not subjected to waves or currents so strong that they scatter the sediment, a delta will be formed. The Greek historian Herodotus applied this term to such deposits as early as the fifth century B.C., when he noted the similarity of the over-all shape of the deposits at the mouth of the Nile River and the Greek capital letter delta (Δ).

Currently, there are a number of large marine deltas, such as those at the mouths of the Amazon, Colorado, Ganges, Hwang Ho, Mississippi, Nile, Paraná, Po, Rhine, and Yangtze rivers. Each of these is different from the others because of its having its own unique set of interdependent controls (fig. 5.3). The main controls are the discharge of the sediment-supplying streams, including the over-all quantity of sediments and their distribution in time; water depth and its variations at the site of deltaic deposition; and the strength and frequency of the currents and waves within the basin of deposition.

The hypothetical delta we shall consider is on a nearly north-south–trending coastline. The stream enters from the west. The drainage basin of the stream includes part of a broad coastal plain and a bordering range of relatively high mountains. Both the plain and the mountains have granitic rocks and marble as their predominant bedrock. The mountains are youthful in appearance: bare rock exposures are common and physical weathering predominates. The coastal plain is rather flat: a thick cover of unconsolidated mantle is present everywhere except in a few stream beds; chemical weathering is dominant. The climate for the area is humid and temperate with the rainfall fairly well distributed throughout the year. The mountains receive winter snow, most of which usually melts during spring thaws. The tributary streams in the mountains are cascading streams that can transport relatively large fragments, especially during the periods when snow is melting and there is a consequent relatively large increase in stream discharge. Each of these tributaries has built up a fairly large sand and gravel deposit on the plain at the foot of the mountains. The tributaries that rise on the plain, on the other hand, are relatively slow-flowing streams that carry small silt-sized and clay-sized particles in suspension and also notable quantities of material in solution. Directly after rains the suspended load is greater and consists of a larger than usual percentage of silt and occasionally

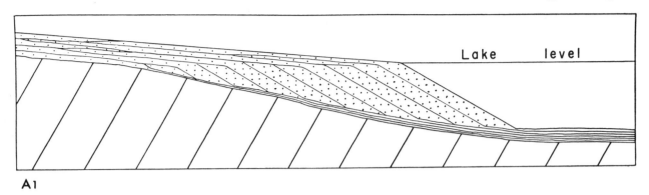

A1

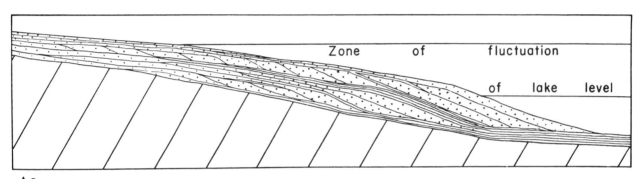

A2

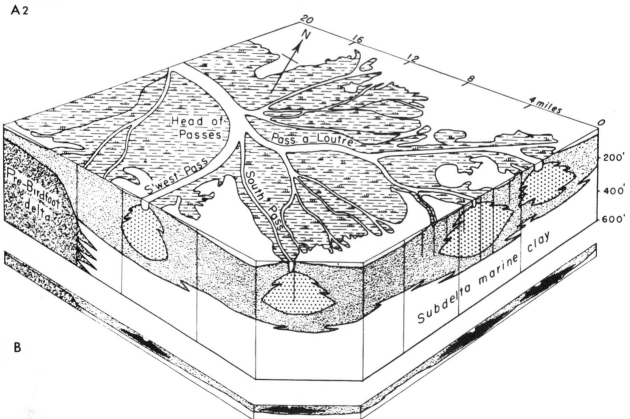

B

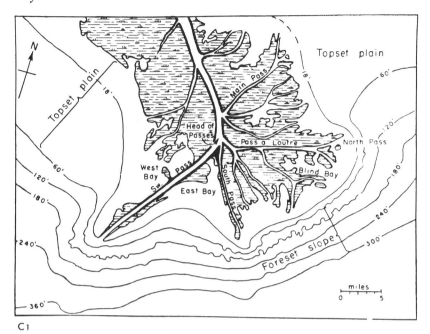

C1

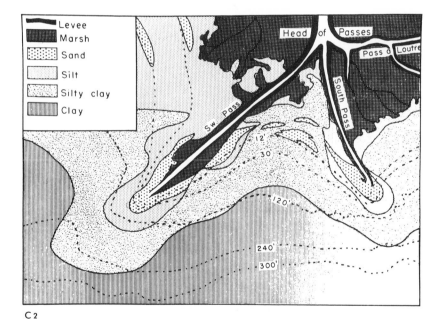

C2

FIG. 5.3. DELTAIC FEATURES: *A*, simple deltas—(*1*) with stable water level,
(*2*) with fluctuating water level; *B*, block diagram of a complex ("birdfoot")
subdelta — linear sand lenses deposited by the chief distributaries are shown in
stipple pattern on main diagram and in black on lower diagram; vertical ex-
aggerations are about 30 and 5, respectively (after H. N. Fisk
et al., 1954, Sedimentary framework of the modern Mississippi Delta, *Jour.
Sed. Petrology*, v. 24, p. 76–99, illus.); *C*, Birdfoot subdeltas—(*1*) of Mississippi
River (after Fisk *et al.*, 1954), (*2*) distribution of sediments of different sizes on
the southwest side of the delta in *C1* (submarine contours give depth in feet). (All
diagrams reprinted, by permission, from C. O. Dunbar and J. Rodgers, *Principles
of Stratigraphy*, © 1963, by John Wiley and Sons)

even some fine sand particles. The master stream is a sluggish, meandering one with a broad floodplain and all of the typical flood-plain features. It generally carries a large suspended load of fine sand, silt, and clay; a relatively smaller bed load chiefly of sand; and a noteworthy solution load. Periodic floods occur, especially when snow melts in the mountains, but a few smaller ones also follow most heavy rainstorms within the drainage basin. During the floods the master stream's physical load is greatly increased in quantity and often also in the size of the materials moved along as bed load.

The part of the ocean basin into which the stream flows was relatively deep at the onset of deltaic deposition. It is a large embayment, not an open coast, and thus is somewhat sheltered from wave activities. Tidal fluctuations range up to several feet. The sea level has been nearly constant since the beginning of deltaic sedimentation. The basin, however, has been undergoing continual sinking (subsidence) throughout the period.

Some of the major features of the delta are apparent in the diagrams of figure 5.3*B* and *C*. A few of the features shown, as well as a number that are not, are worthy of additional note. First and foremost, the delta may be seen to be a complex mixture of features formed in marine and nonmarine environments. Both its physical features and its fossil content present a confusing, interfingering array of characteristics commonly used as criteria for solely marine or solely nonmarine conditions. Nonetheless, there are three less-than-distinct kinds of beds; they are commonly designated as topset, foreset, and bottomset (see fig. 5.3*C*) Some of the topset beds extend outward into the bay for forty to fifty miles; their oceanward slope is about 5 feet per mile. The foresets extend another approximately twenty miles; their slope is about 120 feet per mile. Seawards, the foreset beds grade into bottomset beds, which are sporadically present, with no distinct break in slope. The sediments of any given sedimentation episode grade from coarser to finer seawards. The sediments get younger both upward and seaward because of the subsidence, compaction of the sediments, and seaward migration of the delta. In general, the thicker topset beds contain coarser grained sediments than the thinner ones do. These thicker, coarser layers reflect floods that occurred within the drainage basin of the stream. A few of the larger floods resulted in the deposition of sand on some of the foreset, as well as the topset, portions of the delta. Erosional scour produced local channels on the delta during some of the floods; later, however, these channels were filled to form sedimentary lenses similar in appearance to ordinary stream deposits. Natural levees along the nonmarine parts of the distributaries merge with similar features of the strand zone. Some of the latter outline the channels even during high tide. The delta has subdelta lobes at the ends of the channel extensions of most of the major distributaries. Both the main delta and these smaller lobes serve to modify features of adjacent areas within the basin of sedimentation. The fossil content of the deltaic sediments appears to represent an intermingling of marine, brackish, and nonmarine life. Some of the brackish and marine life forms are stunted. The total fauna is relatively limited in number of species, apparently because of pollutionlike effects involving the introduction of dirt and solutions by the river. There are a few local lenses of chemically precipitated minerals, chiefly calcite and aragonite, where pools of water stood long enough during low tide for evaporation to occur. Swamp litter also occurs sporadically. These, of course, are only a few of the numerous features of the hypothetical delta. A thick tome could easily be written that would include only descriptions, with no interpretations, of the deltaic features.

An additional term, *facies,* would find frequent use in such a description. A facies is any spatially and genetically associated group of rocks of the same age that are formed in essentially one environment. Deltas offer some of the finest known examples of situations in which different sedimentary facies are intimately intermixed.

In addition, it must be recognized that as sediments become part of the stratigraphic record (rock column), their constituents usually undergo changes as the result of compaction, recrystallization, and/or

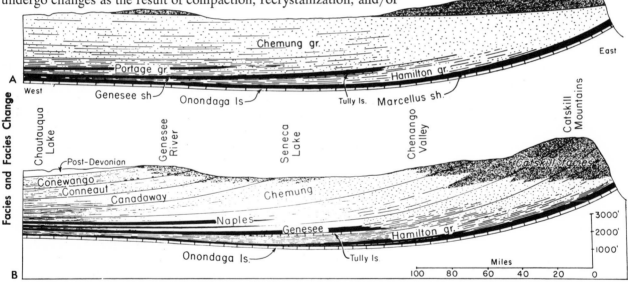

other alterations. Therefore, by the time a delta, for example, becomes exposed for geological field study, it will very likely offer problems much like those that the elephant did to the five blind men.[1] Nonetheless, several large deltas have been recognized within the stratigraphic record. An especially fine example is the Devonian Catskill Delta of New York and Pennsylvania. Before it was finally realized that these deposits represent a deltaic environment, however, the strata were misinterpreted for many decades by some of the finest minds in stratigraphy (fig. 5.4*A* and *B*).

[1] Each "saw" the part of the elephant available to him as follows: tail, a rope; leg, a tree trunk; body, the roof of a tent; ear, a large leaf; and trunk, a large snake.

FIG. 5.4. General east-west cross sections across the Paleozoic Catskill Delta in southern New York. *A*, a former incorrect interpretation; *B*, the current interpretation. Stratification lines indicate probably synchronous deposition. (Reprinted, by permission, from C. O. Dunbar and J. Rodgers, *Principles of Stratigraphy,* © 1963, by John Wiley and Sons)

Up to this point in this chapter, one of the most important aspects of stratigraphy has been almost ignored—the dimension of *time*. Time, of course, must be established if any chronological order of events is to be derived.

Geologists generally recognize two kinds of time—relative time and absolute time. Until the last few decades stratigraphers based most of their work solely on relative time—that is, a time dimension within which one rock is known to be older or younger, but not how much older or younger, than another. Even though methods for determining the "absolute age" of many rocks have more recently been found, relative time continues to serve widespread and extremely useful purposes. Among other things, its determination does not require the sophisticated laboratory equipment necessary for determination of "absolute age." (Suffice it to mention here that "absolute age" may be determined because radioactive isotopes undergo spontaneous disintegration at a constant rate and in such a manner that the ratio between an isotope and its product or products indicates the time elapsed since original incorporation of the parent radioactive isotope within the host mineral or rock.)

William Smith, often called the "Father of Stratigraphy," was one of the first workers to recognize and utilize the fundamentals of sedimentation that permit the geologist to determine the chronology of depositional events recorded in sedimentary rocks. These fundamentals are now referred to rather widely as "laws." The main "laws" pertain to (1) *the original horizontality of strata,* (2) *the original continuity of strata,* and (3) *the original superposition of strata.* They mean that (1) most strata are deposited horizontally, or nearly so; (2) strata are originally continuous over the total area of deposition —that is, they either lens out (thin to nonentity) or abut the boundary of their basin of deposition but do not have original discontinuities like those that might be inferred upon first look at erosion-developed gaps between cliff exposures; and (3) with the exception of cave deposits, more recent beds lie on top of more ancient ones as long as the layers have not been turned over after deposition.

On the basis of these "laws," geologists often try to correlate, or match, rock units from one exposure to another. Several methods and criteria are used. Two examples are: (1) the lateral tracing method, which consists of actually following, from one place to another, the physically continuous parts of a given layer, and (2) the matching of rock characteristics and/or fossil contents of an originally continuous unit which has had its parts separated by structural disruption and/or weathering and erosion processes (fig. 5.5). In the second method the correlation is generally enhanced if the characteristics of the units above and below the unit in question can also be shown to match.

At best, most such methods permit correlation within only a single geologic province. Yet the stratigrapher frequently desires to know the geographic relationships of a given time for a much larger area than a province, perhaps for a continent or even for the whole world.

These relationships are described as paleogeographic. Means for wider-range correlation have been diligently sought. Almost from the onset of these endeavors, it became apparent that fossils might be utilized, but it was equally apparent that their use would be restricted unless they could be used in conjunction with a standard time scale which would serve as a reference.

The utilization of fossils for correlation may involve individual species or groups of animals and/or plants (faunas, floras, or biotas). For an individual species to be of much use, it must have had a widespread geographic distribution but have existed for only a rather short time. When such a fossil is found, it is generally called a guide, or index, fossil. Most guide fossils, however, are not widely enough distributed to be useful in correlating rocks from different provinces. Therefore, groups of fossils are generally of most value. Fortunately, resemblances and similarities in the stage of development of assemblages have been found also to serve rather well for interprovince

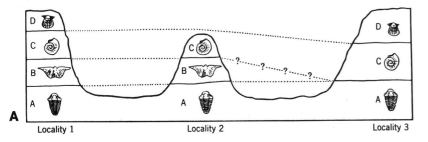

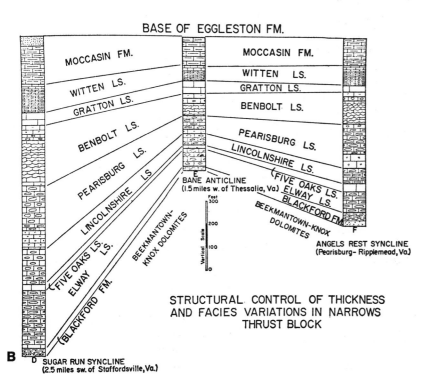

FIG. 5.5. Correlation of strata: *A,* based on fossil content; *B,* based chiefly on rock characteristics. (*A* reprinted, by permission, from C. R. Longwell, R. F. Flint, and J. E. Sanders, *Physical Geology,* © 1969, by John Wiley and Sons; *B* reprinted, by permission, from W. D. Lowry (ed.), *Tectonics of the Southern Appalachians,* © 1964, by V.P.I., Department of Geological Sciences)

correlation. Thus, as more and more data have been accumulated, it has become more and more possible to determine the part of the standard time scale to which just about any group of fossils should be at least tentatively assigned.

The geologic time scale evolved from the early work of Smith. Its development, most of which took place during the mid-nineteenth century, was the subject of much investigation, synthesis, and argument. The standard reference column now recognized by the U.S. Geologic Survey and, with slight modifications, by most geologists throughout the world is given as table 5.1.

The fact that nearly all the names come from the British Isles or western Europe is mainly a reflection of where the early work was done. Even the chief exception, the Permian, which was named for a Russian province, was named by an Englishman, Sir Roderick Impey Murchison, who worked there.

Ages for several of Virginia's stratigraphic units are given on tables 8.1, 8.2, and 8.3 (pp. 168–69, 175, 177). The rock unit names should not, however, be looked upon as time designations. Rock units differ from time units. Rock units are real; they can be delineated and mapped in the field. Time units are artificial; they have been established rather arbitrarily, although each was originally defined as the period during which certain rocks were deposited. The main time units are, from the longest to the shortest: era, period, epoch, and age. The main rock units are, from most to least inclusive: system, series, group, formation, member (tongue, lens, etc.), and bed (layer, stratum, lamina, etc.).

Formations are mappable in that each consists of essentially one kind of rock or of a genetically associated group of rocks that differ from the underlying and overlying units. Each is given a binomial name, such as Waynesboro Shale. The first term gives the name of a place where one can go to see a good exposure of the unit; the second gives the name of the predominant lithology (rock type) that constitutes the unit. The term *Formation* is used for units made up of several lithologies. As mentioned, rock units do not, except coincidentally, correlate with time units (see fig. 5.4*B*).

A third category, time-stratigraphic units, is also recognized by some geologists. These units may be correlated with the time units as follows: system-period, series-epoch, stage-age. Additionally, stages may be subdivided into zones, which have no direct time-equivalent terms. A time-stratigraphic unit may be defined as a rock unit deposited during a given span of geologic time—for example, rocks of the Ordovician system are those deposited during the Ordovician period.

As with all scientific endeavors, questions are frequently raised as to the purposes of stratigraphic investigations. The purposes are of two kinds: (1) those that are economically directed and (2) those that are philosophically oriented. The economically directed studies are based on the fact that a very large percentage of the earth's mineral resources are in sedimentary rocks. (These resources include the natural fuels, several building materials, and some metallic deposits. Some of the economic aspects are given in chapter VII. More than 90 per cent of the Old Dominion's annual mineral-production dollars, which amounted to $295.7 million in 1968, come from sedimentary

TABLE 5.1. Geologic Column and Time Scale

Era	System or Period (rocks) (time)	Series or Epoch (rocks) (time)	Approximate age in millions of years (beginning of unit)
Cenozoic (*recent life*)	Quaternary (an addition to the old tripartite 18th-century classification)	Recent	.01
		Pleistocene (*most recent*)	2.0 to 3.0
	Tertiary (Third, from the 18th-century classification)	Pliocene (*very recent*)	7
		Miocene (*moderately recent*)	25
		Oligocene (*slightly recent*)	40
		Eocene (*dawn of the recent*)	60
		Paleocene (*early dawn of the recent*)	68 to 70
Mesozoic (*intermediate life*)	Cretaceous (*chalk*)		135
	Jurassic (Jura Mountains, France)		180
	Triassic (from three-fold division in Germany)		225
Paleozoic (*ancient life*)	Permian (Perm, a Russian province)		270
	Carboniferous (from abundance of coal)		
	Pennsylvanian*		325
	Mississippian*		350
	Devonian (Devonshire, England)		400
	Silurian (an ancient British tribe, the Silures)		440
	Ordovician (an ancient British tribe, Ordovices)		500
	Cambrian (Cambria, the Roman name for Wales)		550 to 600
Precambrian	Many local systems and series are recognized, but no well-established worldwide classification has yet been delineated.		3500 or more

SOURCES: Approximate ages are from Holmes, 1964; Evernden, Savage, Curtis, and James, 1964; and The Phanerozoic Time Scale of the Geological Society of London, 1964. Reprinted by permission from James Gilluly, Aaron C. Waters, and A. O. Woodford, *Principles of Geology,* 3d ed., © 1968, by W. H. Freeman and Company.

NOTES: Definitions in italics are from the Greek.

Many provincial series and epochs have been recognized in various parts of the world for Mesozoic and older strata. Most of the systems have been divided into Lower, Middle, and Upper Series, to which correspond Early, Middle, and Late Epochs, as the times during which the respective series were deposited.

* Pennsylvanian and Mississippian Systems, named for States of the U.S.A., are not generally recognized outside of North America; elsewhere the Carboniferous System is regarded as a single system.

rocks.) The philosophically oriented studies are undertaken with the objective of learning more about this planet upon which man lives— its history, its relationships to the history of the universe, and so forth.

As noted in the preface, to the present time data are insufficient to permit formulation of a comprehensive geological history of the state. Nonetheless, a general history can be outlined; one is included as the final chapter (VIII) of this book. In addition, several relatively local events and conditions may be reconstructed in some detail. An example is given here in order to acquaint the reader with the kinds of things that may be determined. The example is a brief résumé of conclusions reached as a result of an investigation by C. R. B. Hobbs, Jr., geologist with the Virginia Division of Mineral Resources, W. D. Lowry, professor of geology at the Virginia Polytechnic Institute, and the writer (see Supplementary Readings).

Dolomite, chert, and quartz sand grains in Cambro-Ordovician rocks near Blacksburg and Mountain Lake, Virginia, together with information gained from laboratory investigations, show how, when, and where the dolomite and chert were formed (see table 5.2).

The most complete sequence of formation of any given group of the studied strata was one in which (1) one or more layers of calcium carbonate mud plus sporadic quartz sand grains, probably wind-blown, were deposited; (2) part of the calcium carbonate was

FIG. 5.6. Chert and dolomite relationships. At a locality near Mountain Lake, Virginia.

changed into calcium-magnesium carbonate (dolomite); (3) the dolomitization was interrupted by the introduction of silica, probably in solution, which replaced part of the remaining calcium carbonate but not the dolomite; and (4) another change in chemical environment occurred that resulted in a resumption of dolomitization, which continued until all the remaining calcium carbonate was converted to dolomite. In addition, it is clear that in some cases (5) the dolomite-bearing silica, existing after step 3, became exposed to the atmosphere and was cracked as a result of desiccation and that the resulting fragments were moved around before deposition of the next, overlying layer of calcium carbonate mud.

Certain evidences also suggest: (A) that the carbonates of these

TABLE 5.2. Data and Considerations Relating to Cambro-Ordovician Cherty Dolomite

Fact	Fancy	Remark	Text	conclusion
CaCO₃ pellets are known to form; dolomite and silica ones are not. Rock contains dolomite and silica pellets.	Original sediment was CaCO₃ pellets, which were later replaced by dolomite or silica (chert).	Although unlikely, dolomite and chert pellets could have been originally deposited as such.	1	B
Rock is well laminated.	This may indicate settling in relatively shallow, still water.	A shallow lagoon might be a good guess?!	1	
Sporadic quartz sand grains occur.	These were windblown.	Sporadic distribution is a clue (admittedly ambiguous).	1	
Dolomite crystals occur within chert.	Dolomitization started, was selective, and was interrupted by introduction of silica.	Alternative of formation of dolomite crystals within the chert is extremely unlikely; chert is impervious. Selectivity is indicated by replacement of CaCO₃ but not of silica sand grains.	2 & 3	
Quartz sand adjacent to dolomite is etched; this includes portions of grains only partly within chert. Alkaline solutions will attack silica.	Dolomitization continued after silicification; conditions were alkaline.	These "fancies" seem to be nearly unequivocal conclusions for the data.	4	A
Both dolomite and chert exhibit shrinkage cracking.	Sediments were intermittently exposed to atmosphere.	The type of cracking appears to represent desiccation, thus drying.	5	
A few of the pellets are only fragments. Some pelletiferous rock exhibits cross-bedding.	Some of the pellets were moved and redeposited.	This seems to be another unequivocal conclusion so far as the data are concerned.		C
Upper contacts of some chert beds are regular and parallel to bedding, whereas lower contacts are highly irregular.	Replacement, at least by silica, was close to sediment-seawater interface.	This suggestion is based on the idea that replacement started at the interface and continued downward.		D
Cherty dolomite rock contains no fossils; overlying limestone formation contains fossils.	Conditions during deposition of CaCO₃ and replacement by dolomite and silica were unfavorable to life; later, conditions supported life.	Alternative is that any fossils present in the sediment which is now a cherty dolomite were destroyed during the replacement processes; this seems unlikely considering how faithfully the pellets, lamination, and other minute sedimentary features were replaced.		E & F

rocks were accumulated in shallow oxygenated marine waters which were highly saline, probably abnormally alkaline; (B) that this shallow water environment favored precipitation of calcium carbonate as small pellets and oölites; (C) that after formation some of the pellets were moved about and redeposited; and (D) that the nearly complete conversion of the calcium carbonate to dolomite and/or silica was at or close to the sediment–sea water interface.

It also may be said that (E) the environment under which these activities occurred appears to have been generally unfavorable for marine life. In fact, the environment may be characterized as one that was "naturally polluted." Intermittently, however, changes took place —very likely the water had its salinity sufficiently reduced— to permit the invasion of certain marine animals. Their fossils occur in a few strata of the formation. Later, in fact, the generally unfavorable conditions were supplanted by conditions that supported a relatively abundant marine life (the overlying strata are fossiliferous limestones).

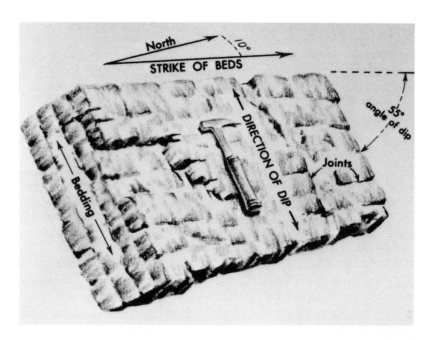

FIG. 6.1. Strike and dip (see definitions in text). (From G. D. Robinson et al., Professional Paper 505, U.S. Geological Survey)

D EFORM a rock(?) —disbelief is the immediate reaction most persons have when they are told that rock has been or may be folded. Nonetheless, there are many kinds of evidence that do, indeed, indicate that many rocks have been folded and/or otherwise deformed (see figs. 6.11–16).

The branch of geology that deals with rock deformation is generally called structural geology. Like most branches of natural science, structural geology has its own jargon. Terms have been introduced to facilitate both the description of deformational features and the consideration of genetic concepts. As a consequence, those who find it necessary or interesting to communicate with structural geologists or to read pertinent reports also find it necessary to familiarize themselves with a special vocabulary. Because of this fact and because consideration of the pertinent vocabulary will serve as a good framework for discussion of rock structures, much of this chapter consists of the introduction of terms commonly used in structural geology. The descriptions and discussions of the nomenclature deal largely with stratified rocks because, in general, they are the rocks which most clearly exhibit the structural features most likely to be encountered and readily recognized.

Although rock strata are typically deposited in more or less horizontal layers, they generally assume some nonhorizontal position as a result of deformation. Because of this fact, it has been necessary to establish standard symbols and designations to indicate the relationships on maps and in reports. Two parameters suffice to define completely the orientation of linear and/or planar features. These measurable values are called strike and dip (fig. 6.1).

The *strike* of a plane may be defined as the compass direction of any horizontal line in that plane. To put it another way, the strike of any nonhorizontal plane may be said to be the compass direction of any line produced by the intersection of any horizontal plane and the described plane. The direction is generally recorded in geological reports as, for example, N 45° E, which would mean that the horizontal line on the plane trends northeast-southwest.

The other parameter, *dip,* may be defined as the angle between the horizontal and the described plane. It is perpendicular to the strike on the measured plane. An additional condition to be imposed wherever possible derives from the fact that the true dip of a sedimentary layer is the angle between the horizontal and the original top of the layer.

As might be guessed, this restriction is necessary because some strata have had their orientations in space changed as a result of folding and/or faulting so that their original bottoms are now above their original tops. In geological reports the dip is generally recorded as the number of degrees in a certain direction, for example, 25° SE.

The map symbol for the plane with a strike of N 45° E and a dip of 25° SE would appear as ⟋$_{25}$. The symbol is placed on the map in such a manner that (1) it is on the location where the measurement was made, (2) the strike line is drawn with the proper orientation, and (3) the dip tick is drawn so it points in the direction toward which the plane slants downward. Other linear and planar features may also have their strikes and/or dips shown on maps. Horizontal and vertical dips are indicated by particular symbols. Frequently used structural symbols are shown in Appendix B, fig. 1, p. 184.

As already stated, strata may be overturned. Therefore, in order to define structures completely, it is necessary to determine which side of a given stratum is the original top and which is the original bottom. Fortunately, certain features commonly formed at the time of deposition of rock units permit the geologist to make such determinations. These features are usually described as geopetal. Some of the more common small-scale geopetal features are shown in figures 6.2 and 6.3.

FIG. 6.2. Geopetal features: *A,* right side up; *B,* overturned, that is, the original tops are toward the bottom of the page. (Reprinted, by permission, from C. R. Longwell, R. F. Flint, and J. E. Sanders, *Physical Geology,* © 1969, by John Wiley and Sons)

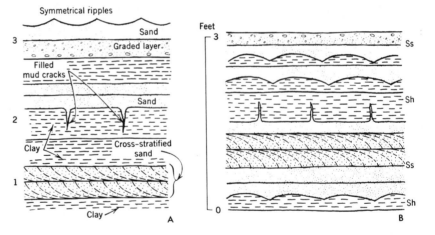

Larger-scale features that permit the geologist to tell stratigraphic tops from bottoms also occur. A relatively common group of these are termed unconformities (fig. 6.4). The formation of an unconformity requires not only a period of nondeposition but also the involvement of some erosional activity. Therefore, the presence of an unconformity usually aids the elucidation of the geological history of the area in which it occurs.

There are two major kinds of deformational structures: folds and fractures.

There are three main kinds of *folds* (fig. 6.5). Anticlines and synclines are relatively abundant in Virginia, especially between the

FIG. 6.3. Ripple marks and mud cracks: *top,* current ripple marks in *Upper* Cambrian dolomite of Tazewell County; *center,* interference ripple marks in Mississippian sandstone on High Knob in Wise County; *bottom,* mud cracks in Middle Ordovician silt-stone in Craig County (*Top,* photo-graph by W. E. Moore; *center* and *bottom,* photographs by T. M. Gath-right, Jr.)

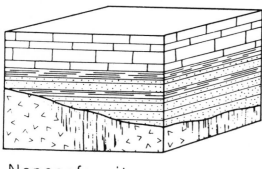

Nonconformity

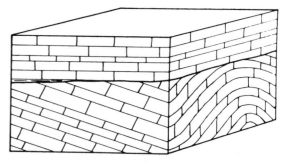

Angular unconformity

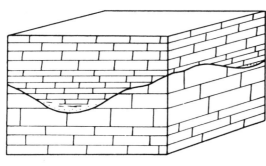

Disconformity

FIG. 6.4. Uncomformities: *A,* a nonconformity — sediments overlie igneous and/or metamorphic rocks; *B,* an angular unconformity — sediments overlie folded and truncated sedimentary rocks; *C,* a disconformity — sediments above and below the surface of erosion have essentially the same strike and dip. (Reprinted, by permission, from C. O. Dunbar and J. Rodgers, *Principles of Stratigraphy,* © 1963, by John Wiley and Sons)

Fall Line and the eastern border of the Cumberland Plateau. Although an anticline is commonly defined as an up-fold and a syncline as a down-fold, strictly speaking a fold cannot be defined on the basis of its position in space. The reason is that either an anticline or a syncline may be overturned, and with the simple up-fold or down-fold definition, an overturned anticline, for example, would be indistinguishable from a syncline. To avoid such possible ambiguity an *anticline* may be defined as a fold with the older strata nearer the center of the fold, whereas a *syncline* would be defined as a fold with younger strata nearer the center of the fold. Terms for different parts of folds are shown in figure 6.6. Plunge is another important parameter (fig. 6.7). As is also shown on figure 6.5, some anticlines and synclines with distinctive configurations or orientations have been given special designations.

Rock *fractures* are of two general kinds: *joints,* which exhibit only

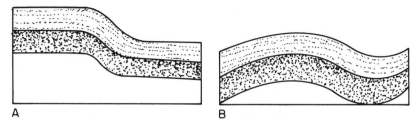

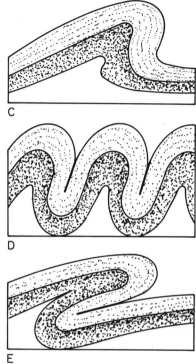

FIG. 6.5. Types of folds: *A,* monocline; *B,* symmetrical anticline and syncline; *C,* overturned anticline and syncline; *D,* isoclinal folds (each of the limbs has approximately the same dip); *E,* recumbent fold (an overturned fold the limbs and axial plane of which are nearly horizontal). (Modified and reprinted, by permission, from W. H. Emmons et al., *Geology: Principles and Processes,* © 1960, by McGraw-Hill Book Company)

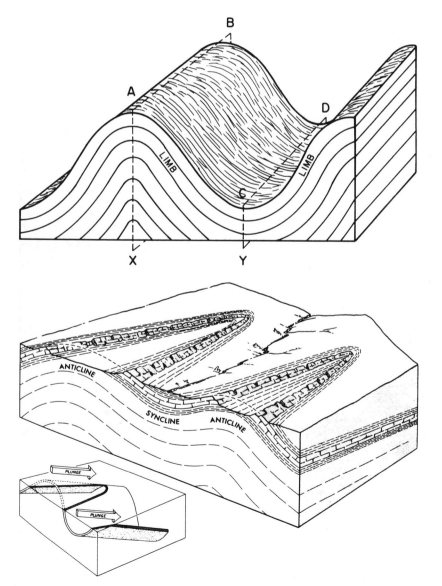

FIG. 6.6. Nomenclature of folds: Plane *ABX* is the axial plane of the anticline; *CDY* is the axial plane of the syncline; *AB* is an axis of the anticline; *CD* is an axis of the syncline. An axial plane bisects a fold; an axis is any line formed by the intersection of the axial plane and a surface of stratification. (Modified and reprinted, by permission, from C. R. Longwell, Adolph Knopf, and R. F. Flint, *A Textbook of Geology,* 2d ed., © 1939, by John Wiley and Sons)

FIG. 6.7. Plunging folds. Plunge may be defined as the dip of an axis. (Modified from G. D. Robinson et al., Professional Paper 505, U.S. Geological Survey)

separation (that is, movement perpendicular to the break), and *faults,* along which there has been lateral movement of the rocks on one side of the break with respect to those on the other.

A group of essentially parallel joints is referred to as a *joint set.* Two or more sets of joints that intersect in such a manner that it is likely they were formed as the result of the same set of stresses are called a *joint system* (fig. 6.8).

Faults are named on the basis of the relative movements of the rocks on either side of the plane or zone of fracture. The movement, commonly called *slip,* may be parallel to either the dip or the strike of the fracture, or at some angle to both of these parameters. The rocks on either side of a fault zone are said to constitute a fault block. In all

FIG. 6.8. Joint set in quartzite in Bedford County near Leesville. Bedding dips from upper left to lower right; smooth-surfaced fractures, like one to left of geologist, are joints. (Photograph by T. M. Gathright, Jr.)

but vertical faults one block is, so to speak, above the other. Because they have often been found to contain mineral deposits, several fault zones were mined long ago. The miners referred to the block above their heads as the hanging-wall block and to the block below their feet as the foot-wall block. This terminology persists even in professional parlance. A fault with a noteworthy dip-slip component of movement is referred to as a *normal fault* if the hanging-wall block moved down dip relative to the foot-wall block (fig.6.9) but as a *reverse fault* when the opposite relative movement occurred. A reverse fault with a

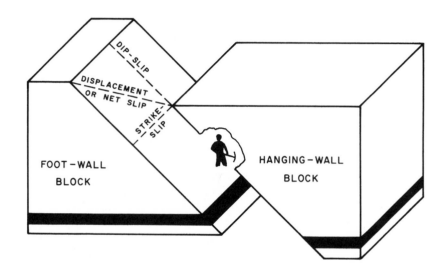

FIG. 6.9. Nomenclature of faults. This is a normal fault with an oblique slip— that is, the displacement had both dip- and strike-slip components. (Modified and reprinted, by permission, from C. R. Longwell, Adolph Knopf, and R. F. Flint, *A Textbook of Geology,* 2d ed., © 1939, by John Wiley and Sons)

dip of less than about thirty degrees is called a *thrust fault.* Particular attention is called to the use of the phrase *relative movement;* in general it is not known whether one block moved up or down while the other remained essentially stationary, whether one moved up while the other moved down, or whether both moved up or down but one over a greater distance than the other. This fact should always be kept in mind.

Some fault zones extend over great distances. The famous earthquake and fire of San Francisco, for example, were the direct and indirect results of movement along a fault that extends from Southern California all the way to San Francisco and thence out into the Pacific Ocean. Faults mapped in the Appalachians of Virginia are known to extend from northern Virginia through the Valley and Ridge Province and into western Tennessee. Some of these faults have had movements that amounted to several miles.

Movements of the rocks along faults and within fault zones have often caused the formation of rocks and features that are termed *mylonite* (material that has been so finely ground that individual fragments are submicroscopic in size), fault *gouge* (finely ground-up rock material), fault *breccia* (ground-up rock material that contains some relatively large angular fragments), and *slickensides* (extremely smooth, slick surfaces along which movement has occurred). Gouge, breccia, and slickensides are relatively common along several of the faults shown on geologic maps of areas within the Old Dominion. Mylonites also occur but are apparently much less common.

There are several other types of rock deformation. Most of these involve the recrystallization or reconstitution of the mineral constituents of the involved rocks. Thus, they are generally considered to have occurred deep within the earth's crust. Under the temperature and pressure conditions there, such changes are believed to occur rather easily, especially when the rocks are also under stress (directional pressure). The rocks formed under these conditions have been described briefly in chapter II, under the heading *Metamorphic rocks*.

Igneous rocks may, of course, also exhibit structural features—foliation, joints, and the like. As with sedimentary rocks, original (often referred to as "primary") and/or deformational structures may occur. Most structures within igneous rocks require such special consideration that simplifications like those that could be given here generally lead chiefly to misunderstanding so nothing more will be said.

The geologist who studies deformed rocks in order to determine what stresses may have been responsible for the internal mineralogical rearrangements and other changes usually does so by plotting the orientation of the minerals so formed or deformed. This branch of geology, which involves both petrology and structural geology, is referred to as petrofabrics. In some cases, a thorough analysis of a rock's fabric may serve as the basis for deducing not only the kinds but also the sequence of different stresses that affected the rock.

Geophysical methods are also frequently employed in structural studies. The methods involve investigation of the effects of natural or artificially produced seismic (earthquake) waves or electrical currents and gravity or magnetic measurements. Some of these methods are particularly helpful in prospecting for structurally controlled mineral resources such as oil. Others are used chiefly for large-scale studies dealing with general relationships among different layers of the earth, with mountain-making movements, and so on. Some of the most basic of all geological questions—such as what causes the movements that are responsible for earthquakes, volcanism, the deformation of rocks, and the formation of mountain ranges—may well be answered when more information of this type becomes available.

One of the more interesting hypotheses dealing with large-scale earth structures is one generally referred to as continental drift. This hypothesis is mentioned only as an example of the kinds of speculations that have been made with regard to the production of mountain ranges and similar major structures. The choice is made because the hypothesis has aspects that may appeal to the interested layman and beginning student as well as to the professional geologist, not because it is generally accepted over other hypotheses.

The similarities in the shapes of the eastern coast of North and South America and the western coast of Europe and Africa have been recognized for at least a century. Speculations as to whether the two continental masses were ever joined were brought to a climax about fifty-five years ago by the German geologist Alfred Wegener. He suggested not only that they were and drifted apart (fig. 6.10)

Late Paleozoic

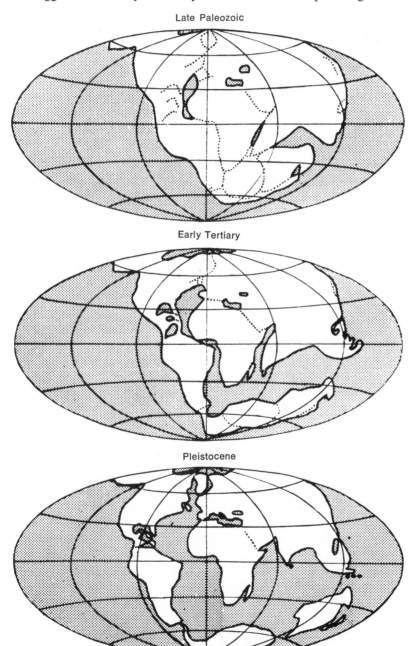

Early Tertiary

Pleistocene

FIG. 6.10. Continental drift. Wegener's concept of continental drift. (Reprinted by permission, from James Gilluly, Aaron C. Waters, and A. O. Woodford, *Principles of Geology,* 2d ed., © 1959, by W. H. Freeman and Company, as modified from A. Wegener, *The Origin of Continents and Oceans,* © 1912, by Methuen and Company)

but also that the drifting would account for several features. He even suggested that the mountain ranges near the western margins of the Americas—the Coast Ranges and Rockies of North America and the Andes of South America—were formed by a buckling in response to frictional drag along the leading edge of the westward drifting continents.

More data are needed to prove unequivocally or to disprove hypotheses like that of continental drift. Furthermore, it seems likely that even with proof, more questions may be raised than answered. For example, if continental drift did take place, what mechanism(s) could have been responsible for such major movements? But this is one of the fascinating aspects of structural geology, in fact of all geology: speculations prompt investigation and discovery, which usually, in turn, promote more speculations.

Several of the diverse structural features that occur within the Commonwealth are among the most interesting known. The various times when some of them may have been formed is mentioned in chapter VIII, which deals with the geologic history of the state. Examples of a few of the more easily accessible and observable structural features are shown in figures 6.11–16.

The general structural patterns from east to west within the state may be briefly outlined: The Coastal Plain Geomorphic Province is underlain chiefly by nearly flat-lying strata, which have undergone little deformation except regional tilting and local arching since being deposited. Most of the Piedmont Province is underlain by rather

FIG. 6.11. Deformed and veined rock. This rock has been metamorphosed, folded, and fractured; the resulting fractures have been filled with white quartz to become veins.

FIG. 6.12. Chevron fold from Floyd County.

FIG. 6.13. Anticline. Several folds like this one occur in Ordovician rocks in Clover Hollow, Giles County, Virginia.

highly deformed metamorphic rocks—the notable exceptions being the Triassic basins, which are underlain chiefly by relatively undeformed sedimentary rocks. The Blue Ridge Geomorphic Province is also underlain to a large extent by relatively highly deformed metamorphic rocks, but along with these rocks it also includes several igneous masses and some only slightly metamorphosed or completely unmeta-

FIG. 6.14. Sharp flexures like this are common in the Ordovician limestone near Peach Bottom near Tazewell. (Photograph by T. M. Gathright, Jr.)

FIG. 6.15. Fold-fault combination in Middle Ordovician sandstone in exposure along road on east side of New River near Eggleston, Giles County; fault zone extends beneath fold and cuts it off near lower right corner. (Photograph by T. M. Gathright, Jr.)

FIG. 6.16. Slickensides. A slickensided fault surface in Triassic rocks at Goose Creek Quarry in Loudoun County. (Photograph by T. M. Gathright, Jr.)

morphosed volcanic-sedimentary sequences. Most of the Valley and Ridge Province is underlain by sedimentary rocks that have been folded and/or faulted. The Plateau Area of Virginia is underlain chiefly by relatively undeformed flat-lying sedimentary rocks. A highly generalized geological cross section of the state is given as figure 6.17.

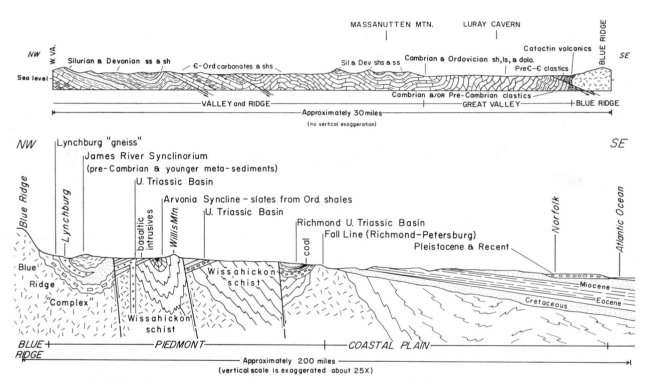

FIG. 6.17. Schematic geological cross sections across Virginia. *Notice that the two sections have different scales.*

GEOLOGISTS who apply their knowledge to the resolution of practical problems are employed by oil, geophysical exploration, and mining corporations; by numerous federal, state, and municipal governments; by many transportation, communication, and industrial firms; and by a number of other organizations. Nearly all of the activities of these geologists fall into two broad fields: Economic Geology and Environmental Geology. This utilization of the adjectives *economic* and *environmental* is quite appropriate. Economic geologists deal mainly with the discovery and development of mineral deposits; environmental geologists concern themselves with planning for and control of land use, with geological aspects of environmental health, and with resource management.

Minerals and rocks are the basis of modern civilization. The power and economy of nations and the standard of living of their citizens depend upon mineral resources. Today's American suburbanite, for example, is unable to go through a single day without utilizing many mineral and rock products. Furthermore, he depends upon several other commodities that require minerals in their production or manufacture. A few examples of man's dependency on minerals may be noted: Soil, the supporter of all plant life upon which man and other animals depend, is composed chiefly of mineral and rock fragments. Water, one of man's greatest personal needs as well as an industrial necessity, is a mineral resource. Metals and alloys are derived from minerals and rocks. Roads and numerous building materials are made of minerals and/or rocks. Most homes are heated and most vehicles are propelled by mineral fuels. This book could not have been printed were it not for minerals.

FIG. 7.1. Indians used Virginia rocks long before the arrival of the English colonists.

Virginia has had a varied and interesting history in developing her mineral and rock resources. And, the future is bright for her continuing to use these and other mineral commodities that will doubtless be needed to support further technological advances.

Relics found within the state indicate that prehistoric man used minerals and rocks for tools and weapons as long ago as the Great Ice Age of the Pleistocene Epoch. Thousands of years later Indians also used them for implements and for adornment (fig. 7.1).

Both the discovery and the settling of America by Europeans were prompted by the search for gold and other precious substances. In 1609, only two years after the first Jamestown settlement, bog iron was shipped to England by Virginia colonists.[1] This same kind of iron ore led to the establishment in 1619 of an ironworks at Falling Creek, a few miles south of the present site of Richmond. Two years later lead was mined and smelted to make shot, also at Falling Creek. The furnaces were destroyed during an Indian massacre in 1622. There is no further record known about Virginia's mineral wealth until 1669. In that year, in an article printed in London, Nathaniel Shrigley cited Virginia occurrences of "Fullers-Earth, Marle, Salt-Peter, Iron, Stone, Lead, Tin, and Silver Oar."

In the first decade of the eighteenth century coal from the Richmond Triassic Basin was mined and used locally. This was apparently the first coal mined in the Western Hemisphere. During the next decade a number of new iron furnaces were built. For example, Governor Spotswood had one built in 1714 beside the Rappahannock River near the present site of Fredericksburg. Lead was mined in the 1750's at the Chiswell mines in Wythe County. A Quaker church built in 1763 at what is now Lynchburg had a greenstone foundation. Copper was mined at the Phoenyx Mine in Fauquier County more than a decade before the Revolutionary War. Coal was mined west of the Blue Ridge, near Blacksburg, as early as 1768.

Thomas Jefferson in his *Notes on the State of Virginia* (1782), cited sources of gold, lead, copper, iron, graphite, coal, marble, limestone, millstone, mica, magnetite, asbestos, ocher, salt, and some gemstones. Silica-cemented sandstone from Aquia Creek, Stafford County, was used between 1791 and 1840 for construction of the White House, the older parts of the Capitol, the Treasury, and other buildings in the District of Columbia.

Salt from southwestern Virginia, although known even before Jefferson's report, was not taken in notable amounts from the salt marshes of the Saltville area in Smyth County until the time of the War of 1812. Later, in 1840, wells were dug in an attempt to tap the source of the salt. According to the records of the U.S. Mint, gold was first produced in the Old Dominion in 1829. Early in the next decade the well-known Vaucluse Mine of Orange County was opened. It became a major producer of the more than a million and a half dollars' worth of gold produced within the state during the next forty or so years. In the 1830's: manganese was mined in Frederick County; the Arminius Mine of Louisa County, a producer at different times of iron, copper, and pyrite, was opened; cement was produced in Rockbridge County in conjunction with canal building; and natural coke from the Richmond Basin was described by William Barton Rogers, a one-time Virginia resident who later founded the Massachusetts Institute of Technology. Barite production started near Catlett, Fauquier County, in the 1850's. The sulfide "leads" of the

---

[1] Many dates dealing with Virginia's mineral production are not well established. Those cited here were chosen because they occur in articles which are accurate in respect to other dates or which were written soon after the period involved.

southern part of the Blue Ridge and the copper mines of the Virgilina District were discovered between 1854 and 1859.

At the beginning of the Civil War, Virginia was the major mineral-producing state in the South (fig. 7.2). Lead and iron were the state's chief mineral contribution to the Confederacy, but salt, saltpeter, and coal were also important. Oriskany iron ore from the Grace Furnace

FIG. 7.2. Old woodcut depicting the furnace of the Shenandoah Iron Company, Shenandoah, Virginia. This operation, begun in the early 1800's, was one of the leading producers in the state immediately before the Civil War. (Courtesy of Norfolk and Western Railway)

FIG. 7.3. The Confederate ironclad *Merrimac*, or *Virginia* (*right*), faces its Union opponent the *Monitor*. (Photograph courtesy of Norfolk and Western Railway)

Mines in Botetourt County was used by the Tredegar ironworks of Richmond to produce the armor of the ironclad *Merrimac*. Coal from mines in Montgomery County propelled the craft (fig. 7.3).

After the Civil War the Bertha Zinc District of Wythe County was discovered in 1866; manganese was found in the Crimora District of Augusta County in 1867; and mica was mined at the Hewlett Mine of Hanover County in 1867 and at the Jefferson Mine of Amelia County in 1873. Despite these important discoveries mineral production in Virginia declined for about ten years after the war. Recovery from this temporary slump was not signaled until the opening of several new iron mines in 1878 and the beginning of zinc mining at Bertha the following year.

More recently: the now-abandoned Crimora Mine in Augusta County, at one time the largest open-pit mine in the eastern United States, produced enough manganese to rank as the country's all-time leader in the production of high-grade manganese oxide; a total of more than 25 million tons of iron were produced from about thirty-five counties of the Old Dominion; pyrrhotite and pyrite mined in Carroll and Grayson counties served as the basic raw material for a sulfuric acid-manufacturing plant in Pulaski; scrap mica was mined at numerous places on the Piedmont; sheet mica has been obtained from pegmatite bodies near Amelia and from other bodies in the vicinity of Ridgeway in Henry County (fig. 1.21); and small amounts of asbestos, barite, diatomite, and emery have been recovered within the state.

During 1968 Virginia's mineral production was worth approximately $295,663,000 (see table 7.1).

With more than 50 minable seams, the Commonwealth boasts coal that is as good as any available in the United States in quality and diversity of use (fig. 7.4). Production during 1968 was from eight counties of southwestern Virginia, with 96 per cent from Buchanan, Dickenson, Russell, and Wise counties. Included were coking coal, steam coal, metallurgical coal, domestic coal, and by-product coal.

As is indicated in the table, various kinds of stone along with sand and gravel production accounted for slightly more than $67 million of the value of the state's 1968 mineral production. Among the numerous kinds of stone which were quarried or mined during the

FIG. 7.4. Coal mining is Virginia's major mineral industry: *preceding page,* examining a coal "seam"; *top,* a six-ton "buggy" is loaded in about one minute; *bottom,* coal ready to go to market. (Photographs courtesy of Norfolk and Western Railway)

year were amphibolite, basalt, diabase, dolomite, granite, "green-stone," limestone, sandstone, soapstone, and slate. Although more than 99 per cent of the bulk of the stone was used as construction aggregate, noteworthy amounts were also used for such things as

TABLE 7.1. Mineral Production in Virginia during 1968*

Mineral or Product	Quantity†	Value‡
Clays	1,462	$ 1,714
Coal	36,966	178,946
Gemstones	?	7
Lead	3,573	944
Lime	919	11,138
Natural gas	3,389	1,013
Petroleum	3	withheld
Sand and gravel	10,859	13,644
Soapstone	3,928	10
Stone	217	53,533
Zinc	19,257	5,199
Others§		29,515
		$295,663

* Slightly generalized from volume 15, no. 4, of *Virginia Minerals*.
† Thousands of short tons except for petroleum (in thousands of 42-gallon barrels) and natural gas (in millions of cubic feet).
‡ In thousands.
§ Includes "aplite," cement, feldspar, gypsum, iron pigment, kyanite, salt, titanium concentrate, and petroleum (in value column).

agstone, ballast, dimension stone, riprap, and roofing granules. Most of the state's sand and gravel was produced by open-pit mining and dredging. About 85 per cent of it was used in paving and building construction; the rest was used for such diverse purposes as glass manufacture and engine sand.

Of the state's 1968 total lime production, more than 60 per cent was shipped out of Virginia, principally to Georgia, Kentucky, Maryland, North Carolina, Ohio, Pennsylvania, South Carolina, West Virginia, and Wisconsin. High-calcium limestone, dolomitic limestone, and oyster shells were used to produce the primary lime that was finally marketed as quicklime or hydrated lime. Both products found their greatest use in several chemical and metallurgical industries.

Although zinc and lead have been mined in several of the Commonwealth's counties in the past, only two mines in southern Wythe County were in production during 1968. The value of zinc and lead taken from these mines has exceeded $6 million for each of the last few years.

Virginia clays, used chiefly in the manufacture of brick, have also been used in the manufacture of portland cement, lightweight aggregate, pottery, sewer tile, clay dummies (shothole tampers), and other less common clay products.

In 1968 in Tazewell, Buchanan, Dickenson, and Wise counties

3,389 million cubic feet of natural gas were produced from a few more than a hundred wells.

Other mineral products totaling some $29,532,000 in value for 1968 may be summarized briefly:

Cement, both portland and masonry, is produced from low magnesium limestone, shale, clay, and/or calcareous marl of Augusta, Botetourt, and Warren counties and the city of Chesapeake. Although approximately three-quarters of the portland cement is used within the state, some of it is shipped as far as South Carolina. Virginia-produced masonry cement is used in thirty-one states and the District of Columbia.

Feldspar, including "aplite," is obtained in Bedford, Hanover, and Nelson counties. It is used in the manufacture of glass, ceramic enamel, and pottery and also in such things as soap and abrasives as well as for aggregate.

As mentioned in chapter I, several gemstones have been found in Virginia (fig. 7.5). It is estimated that gems worth a few thousand dollars continue to be collected within the state each year.

FIG. 7.5. Gem faceting. John Sinkankas, well-known gemologist, formerly of Arlington, Virginia, cuts faces on a mineral on his diamond dust—impregnated wheel. (Photograph courtesy of Washington *Star* Pictorial Magazine)

Gypsum, mined in Smyth and Washington counties, is processed at Plasterco in Washington County to produce plasterboard.

Natural earthy iron oxides, both raw and burnt, are combined at a plant near Hiwassee, Pulaski County, to produce more than a hundred different-colored pigments. The pigments are used in such diverse products as cement, ink, linoleum, magnetic tape, and paint.

Kyanite for high-temperature refractories and other ceramic products is recovered from three open-pit mines in Buckingham and Prince Edward counties. Virginia is North America's foremost producer of this mineral.

Petroleum has been produced in Lee County since 1941. During 1968 the Rose Hill and Ben Hur fields in the county yielded 2,583 barrels of crude petroleum.

Salt, used in the production of caustic soda, chlorine, soda ash, and a few other chemicals, has been recovered from brine wells in the vicinity of Saltville, Smyth County, for many years (fig. 7.6).

Titanium concentrates, consisting of ilmenite and/or rutile, are produced in Amherst and Hanover counties. They are used in the production of titanium dioxide pigments. These pigments find wide utilization in the manufacture of such things as paints, plastics, and textiles.

The mineral industries scattered throughout the state increase the economic benefits of mineral and rock production.

It must never be forgotten, however, that the earth's mineral heritage—the cumulative result of extremely slow-acting geologic processes that have been going on intermittently for more than a billion years—has been undergoing extremely rapid depletion during the last few decades. More minerals have been used by man since the beginning of World War I than in all previous history, and these resources are not renewable. In general, once the sought-after materials are removed, only holes and scrap heaps remain.

On the brighter side, there are deposits yet to be discovered; a few resources have reserves that should last for centuries; technological advances will undoubtedly make some minerals and rocks which are now considered useless become valuable assets; and substitutes may be found for some mineral products. The future discovery of more mineral resources and the alluded-to technological advances, in particular, will depend upon increased geological field and laboratory research.

As already mentioned, however, the discovery and extraction of minerals constitute only a fraction of the benefits that accrue to man through the application of geological knowledge and thought. Consider how engineers who are responsible for the construction of transportation routes, impoundment dams, and many buildings de-

FIG. 7.6. "Christmas tree" for brine well at Saltville, Virginia. Rock salt beneath the surface near Saltville is "mined" as follows: Water is pumped, under high pressure, into the salt; the water dissolves the salt; the brine solution comes to the surface; the solution is evaporated; and salt is recovered as a precipitate. (Photograph by W. E. Moore)

pend on geological data and predictions; how those who require water often need geological advice; how municipalities and industries which are having to face the numerous problems of safe waste disposal must seek geological information. These and other aspects of "environmental geology" are becoming increasingly important every day as the world's population increases and as individual man's needs and desires grow. There can be little doubt that the benefits from the application of geological know-how to man's environmental problems will surpass even optimistic present-day expectations.

In order to choose an appropriate site for a structure and to determine how best to design, build, and maintain the structure, the engineer and/or architect often needs geological advice. Engineering works may succeed or fail on the basis of how well they fit their geological environments. Major tragedies like the 1959 failure of the Malpasset Dam in southeastern France have drawn attention to the fact that engineers can no longer afford to be ignorant of the geological features that exist where they build (figs. 7.7–9). Even

FIG. 7.7. Earth slide: this macadam road was put on top of filled ground, which is slowly slipping away as the result of uncontrolled drainage and surface water run-off. (Photograph courtesy of C. F. Withington, U.S. Geological Survey)

FIG. 7.8. Earth slides may be expensive. The estimated cost of removal of materials deposited by slides on the highways of south-western Virginia alone was more than one million dollars in 1968. (Photograph by H. C. Porter)

FIG. 7.9. Earth slip. This is one of several homes which were badly damaged as a result of slippage of a relatively large mass of clayey sediments on the Coastal Plain of Virginia. (Photograph by H. C. Porter)

when disastrous outcomes are not likely, the lack of geological information may still result in costly delays, faulty performance, and unnecessary expense. Essentially all building and dam foundations, all grading and straightening operations for transportation routes, all bridge and tunnel construction, and the like depend directly on geological environments and their bearing on feasibility of initiation, costs of both construction and subsequent maintenance, and ultimate safety.

Geologists with different specialties may cooperate with construction engineers to predict the identities, distributions and behavioral characteristics of the geological materials to be encountered at given locations. Those who so direct their studies and thoughts are often called engineering geologists. Among the more obvious questions that geologist-engineer teams may consider are: Will the rock afford an adequate support for the proposed structure? Will the desired grading disturb relations so much that erosion or landslide hazards will be created? Is any of the material that has to be moved of such character that it may be used in the construction?

It is estimated that approximately 750 gallons of water are used each day to fill the needs and desires of each mid-twentieth-century American: 50 to 60 gallons are used for drinking, cooking, sanitation, and so forth, and approximately 700 gallons more are utilized by industry in manufacturing and processing goods for him. (For example, about 10 gallons of water are needed to produce a gallon of gasoline, at least 100 gallons are used to produce enough rayon fiber for a lightweight summer dress, and more than 65,000 gallons are utilized in the production of a ton of steel.)

Water, unlike most mineral resources, is a renewable resource. Thus even though future increases in both population and the per capita use of water appear to be virtual certainties, no impossible situation needs to be reached. As a renewable resource, water can be managed. In order to manage water resources wisely, however, several professionals may need to collaborate. A good management team should include representatives of the biological, chemical, and engineering fields and perhaps even an economist, a demographer, and/or a psychologist, along with one or more geologists.

The basic data are geologic. They generally include information relating to both present-day and future availability, as well as to the occurrence and quality of the water under consideration. Availability inventories are usually broken down so that surface and subsurface supplies may be distinguished. Predictions relating to future availability are hazardous; they depend on climatic conditions. Occurrence information, especially for subsurface water, which as noted is commonly called groundwater, may prove to be extremely useful. For example, certain groundwater supplies may be replenished artificially and the containing areas thereby be used as underground storage reservoirs. Such reservoirs, by the way, have several advantages over surface impoundments: they may require no or little construction; they do not cover and thus preempt any surface area; they do not silt up; they lose very little if any water by evaporation; they yield water of predictable temperature and quality.

As already mentioned, geologists should also be involved in feasibility studies and construction planning if impoundments are found to be necessary (fig. 7.10).

FIG. 7.10. Claytor Dam. Built in 1939 near Radford, Virginia, this dam serves to impound the water of New River; the impounded water offers flood control, a large recreational area (lake), and a means of producing large quantities of electricity. (Photograph courtesy of Appalachian Electric Power Company)

Pollution is usually repulsive and often noxious to man, to other animals, and even to plants. Both water and air pollutants are becoming more voluminous and varied as manufacturing, processing, mining, and the human population grow. The waste materials, the disposal of which causes pollution, consist of organic substances, inorganic chemicals, insoluble sediments, and heat. Radioactive wastes, which may become commoner with the increase in nuclear power plants, present special problems. The treatment and disposal of pollutants pose economic and social dilemmas as well as operational difficulties. Geologic data will be of particular value whenever the best procedure seems to be underground disposal or surficial disposal involving lagoons or landfill.

The application of geologic investigations and considerations to the planning, design, and development of both urban and nonurban areas, as already mentioned, is also a function of environmental geology (figs. 7.11 and 7.12). Actually, most so-called environmental geologists differ from other geologists only in their attitudes, that is, in the objectives they seek. As in nearly all geological investigations, their efforts range from relatively simple to highly complex field and laboratory studies. For example, the studies may involve only topographic and/or geologic map and literature analyses; they may utilize such things as bore holes and geophysical methods (in which principles of physics are applied to the determination of the depths, the forms, and perhaps even the compositions of buried rocks); and/or

FIG. 7.11. "Swell-shrink soil." Soil like this one in Clark County may cause problems; when dry (as shown) these montmorillonitic soils "swallow up" materials such as those that might be dumped on them during excavation for construction; later, upon becoming wet they reswell, sometimes creating pressures of up to 10,000 pounds per square foot. Such pressure is sufficient to cause damage to structures such as house foundations. (Photograph by H. C. Porter)

they may require use of highly sophisticated laboratory equipment. In any case, the resultant findings often permit the reaching of better decisions relating to land use (including the proper scheduling of multiple and/or sequential use), more intelligent zoning, the avoidance of hazardous undertakings, and so forth. All this serves mainly to help man to adapt better to his geological environment.

These brief reviews are indicative of the many and diverse ways in which geology may be applied to help satisfy man's needs and desires. Even though they are strictly historical, they also show by inference that new applications have developed as new needs have arisen. This warrants emphasis. It bodes well for an exciting, ever-changing future for geology and for the geologists who will take part in that future.

A majority of the currently predictable needs can be filled by merely increasing and broadening geological coverage and research. For example, in Virginia there doubtless will be an ever-increasing need for detailed mapping of both the state and its adjacent offshore areas. Topographic, soil, geologic, geochemical, and geophysical maps with more and more details will be a continuing, basic need for many years to come. In addition, many more analyses of geologic materials will be required; to be of value, most of these analyses will have to include physical as well as chemical data (that is, they must include the determination of engineering properties, and the like). Perhaps of primary importance is the fact that special care will have to be taken in preparing the formats of the resulting maps and accompanying data. Most should be drawn so that they may be understood by nongeologists as well as by geologists if they are to fulfill their real purpose.

The dividends that will accrue to Virginia and its citizens as a result of such an increase and broadening of geologic studies within the state can hardly be imagined.

FIG. 7.12. Mutilated land. On top of shale bedrock in central Scott County. (Photograph by H. C. Porter)

VIII *Geological History*

THE quest for knowledge about geological history began when man first wondered about his environment. Some historians think the biblical story about the Great Flood may even have been framed in answer to questions dealing with man's finding fossil seashells on high and dry land.

In order to place the sketch of Virginia's geological history in the proper perspective, a review of the structural framework of North America is needed. North America, as shown in figure 8.1, exhibits a roughly symmetrical over-all pattern. From the center outward are the Canadian Shield, the Stable Interior, and Linear Orogenic belts (defined below). In addition (not shown on the map), on the east and south there is a Coastal Plain area, which has been receiving sediments more or less continuously since Late Cretaceous time.

FIG. 8.1. Structural framework of North America.

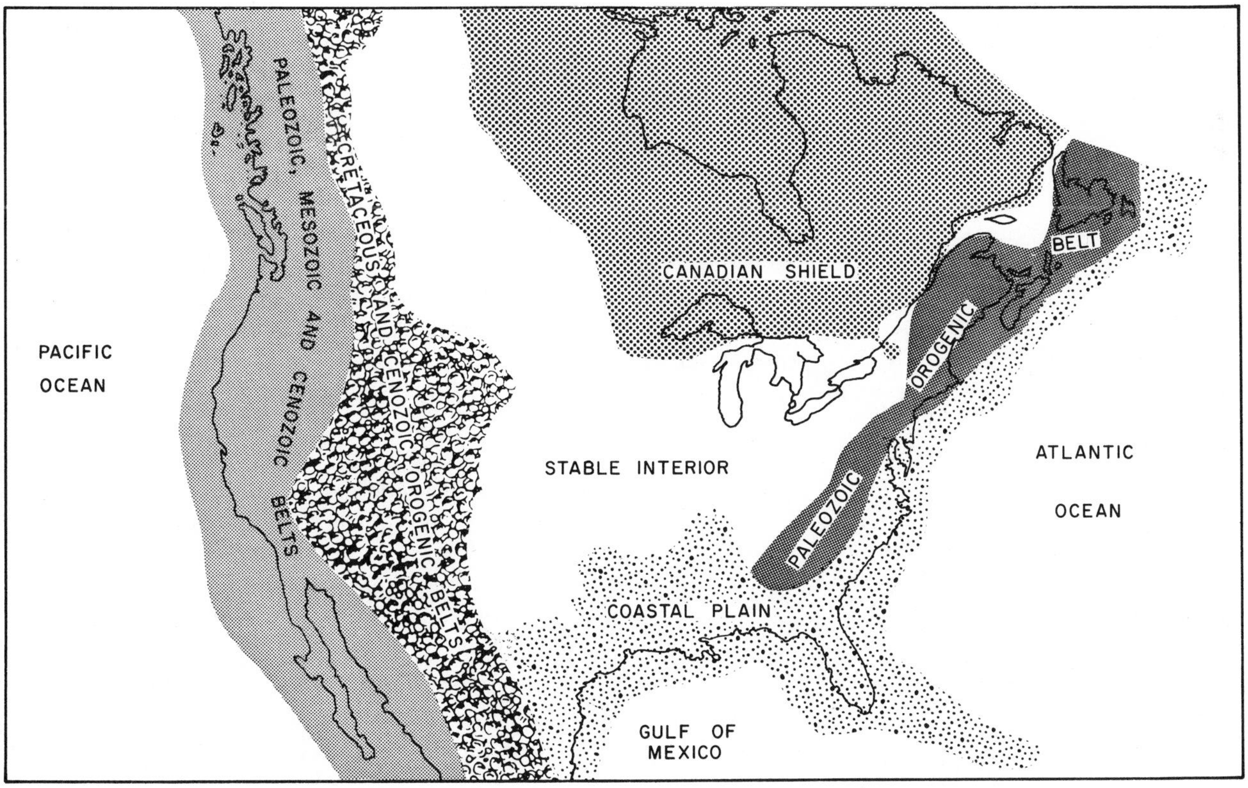

These sediments overlie the eastern part of the orogenic belt and extend oceanward to form the present-day continental shelf.

The Canadian Shield is an area of some two million square miles which constitutes most of the north-central part of North America. The bedrock of the shield is predominantly Precambrian granites and gneisses, but it also includes local belts of metamorphosed sedimentary and volcanic rocks. Most of these rocks appear to have gone through several episodes of deformation. Since at least Early Paleozoic time, however, the shield seems to have been fairly stable: it appears to have undergone only broad uplift and/or subsidence. It is also noteworthy that at least part of the shield appears to have had its over-all gently rolling landscape since Late Precambrian time.

The surface of the shield passes beneath the sedimentary bedrock of the surrounding Stable Interior. This Stable Interior, also known by such names as the Central Lowland, differs from the shield mainly in having a sedimentary cover. East of the Mississippi River the cover, ranging up to a few thousand feet thick, consists essentially of flat-lying sedimentary rocks deposited in shallow Paleozoic seas. Relatively extensive highs (such as the Ozark Dome) and lows (such as the Michigan Basin) were present on the surface during part or all of the period of deposition. Currently the area is relatively flat except where it is dissected. Nonetheless, it does rise, albeit gradually, both to the east and to the west to constitute geomorphic provinces like the Colorado and Allegheny plateaux.

Linear orogenic belts of diverse ages border much of the Stable Interior. (An orogenic belt may be defined as a belt which has undergone folding and faulting, commonly accompanied by metamorphism and/or igneous activity. Most, if not all, such belts appear to have been developed from sediments deposited in geosynclines. A geosyncline is generally defined as an elongate belt, in the earth's crust, which subsided while many thousands of feet of predominantly shallow-water marine sediments accumulated within it. Many geologists, however, believe the term also implies a concept which involves not only the initial formation, the subsidence, and the sediment accumulation but also the formation of folded, faulted, or complex mountains as a result of deformation of the sediments. With respect to this concept it is noteworthy that in the language of geologists orogenic mountains do not have to be expressed by topographic mountains. The designation orogenic mountains indicates only that the bedrocks in question have undergone deformation of the kind generally referred to as mountain-making activities. Within present-day Virginia, both the Valley and Ridge and the Piedmont provinces may be said to be underlain by orogenic mountains whereas only the Valley and Ridge may be considered to contain more than a very few topographic mountains.)

The Appalachians of eastern North America are a fine example of orogenic mountains formed as the result of deformation of geosynclinal sediments. This mountain system, which extends from Newfoundland to Alabama (and may in subsurface join the Ouachita System of Arkansas and Texas), may be divided into two main parts, the sedimentary Appalachians on the west and the crystalline (or metamorphic) Appalachians on the east. The sedimentary Appalachians of Virginia underlie the Valley and Ridge and the adjacent part of the Blue Ridge geomorphic province. They consist of a thick sequence of Late Precambrian and Paleozoic sedimentary rocks that passes westward into the rock sequence of the Stable Interior. The rocks within the sedimentary Appalachians have undergone much folding and/or faulting, apparently as a result of stresses directed from the southeast toward the northwest. The crystalline Appalachians of the Piedmont and parts of the adjacent Blue Ridge geomorphic province consist of Late Precambrian and Paleozoic metamorphic and intracrustal igneous rocks. The metamorphic rocks have undergone not only metamorphism but also folding and faulting. The zone that underwent the most intense metamorphism is nearer to the Blue Ridge than it is to the edge of the overlapping Coastal Plain sediments. In some places, such as in central Virginia, an intervening belt of more ancient igneous and metamorphic rocks occurs between the sedimentary and crystalline Appalachian subdivisions. These older rocks appear to have acted as a barrier between the two regions during at least part of the period of Late Precambrian and Paleozoic sedimentation. (In the terminology of some geologists, the rocks of the western belt would be described as miogeosynclinal and those of the eastern belt, as eugeosynclinal. These terms draw attention to the absence versus the presence of significant amounts of volcanic materials.)

As mentioned, there is an area along the eastern border of the continent extending from at least New England southward which is underlain by relatively recent sediments. These sediments constitute a southeastwardly thickening wedge of Cretaceous to Recent detritus that ranges up to at least ten thousand feet thick beneath the continental shelf. Sedimentation is still taking place on the off-shore parts of this sequence. The Gulf of Mexico portion of this border area may be a geosyncline "in the making." In fact, some geologists consider the entire Coastal Plain sequence to be a marginal geosyncline in the process of formation.

Virginia contains parts of all of the structural units mentioned above except the Canadian Shield. The Cumberland Plateau of southwestern Virginia is an eastern edge of the Stable Interior. The Valley and Ridge and western edge of the Blue Ridge geomorphic provinces are a part of the miogeosynclinal, sedimentary Appalachians. Most of the Piedmont and some of the eastern part of the Blue Ridge geomorphic provinces are part of the eugeosynclinal, crystalline Appalachians. The Coastal Plain of the state is part of the over-all eastern North American Coastal Plain. In addition, parts of the western Piedmont and Blue Ridge geomorphic provinces belong to the structural unit often called the Blue Ridge anticlinorium. (An anticlinorium is generally defined as a complex anticline that consists of subordinate folds, the whole having an archlike form.) This anticlinorium, as already noted, is believed to have existed as a local topographic high and thus a barrier during most, if not all, of the Late Precambrian–Paleozoic sedimentation period. In fact, it probably supplied sediment to both the bordering miogeosynclinal and eugeosynclinal troughs.

Within this framework, the over-all geological history of the state of Virginia from the Late Precambrian to the present may be briefly summarized:

In Late Precambrian time, volcanism from sporadic centers along the Blue Ridge anticlinorium was waning, and sedimentation was taking place over much of the remainder of the state. Sedimentation of a miogeosynclinal character continued intermittently and sporadically to the west of the anticlinorium until at least Middle Pennsylvanian time. Sedimentation of a eugeosynclinal character took place, perhaps with major periods of interruption, to the east of the anticlinorium until at least Devonian time. Furthermore, during and following the sedimentation, both areas were undergoing deformation: the miogeosynclinal rocks were folded and faulted into orogenic mountains; the eugeosynclinal rocks were folded, faulted, metamorphosed, and intruded by magma to form highly complex orogenic mountains. Subsequently, erosion acted upon the rocks so that by Early Triassic time the eastern part at least of the crystalline Appalachians was worn down to a relatively flat erosion surface. During Late Triassic time, the crystalline rocks were locally normal-faulted to form troughs, and the troughs were filled with nonmarine, chiefly detrital sediments. There also was local, near-surface intrusion of basaltic magma in Virginia and simultaneous volcanism to the northeast in New England. After the Triassic, the Late Cretaceous is the first period for which evidence has been definitely recognized within the state. During Late Cretaceous time all of Virginia eastward from a few tens of miles west of the present Fall Line was submerged beneath the ocean and received sediments from rivers and streams draining the nearby crystalline rock terrain. At the same time western Virginia, including not only the area of the present Cumberland Plateau and Valley and Ridge provinces but also the present-day Blue Ridge and even some of the western Piedmont, was drained to the west. Thus, the Late Cretaceous may be considered to be the beginning of the state's late geological history, which has progressed in a relatively normal way to the present. This progression has consisted chiefly of continual sedimentation in eastern Virginia and/or in the adjacent offshore area coupled with a migration of the Atlantic-Gulf divide to the west. The drainage basin of the Atlantic has consequently become larger, while that of the Gulf has become smaller until it now includes only the southwestern part of Virginia.

The succeeding sections of this chapter elaborate upon this brief statement. The events suggested are based on currently available information interpreted in line with the uniformitarianism principle. Because insufficient data are available, this suggested history is equivocal as well as incomplete. Qualifying terms such as *probably* and *apparently* should be added to many of the remarks. It also needs to be kept in mind that some of the data used to help formulate this sketch have come from areas outside Virginia. This is a quite sound procedure because the different geological belts within Virginia extend both to the northeast and the southwest well beyond state boundaries.

Blue Ridge–Piedmont "Crystalline" Rock Terrain

With a few notable exceptions, the Blue Ridge and Piedmont areas which are underlain by crystalline (igneous and metamorphic) rocks constitute a *terra incognita* so far as geological history is concerned. Although in some places one rock unit may be shown to be younger than another, even most evidence of the order of events within the area has become obscured or rendered ambiguous by metamorphism. Rock units in the vicinity of Lynchburg are a prime example of such ambiguity: four geologists who have worked there have come up with two diametrically opposed views regarding the time sequence in which the major bedrock units were deposited.

Not the least of the several difficulties relating to the understanding and synthesis of the geology of this terrain lies in the fact that, in general, the designations Blue Ridge and Piedmont have been used indiscriminately and inconsistently. Each of these terms has been applied to both geomorphic and geologic provinces despite the fact that their boundaries are not coincident (compare fig. 4.16 and Appendix C). In the following discussion a clear distinction is made. The provinces designated as the Blue Ridge and Piedmont geomorphic provinces are defined in accordance with the descriptions in chapter IV and the map, figure 4.16. The Blue Ridge Geologic Province is called the Blue Ridge Complex and includes only the ancient metamorphic and igneous rocks that predate the Late Precambrian-Paleozoic geosynclinal rocks. The Piedmont geologic province is referred to as the Piedmont Eugeosynclinal Belt and includes only the Late Precambrian-Paleozoic eugeosynclinal rocks. This, of course, means (1) that some of the bedrock of each of the geomorphic provinces cannot, on the basis of presently known data, be unequivocally related to one or the other geological province; (2) that whereas most of the bedrock of the Piedmont geomorphic province belongs to the Piedmont Eugeosynclinal Belt, some of it belongs to the Blue Ridge Complex; and (3) that whereas southwestward from Nelson County the bedrock of the Blue Ridge geomorphic province does include Blue Ridge Complex rocks, it also includes sedimentary rocks of the miogeosynclinal, sedimentary Appalachians and metamorphic rocks of the Piedmont Eugeosynclinal Belt. Notice on the geologic map (Appendix C) that Blue Ridge Complex rocks constitute much of the bedrock of the western Piedmont geomorphic province northeastward from Franklin County and that Piedmont Eugeosynclinal Belt rocks underlie several square miles of the upland part of the Blue Ridge geomorphic province of Floyd, Carroll, and Grayson counties. (It also should be noted, that the geologic map is misleading in that it fails to indicate that a large area in Carroll and Grayson counties is underlain by rocks of the Blue Ridge Complex.)

Despite these geographic problems, there are several major items of agreement: It is generally agreed, for example, that the rocks which make up the Blue Ridge Complex are the oldest rocks in the state. These rocks consist of highly metamorphosed sedimentary and igneous rocks. (Some of the igneous rocks probably represent ancient sedimentary rocks that have undergone melting.) Isotopic data suggest that some of the rocks of the complex attained essentially their present metamorphic character at least 1.8 billion years ago. Local infolds of younger rocks and intrusives that are probably genetically related to the rocks of the eugeosyncline further complicate this "complex" area.

It is also generally agreed that many of the metamorphic rocks east of the Blue Ridge Complex are younger sedimentary and volcanic rocks that have undergone different degrees of metamorphism since they were deposited. So far as the ages of these rocks are concerned, isotopic data suggest that some of them are at least 800 million years old, which is Precambrian in terms of the geologic time scale. Fossils in the Arvonia and Quantico slates, however, indicate those units to be of Late Ordovician age and support the suggestion that some of the other metamorphosed sediments and volcanics are of even more recent Paleozoic age.

In any case, all of the rocks of both of these crystalline rock provinces have undergone changes at temperatures, and perhaps pressures as well, that were greater than those sustained by rocks of the sedimentary rock province to the west. The former are metamorphosed; the latter are not. Furthermore, it is clear that at least some of the metamorphism took place well after many of the sediments of the miogeosyncline were deposited. Evidence for this fact is the slates containing Ordovician fossils. It seems very likely that at least some of the metamorphism occurred essentially simultaneously with folding and faulting of the miogeosynclinal sedimentary rocks. If this is true, it might indicate a greater intensity and/or depth for the deformational activities east of than west of the Blue Ridge Complex. On the other hand it could instead reflect the escape of the sedimentary rocks west of the Blue Ridge Complex from metamorphism because the chiefly quartzose rocks near the bottom of the miogeosynclinal sequence acted like a furnace jacket to insulate the overlying rocks from temperatures high enough to promote metamorphism.

From the time standpoint, Virginia's recognizable geologic history started with rocks that were formed at least two billion years after the birth of this planet. The most ancient rocks in the Blue Ridge Complex appear to represent sedimentary rocks which were deposited in ancient waterways and were subsequently deformed and metamorphosed, in general more than once, by high temperatures and pressures like those that now exist several thousand feet beneath the earth's surface. The complex also contains igneous rocks, some of which were injected into the metamorphic rock, others of which were formed essentially *in situ* when preexisting rocks were subjected to such high temperatures that they underwent partial to complete melting and took on their igneous characteristics upon reconsolidation.

As rocks of the Blue Ridge Complex were uncovered by weathering and erosion, they served as a source of sedimentary material. Some of the sediments that accumulated on each side of the ancestral Blue Ridge were derived from these rocks.

Pre-Triassic eugeosynclinal sedimentation and volcanism occurred to the east of the complex, at least intermittently, from Late Precambrian (approximately one billion years ago) until Middle Paleozoic (300±50 million years ago). The rocks of this sequence were subjected to temperatures and pressures that induced metamorphism sometime before Late Triassic time. Although the number of periods of sedimentation and metamorphism that may have taken place is not clear, there is widely accepted evidence for at least two periods of sedimentation plus or minus volcanism and for at least three periods of metamorphism, if the bringing of radioactive elements to equilibration is considered a consequence of metamorphism. Actually there may very well have been more.

The zone of most intense deformation was not near the eastern edge of the eugeosynclinal belt, as some geologists have suggested. On the contrary, data obtained from drilling suggest that the eastern part of the belt, now buried beneath Coastal Plain sediments, has undergone little or no metamorphism. In addition, as might be expected, there apparently was no fixed zone that repeatedly underwent the most intense deformation. Nonetheless, if grade of metamorphism is taken as an indicator, it is worthy of repetition that most of the areas that underwent relatively high-grade metamorphism are rather near the Blue Ridge Complex at the present level of exposure—in, for example, central Pittsylvania County.

Just as it is not clear how many episodes of deformation occurred, it is not known how many periods of igneous intrusion, pegmatite formation, and mineralization took place. Isotopic data do show, however, that some of these activities did occur during the Paleozoic rather than later. Examples of the manifestations of such activities are the Striped Rock "granite" of Grayson County (this mass is within the Blue Ridge Complex rocks at the present level of erosion), the pegmatites of Bedford and Amelia counties, and the gold and sulfide deposits of the central Piedmont.

By the end of the Paleozoic, weathering and erosion exposed these rocks. They probably appeared much as they do today in areas of exposure. The events of the Triassic which interrupted the general history of the area are outlined later.

Valley and Ridge–Plateau Sedimentary Rock Sequences

The history of miogeosynclinal sedimentation that is reflected in the rocks west of the Blue Ridge Complex in Virginia started late in the Precambrian era and continued until at least Middle Pennsylvanian time, that is, for approximately 500 million years. But, the sedimentary record is incomplete. There were several periods of nondeposition and a few periods when the sea actually withdrew and there was subaerial erosion of the exposed sediments. Nonetheless, a composite thickness of nearly 40,000 feet of rocks was deposited in western Virginia during this period. (This is more than seven times the thickness of the rock sequence between the bottom and the top of the Grand Canyon!)

This Late Precambrian-Paleozoic sedimentation sequence of western Virginia was heralded by volcanism. In Grayson, Smyth, and Washington counties in the vicinity of Mt. Rogers, the volcanism consisted of both flows and explosive activities that resulted in the formation of rocks of rhyolitic composition. There is ample evidence that this volcanic activity took place in an area that was also undergoing more "normal" sedimentation; the volcanic rocks are interbedded with detrital, chiefly coarse-grained sediments. There is also evidence suggesting that the area was subject to local valley glaciation, mudflow, or submarine high-density, turbidity-current activity. The possibility of glaciation is inferred by some geologists because of the presence of presumed varved lake deposits similar to those that are often formed in regions with glacial or subglacial climates. Along the present Blue Ridge Geomorphic Province in central and northern Virginia and northeastward into Maryland and Pennsylvania there was also volcanism, but of a different kind. This volcanism resulted mainly in the formation of basaltic rocks, now called the Catoctin greenstones. These greenstones, like the Mt. Rogers Volcanics, are also interbedded with detrital sedimentary rocks.

As the volcanic activities waned and finally ceased, sedimentation continued and became the dominant process. The earliest sediments now exposed on the western side of the Blue Ridge and along the eastern edge of the Valley and Ridge were of the same general character as those interbedded with the volcanics; that is, they were largely arkosic conglomerates and sandstones. These sediments (Unicoi-Weaverton; see Table 8.1) were probably derived from a fairly nearby land mass to the southeast, perhaps an ancestral Blue Ridge, which was undergoing chiefly physical weathering.

During deposition of the Unicoi sediments southwest of Roanoke there were two or three periods during which basaltic lavas were poured out within the basin of sedimentation. (These flows may be of the same general age as the Catoctin greenstones to the northeast.) As sedimentation continued, the source area was becoming lower and lower in relief and thus supplying finer and finer sediment. The Hampton and Harpers formations, which overlie the Unicoi and Weaverton, respectively, reflect this change. They consist chiefly of relatively fine-grained sands, silts, and clays.

The overlying Erwin and Antietam formations consist in a large part of extremely pure fine-to-medium-grained quartz sandstone (fig. 8.2). Large quantities of such pure quartz sand always pose several questions about both the source area and the area of deposition. Three conditions must be met: (1) a source for the sand is required; (2) other materials must be absent at the source or subsequently eliminated; and (3) sorting of the grains as to size must be extremely efficient. Let us consider each of these: (1) A plausible source would be a preexisting sand; an upfolded or upfaulted portion of the older Unicoi-Weaverton unit seems to offer a good possibility. (2) Even with such a source, some materials would have to have been elimi-

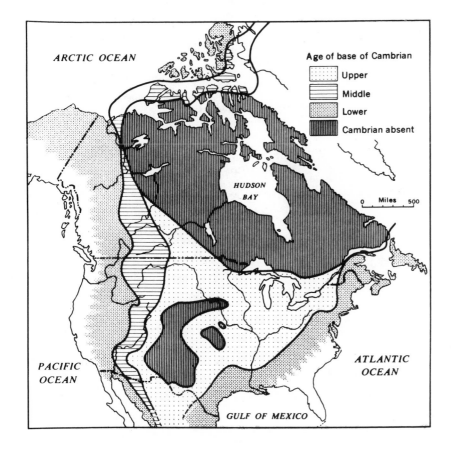

FIG. 8.2. Rocks at base of Cambrian in the interior of North America. The area indicated by vertical hatching appears to have been land above sea level throughout the Cambrian (at least the area has retained no Cambrian sediments). Late (Upper) Cambrian seas, as now represented by sedimentary rocks, extended farther onto the land mass than the Middle and Early (Lower) Cambrian seas did. (Reprinted, by permission, from G. M. Kay and E. H. Colbert, *Stratigraphy and Life History*, © 1965, by John Wiley and Sons)

TABLE 8.1. Generalized Stratigraphic Sequence West of the Blue Ridge Complex

		NAMES	DESCRIPTION
Pennsylvanian	Lower	Harlan Ss. Wise Fm. Gladeville Ss. Norton Fm. Lee Fm.	In general: ss, locally arkosic and/or conglomeratic, and sh with intercalated coal beds; a few thin ls strata occur locally near base; plant fossils are abundant locally; largely nonmarine
Mississippian	Upper	Bluestone Fm.	ls, various colored limy shs, ss, cg and local coal; fossiliferous—includes land plants
		Princeton Ss.	conglomeratic ss & graywacke with some ls pebbles
		Hinton Fm. (also called Pennington Fm.)	red sh, ss, local beds of impure ls; moderately fossiliferous
		Bluefield Sh. (formerly Glen Dean Ls.)	interbedded ls and red, yellow, and blue shs; fossiliferous
	Middle	Greenbrier Ls. (includes Little Valley Ls., Warsaw Fm., Hillsdale Ls. [=St. Louis Ls.], Ste. Genevieve Ls., Gasper Ls., etc.)	chiefly ls—some shaly, some cherty, some oölitic; local mudstones; locally fossiliferous
		Maccrady Sh.	red shaly siltstones and sandy mudstones: local salt and gypsum
	Lower	Price Fm. (formerly Pocono Fm.; locally has Parrott and Cloyd cgs. near base)	sh, ss, local coal beds; conglomerates locally near base; mixed marine and nonmarine
Devonian	Upper	Hampshire Fm. "Chemung" Fm. Brallier Sh.	red arkosic ss & mudstones; nonmarine arkosic ss, sh & thin cgs; fossiliferous sandy, micaceous green sh; fossiliferous
	Middle	Millboro Sh.	black sh; commonly contains "cannon-ball" concretions
	Lower	Huntersville Cht. (equals part of Needmore Sh.)	phosphatic, limy ss & chert; Needmore is calcareous sh
		Ridgeley Ss. (formerly Oriskany Ss.)	coarse friable ss, locally iron carbonate-cemented; fossiliferous
		Licking Creek Ls. (Rocky Gap Ss. is. laterally equiv.; formerly called Becraft Ls.)	cherty ls, sandy to southwest; fossiliferous
		New Scotland Ls.	cherty ls; fossiliferous
		Coeymans Ls.	crinoidal ls
		Keyser Ls.	ls, local ss interbeds; fossiliferous—some "reef-like" masses
Silurian	Upper	Tonoloway Ls.	laminated black ls; fossiliferous
		Wills Creek Sh.	clayey & sandy ls & sh; local salt
	Middle	"Keefer" Ss.	white ss, calcareous to northwest
		Rose Hill Fm. (formerly called Clinton Fm.)	variegated sh & ss, some highly ferruginous sparsely to highly fossiliferous
	Lower	Tuscarora Ss. (also called Clinch Ss.)	pure quartz ss

TABLE 8.1 (*cont.*)

		NAMES	DESCRIPTION
Ordovician	Upper	Juniata Fm.	red sh & ss; at least in part nonmarine
Ordovician	Middle	Martinsburg Fm. (part Late and part Middle Ordovician)	calcareous sh & siltstone; fossiliferous
Ordovician	Middle	Middle Ordovician Fms. (includes Liberty Hall Sh., Moccasin Fm.—a limy mudstone, Mosheim Ls., and several other chiefly limestone units)	heterogeneous as names indicate; locally cherty; includes bentonites; locally fossiliferous—some "reeflike" accumulations
	Lower		
Cambrian	Upper	Knox Dolo. Group (constituted by Copper — — Ridge Dolo., Conococheaque Ls., Chepultepec Ls., Longview Ls., etc.)	pure & impure dolo & ls, some is cherty, some is sandy; sparsely fossiliferous
Cambrian	Upper	Nolichucky Sh.	alternating sh & ls, locally glauconitic; fossiliferous
Cambrian	Middle	Elbrook Dolo. (Honaker Dolo. is laterally equivalent)	laminated and/or brecciated dolo & ls, locally shaly

		SW of Roanoke	NE of Roanoke	
Cambrian (Lower)	Rome Fm.	Waynesboro Fm.	red & green sh, dolo; local ls; sporadic fossils
	Shady Dolo.	Tomstown Dolo.	dolo, local ls; local "reeflike" fossil accumulations
	Erwin Qtzt.	Antietam Ss.	clean, quartz ss & qtzt; sporadic fossils
Precambrian	Hampton Fm.	Harpers Sh.	siltstone & sh
	Unicoi Fm.	Weaverton Ss.	coarse arkosic ss & cg; basalt flows in Unicoi
	Mt. Rogers Vols.	Catoctin Fm.	Catoctin—basaltic vols, coarse ss, & cg Mt. Rogers—silicic vols, coarse ss, & cg
	Blue Ridge "Complex"		metamorphic & igneous

NOTE: Wavy line represents widespread unconformity; abbreviations used are cg, conglomerate; cht, chert; dolo, dolomite; fm, formation; ls, limestone; qtzt, quartzite; sh, shale; ss, sandstone; and vols, volcanics.

nated; chemical destruction of all but the quartz in the source area, or repeated winnowing out by water of all extraneous material in the area of deposition, or a combination of these two seem to be good possibilities. (3) The very efficient sorting could have been accomplished in several ways: actually the suggested source (1) and the possible elimination processes (2) would each tend to accomplish such sorting. Although several questions remain to be answered, two conditions appear to be reflected by these sediments no matter what the additional nuances: (*A*) the source area must have been undergoing predominantly chemical weathering, and (*B*) both the source area and the basin of deposition must have been quite stable during the period.

Marine animals, whose remains constitute the oldest identified fossils within this sedimentary pile, inhabited the area while the Erwin-Antietam sediments were being deposited. The included trilobite fossils are characteristic of Early Cambrian time; hence geologists generally consider this unit to be the oldest Paleozoic rock within the miogeosynclinal part of the Appalachians.

During the late stages of Erwin-Antietam sand deposition, fine silts and clays were introduced into the basin, and carbonate sediment made its first appearance. The top few feet of the formation are typically cemented by dolomite.

The overlying Shady Dolomite unit consists almost wholly of dolomite and limestone. Neither the source of the carbonate nor the change in conditions that caused carbonate deposition are well understood. In a few localities during this period of sedimentation there were reeflike accumulations of fossils. A fine example of such a reef occurs at Austinville in southern Wythe County.

After several hundred feet of carbonate sediments were deposited, there was an influx of clay-bearing waters into the basin of deposition. The shale formed from these clays marks the beginning of Rome-Waynesboro sedimentation. The complete Rome-Waynesboro unit, however, consists not only of shales but also of numerous carbonate units. Most of the shales are red, but a few are buff, greenish, bluish, or gray. Most of the carbonate rocks are dolomite, but a few are limestone lenses. The presence of mud cracks, ripple marks, and other such features within several of the shales suggests deposition on tidal flats and in other shallow-water, near-shore environments.

It is noteworthy that the dolomite strata in the lower part of this unit are essentially indistinguishable from dolomite layers in the underlying Shady Dolomite and that dolomite strata in the upper part of the Rome-Waynesboro unit are quite similar to some of the dolomites in the overlying Elbrook and Honaker formations. Furthermore, some of the Elbrook dolomites are essentially indistinguishable from those in the overlying Knox Group. Therefore, in the over-all history it seems that the Rome Formation detrital units may be considered to be only examples of the sporadic and intermittent interruptions that took place during the period of predominantly carbonate sedimentation that began with the Shady dolomites and continued until the late part of the Middle Ordovician (Martinsburg). It is also interesting that the detrital deposition initiated in the Late Precambrian time and which included the sedimentary part of the Mt. Rogers and Catoctin sequence, the Unicoi-Weaverton, the Hampton-Harpers, and the Erwin-Antietam units could quite logically have evolved into the kind of detrital sedimentation that is characteristic of the Rome-Waynesboro unit. A rather stable landmass undergoing progressive lowering because of weathering and erosion might be expected to supply detritus in the sequence reflected in these rocks.

After deposition of the Rome-Waynesboro unit, carbonate deposition predominated in the geosyncline throughout Middle and Late Cambrian and Early and Middle Ordovician time. However, even though a large percentage of the rocks of that period are generally similar, several different environments are indicated, for example, the one involving the "natural pollution" described in chapter V. Other especially noteworthy environmental conditions, listed chronologically, are quiet lagoonal conditions (laminated Elbrook); conditions conducive to glauconite formation (Nolichucky); near-shore marine environments which were intermittently hypersaline, normally saline, and silica rich and which were also intermittently receiving wind-blown and/or water-transported sand (Knox); terrestrial exposure of the sediments to subaerial erosion with production of a relief of up to 400 feet (post-Knox-lowest Middle Ordovician interval); putrid and muddy marine waters (Liberty Hall Shale); sporadic conditions permitting reeflike accumulations of fossils (Middle Ordovician); and the showering down of windblown volcanic material (Middle Ordovician bentonites).

This Late Cambrian–Early and Middle Ordovician deposition of the chiefly carbonate sequence was brought to a close with the influx of sand, silt, and clay in Late Middle Ordovician time. Most of the Moccasin-Martinsburg detrital sedimentation represents a relatively near-shore environment. Marine life became especially plentiful during the deposition of Martinsburg sediments.

The overlying Juniata, which consists chiefly of red beds, appears to represent a nonmarine environment throughout most of Virginia.

A large part of the next younger Early Silurian sedimentation within the region also consisted of clastic material (fig. 8.3). One rather peculiar environment, however, existed for a while during the lower Middle Silurian when highly ferruginous sands of the Rose Hill Formation were deposited. These iron-rich beds have been used in central New York and in the Birmingham district of Alabama as iron ore. A few calcareous beds occur in the lower part of the Upper Silurian section. From the Tonoloway unit upward through much of the Lower Devonian, limestone deposition again predominated. Reeflike masses occur within the Keyser Limestone that straddles the Silurian-Devonian boundary. These, like several other reeflike accumulations and even some of the individual fossils within the over-all

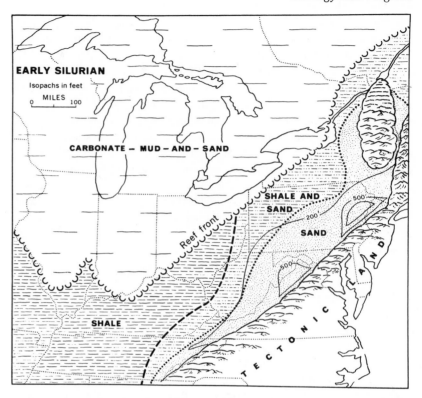

FIG. 8.3. Early Silurian paleogeography of central eastern North America. Map is schematic and highly interpretive because of lack of data. As may be seen, the interpretation given is that highlands on the east supplied the sediments; embayments existed in areas such as northeastern Pennsylvania and northwestern Virginia; and a reef front was present to the west and northwest. (Reprinted, by permission, from G. M. Kay and E. H. Colbert, *Stratigraphy and Life History,* © 1965, by John Wiley and Sons)

section, indicate that conditions within the Paleozoic sea of this region were similar to those of the shallow, subtropical oceanic areas existing today.

The overlying Devonian Coeymans Limestone consists to a large extent of crinoid columnals. In eastern belts south of the James River, Early Devonian rocks and most of the Silurian formations were removed by erosion or not deposited. In places, the Ridgeley Formation rests directly on top of "Keefer" or Tuscarora Sandstone. From the middle part of the Early Devonian up to the uppermost formation that represents the Devonian in this region, sedimentation was again predominantly fine sand, silt, and clay. The exceptional, locally phosphatic Huntersville chert probably represents a rather peculiar, stagnant, oxygen-deficient environment. The Millboro carbonaceous shales may reflect similarly stagnant, perhaps even putrid environments into which clay was carried and deposited. Above the Millboro the conditions were more nearly normal. The latest part of the Devonian, however, was a time when the sea was withdrawing from the area; the Hampshire Formation consists of nonmarine red beds.

The overlying lower Mississippian consists of a mixed group of marine and nonmarine deposits, including coal. The rest of the Mississippian, however, consists chiefly of interbedded detrital materials and limestones, all of which were apparently deposited under marine conditions. Exceptionally, within the Middle Mississippian (in the Maccrady Shale interval), salt and gypsum were deposited here and there. This deposition probably took place within lagoons or other more or less isolated, closed basins.

Near the end of Mississippian time, the sea again retreated. Thus, most of the sedimentation within western Virginia and adjacent areas during Pennsylvania time was under nonmarine, in part possibly brackish, conditions. The coal beds within this part of the section represent growth and decay in fresh water or tidal swamps relatively near a seacoast.

All the rocks of the miogeosynclinal basin of Virginia, except some of the Mississippian and Pennsylvanian strata, have been folded and/or faulted since their deposition. There are two general schools of thought with regard to the time or times when the structural deformation took place. Some of the geologists who are most familiar with the rocks of the region believe that the available evidence best supports the hypothesis that deformation was going on almost continuously throughout the period of sedimentation. Other geologists think that the deformation was spasmodic. Several of the latter group favor the idea that there were two or three periods of major deformation.

In any case, the major structures of the miogeosynclinal Appalachians appear to have been formed as the result of stresses that acted in a manner such that the rocks appear to have been compressed as the result of a pushing from the southeast toward the northwest. In addition, although it is commonly suggested that the rocks of the Blue Ridge Complex acted as the plunger which caused the compression, it is now known that at least some rocks of the complex were also thrust up to several miles out over the deformed sedimentary rocks of the miogeosynclinal sequence.

Two additional kinds of geological events not mentioned previously in this section but known to have occurred within the sedimentary Appalachians are the formation of some small igneous intrusive masses and local deposition from mineralizing solutions. There are small igneous masses in Augusta, Highland, and Rockingham counties. Sporadic zones of mineralization are well exemplified by the sulfide deposits of the Timberville Area of Rockingham and Shenandoah counties and of the Austinville-Ivanhoe District in southern Wythe County. The chronology of these events has not been well established.

Triassic Basin Sedimentation

As already mentioned, the deformation that resulted in the folding and faulting of the eugeosynclinal rocks was followed by weathering and erosion, which resulted in the formation of a rather mature erosion surface. This had happened prior to the block faulting and sedimentation that characterized the Late Triassic of eastern North America. In Virginia, Triassic sediments and near-surface intrusive rocks fill the basins which occur here and there on the presently exposed Piedmont geomorphic province and also beneath the Coastal Plain sediments. Similar Triassic basins occur sporadically from the Maritime provinces of Canada to at least South Carolina (fig .8.4).

The Triassic sedimentary rocks are chiefly red arkosic conglomerates and sandstones and shales, but they also include sparse limestone lenses and sporadic coal beds (table 8.2). Here and there the rocks contain nonmarine aquatic fossils and/or dinosaur tracks. The characteristics of most of the Triassic sediments suggest (1) that they were derived from an area that was undergoing chiefly physical weathering, (2) that the detritus was carried either rapidly or (and?) for only relatively short distances before deposition, and (3) that the

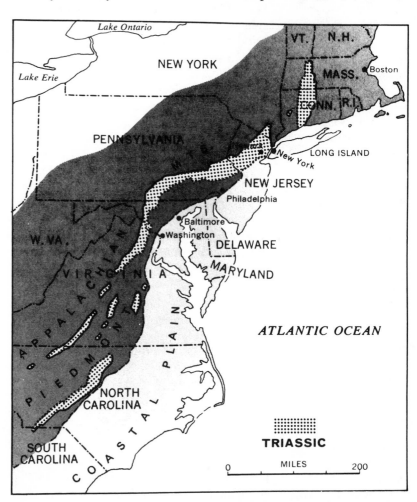

FIG. 8.4. Late Triassic rocks in eastern North America. Nonmarine sediments and volcanic rocks of late Triassic age make up the bedrock not only in the areas indicated on this map but also in the Bay of Fundy area of Nova Scotia and New Brunswick. (Reprinted, by permission, from G. M. Kay and E. H. Colbert, *Stratigraphy and Life History,* © 1965, by John Wiley and Sons)

basin of deposition was an area of rather poor, continually changing drainage. The diverse rock types also have spatial interrelationships that indicate that there were intermittent movements along the border faults of the basins during the period of sedimentation.

The characteristics of the basaltic intrusive bodies within the sedimentary sequence are such that it is clear that the magma from which they consolidated was intruded at shallow depths during the general period of Triassic sedimentation. This is corroborated by the fact that lavas of similar composition were extruded during the Late Triassic within some of the basins outside Virginia.

TABLE 8.2. Triassic Strata in Virginia

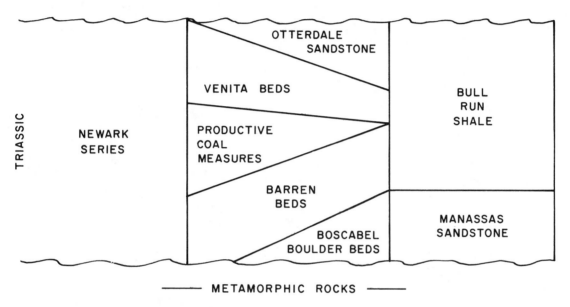

SOURCE: McKee et al., "Paleotectonic Maps of the Triassic System," U.S. Geol. Survey, Misc. Geol. Invest., Map I-300.

Coastal Plain Sediments

By Cretaceous time at least the eastern part of the Piedmont geomorphic province was again reduced to a relatively flat erosion surface. In Late Cretaceous time the ocean invaded eastern Virginia, at least as far west as the Fall Line, and sediments, chiefly from the west, were fed into the area (fig. 8.5).

According to the rock record thus far studied, the Late Cretaceous sediments were the first to be deposited during this general sedimentation period. Subsidence and sedimentation, interrupted several times by withdrawal of the sea from at least part of the area where Coastal Plain sequence sediments are now exposed, continued until the end of Miocene time. A sedimentary wedge that thickens from the Fall Line to at least 20,000 feet some 70 to 80 miles offshore was deposited. The general sequence is shown in table 8.3.

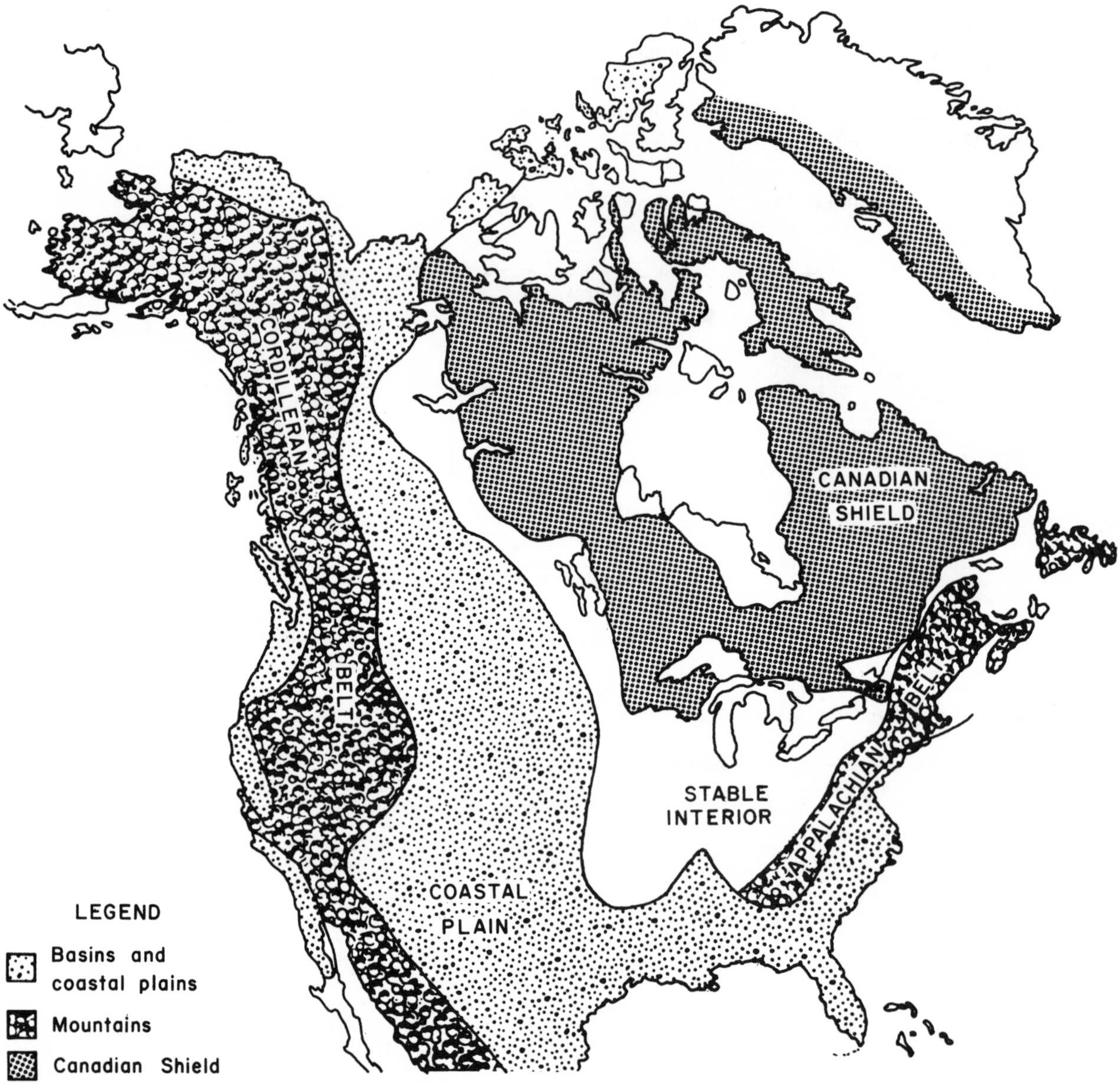

FIG. 8.5. Late Cretaceous of central North America

The present Fall Line is probably relatively near the strand line that existed during the deposition of these formations. Alternating transgressions and regressions of the ocean or subsidence and uplift of the land are indicated by the presence of several unconformities within the sequence. Some of the fossils present in, for example, the Patapsco formation indicate fresh or brackish, probably estuarine conditions. All the formations have characteristics, including fossil contents, that suggest deposition under climatic conditions more like those of the present-day Georgia and Florida coast than like those currently existent along the Virginia coast.

TABLE 8.3. Coastal Plain Sequence

Recent		Alluvium, soils, travertine	
Pleistocene		Terrace sands and gravels	
Pliocene		Upland gravels	
Miocene	Chesapeake group	Yorktown Formation	coquina, sd, clay, shell marl; highly fossiliferous
		St. Marys Formation	sd, some glauconitic, and blue-gray clay; locally fossiliferous
		Choptank Formation	dk brown sd & ss; mollusks
		Calvert Formation	sdy & diatomaceous clay; "diatomaceous earth"; fossil flora
(No Oligocene)			
Eocene	Pamunkey group	(Chickahominy Formation subsurface only)	glauconitic & pyritic clays
		Nanjemoy Formation	clayey greensds, pink clay near bottom, local gypsum
Paleocene(?)		Aquia Formation	limy greensds, some silica-cemented; fossiliferous
		(Mattaponi Formation subsurface only)	variegated, commonly mottled clays, greensds; abundant fossils
Cretaceous		Patapsco Formation	variegated clays and light-colored sdy clays; brackish water mollusk
		Patuxent Formation	gray to buff arkosic sd & ss, chloritic clay & gvl lenses; fossil flora in clay
Paleozoic(?), metamorphic rocks and Triassic rocks			

Later History

The late geological history of Virginia is largely unknown. The evidence is either lacking or has not been recognized. Nonetheless, at least the following must have been involved: (1) the formation of upland gravel deposits of Pliocene (?) age; (2) the deposition of beach sands and gravels *and* terrace formations atop the Coastal Plain sediments during periods of relatively high sea level during the Pleistocene; and (3) local alluviation, soil formation, cave excavation and deposition, and diverse weathering and erosion throughout at least post-Miocene time.

A few geologists have thought that they could recognize three or more episodes in which distinct erosional surfaces were developed in the eastern United States. The main surfaces conceived by these geologists are believed to have been developed in pre-Cretaceous, Middle Tertiary, and Late Tertiary time.

Several other kinds of events are generally thought to have occurred fairly recently. Examples, with possible dates given in parentheses, are: (1) the formation of bauxite and manganese nodule-bearing clay deposits in the Great Valley and along the western front of the Blue Ridge geomorphic province (Eocene ?), (2) the formation of lignite deposits on the Blue Ridge geomorphic province (Cretaceous ?), and (3) drainage changes such as capture of certain New River Basin streams by Roanoke River Basin streams (Late Paleozoic to Late Pleistocene ?).

As is quite evident, interpretations of the geologic history of Virginia have advanced a long way since Thomas Jefferson attributed the formation of Natural Bridge to "sudden convulsions in nature" and even since the nineteenth-century geologists Henry D. and William B. Rogers ascribed the folding and faulting in the Valley and Ridge Province and the intrusions of the Blue Ridge Province to "catastrophic explosions . . . [of] subsurface gas-charged lava." Nonetheless, as already mentioned, many data remain to be gathered before any truly comprehensive geologic history of the Old Dominion can be written with assurance of its validity. It is hoped that some of the readers of this brief sketch of Virginia's geologic history will help fill in some of the gaps and thus hasten the correct formulation of the Commonwealth's long and spectacular geologic history.

THESE tables are given to help identify some of the more common minerals. The minerals are divided into two main groups according to luster—nonmetallic and metallic. Minerals within each of these main groups are divided into smaller groups on the basis of color. Within the color groups the minerals are arranged in order of Mohs's hardness scale and each mineral name is followed by a remark, or "key test," a simple and reliable test that will usually pin down identification. Nearly all of the known minerals are given on tables similar to these in *Mineral Tables (Hand Specimen Properties of 1500 Minerals)* by the author.

TABLE A.1. Nonmetallic Minerals

Color	Hardness	Mineral	Key Test
Colorless or white	1	Talc	Soapy feel
	1	Kaolinite	Smells like clay when breathed upon
	1–3	Bauxite	Earthy; commonly in rounded grains
	2	Niter (saltpeter)	In crusts or needlelike crystals; soluble in water; cooling taste
	2	Gypsum	Transparent to translucent; one perfect cleavage
	2.5	Halite	Has salty taste
	2.5	Muscovite	Cleaves into thin elastic plates
	3	Barite	Heavy for a white mineral
	3	Calcite	Cleaves into blocks with diamond-shaped faces; effervesces with cold dilute hydrochloric acid
	3	Anhydrite	Massive; common associate to gypsum
	3.5	Aragonite	No cleavage; commonly stalactitic
	3.5	Dolomite	Effervesces with cold dilute hydrochloric acid when freshly powdered
	4	Fluorite	In cube-shaped crystals; cleaves into octahedrons (8-sided figures)
	5	Apatite	Commonly in hexagonal prisms with rounded edges; poor cleavage perpendicular to length
	5	Smithsonite	Typically in colloform, honeycombed crusts; effervesces in cold hydrochloric acid
	5	Hemimorphite	Similar to smithsonite but does not react with hydrochloric acid
	5–6	Amphibole (tremolite)	Two cleavages at about 55° and 125°
	6	Orthoclase	Two cleavages at right angles
	6	Plagioclase	Two cleavages at nearly right angles; apparent striations occur on better cleavage
	7	Quartz	Conchoidal fracture; vitreous
	8	Topaz	One perfect cleavage
	10	Diamond	Extremely high luster
Yellow to brown	1–5.5	Limonite	Yellow-brown streak
	2.5	Phlogopite	Brown mica; cleaves into elastic sheets
	2.5–4	Serpentine	Feels smooth; looks greasy
	3	Calcite	Three good cleavages yielding six-sided blocks with diamond-shaped faces; effervesces with cold dilute hydrochloric acid

(*Continued on next page*)

Nonmetallic Minerals (cont.)

Color	Hardness	Mineral	Key Test
Yellow to brown (*cont.*)	3.5	Sphalerite	Resinous; rotten egg odor when scratched
	4	Fluorite	Cubic crystals; cleaves into octahedrons
	4	Siderite	Cleaves into blocks with diamond-shaped faces
	5	Apatite	Commonly in hexagonal prisms with rounded edges; poor cleavage perpendicular to length of crystals
	5	Smithsonite	Typically in colloform, honeycombed crusts; effervesces in cold hydrochloric acid
	5	Hemimorphite	Similar to smithsonite but does not react with hydrochloric acid
	5.5	Hematite	Red-brown streak
	6	Rutile	Reddish-brown to black; very high luster
	6–7	Cassiterite	Brown to black; very high luster; very heavy
	7	Quartz	Conchoidal fracture
	7	Staurolite	Commonly in crossed twins
	7	Tourmaline	Typically long, slender, triangular-shaped crystals that are striated; high luster
	7–8	Zircon	Extremely high luster
Red to violet	1–3	Bauxite	Earthy; commonly in rounded grains
	3	Calcite	Effervesces with cold dilute hydrochloric acid
	4	Fluorite	Cubic crystals; cleaves into octahedrons
	5.5	Hematite	Red-brown when powdered
	6	Orthoclase	Salmon color; two cleavages at right angles
	6	Rutile	Reddish-brown; very high luster
	7	Garnet	Brittle; typically in 12- or 24-face crystals
	7	Quartz	Conchoidal fracture
	7.5	Spinel	Typically in 8-sided crystals (octahedrons)
Green or blue	1	Talc	Soapy feel
	2	Chlorite	Cleaves into thin nonelastic sheets
	2	Glauconite	Olive to dark green; commonly in small rounded grains
	2.5–4	Serpentine	Feels smooth; looks greasy
	3	Calcite	Effervesces with cold dilute hydrochloric acid
	3.5	Azurite	Dark or pale blue
	3.5	Malachite	Dark to light green
	3.5	Aragonite	No cleavage; commonly stalactitic
	4–7	Kyanite	Blue; bladed; H-7 across crystals; H-5 along length of crystals
	5	Apatite	Commonly in hexagonal prisms with rounded edges; poor cleavage perpendicular to length
	5–6	Amphibole	Two cleavages at about 55° and 125°
	5–6	Pyroxene	Two cleavages at nearly right angles
	6	Microcline (Amazon stone)	Blue-green; two cleavages at nearly right angles
	6–7	Epidote	Pistachio or yellow-green
	6–7	Olivine	Bottle-green; typically in sugarlike masses
	7–8	Beryl	Six-sided prisms; light blue-green
Gray or black	1	Graphite	Greasy feel; marks paper easily
	1–2	Pyrolusite	Rubs off on fingers; fibrous aggregates common
	1–6	Wad	Dull, earthy; commonly colloform; commonly called "bog manganese"
	1–6	Limonite	Yellow-brown streak
	2.5	Biotite	Cleaves into thin elastic sheets
	3	Anhydrite	Massive; common associate to gypsum
	3	Calcite	Effervesces in cold dilute hydrochloric acid
	5–6	Amphibole	Two cleavages at about 55° and 125°
	5–6	Pyroxene	Two cleavages at nearly right angles
	6	Psilomelane (and crypto-melane)	Commonly in colloform groups
	6–7	Cassiterite	Brown to black; very high luster; very heavy
	7	Garnet	Brittle; typically in 12 or 24 face crystals
	7	Quartz	Conchoidal fracture; vitreous
	7	Staurolite	Commonly in crossed twins
	7	Tourmaline	Typically long, slender, triangular-shaped crystals that are striated; high luster

TABLE A.2. Metallic and Submetallic Minerals

Color	Hardness	Mineral	Key Test
Black or dark gray	1	Graphite	Greasy feel; marks paper easily
	1–2	Pyrolusite	Rubs off on fingers; fibrous aggregates common
	1–6	Wad	Dull, earthy; commonly colloform; commonly called "bog manganese"
	2.5	Galena	Good cubic cleavage
	3	Chalcocite	Can be cut with a knife; brittle
	4	Manganite	Water given off when heated; common associate of pyrolusite
	5	Wolframite	Heavy; one perfect cleavage
	6	Magnetite	Magnetic
	6	Psilomelane (and crypto-melane)	Commonly in colloform groups
	5.5–6	Ilmenite	Massive granular; platy crystals; may be slightly magnetic
Light gray or silvery	5.5	Arsenopyrite	Garlic odor given off when broken
	6	Marcasite	Radiating masses common; decomposed readily to white power
Yellow to brassy	2.5	Gold	Malleable (flattens with hammer)
	3.5	Chalcopyrite	Yellow-brass color; commonly tarnished (peacock colors)
	3.5	Pyrrhotite	Slightly magnetic
	6	Pyrite	Massive or in equidimensional crystals
	6	Marcasite	Radiating masses common; readily decomposes to white powder
Red or brown	1–5.5	Limonite	Yellow-brown streak
	2.5–3	Copper	Malleable (flattens with hammer)
	3.5	Sphalerite	Resinous; rotten egg odor when scratched
	6	Hematite	Red-brown when powdered
	6	Rutile	Reddish-brown to black; very high luster; lighter than cassiterite
	6–7	Cassiterite	Brown to black; very high luster; very heavy

Topographic and Geological Maps

IN GEOLOGY, a good base map is a primary need, and a good geological map is a desired product. Therefore, it is necessary for anyone interested in geology to have a basic understanding of maps and how to use them.

Most maps are representations on a flat piece of paper of an area on the earth's surface. (The commonest exception is a map of some buried surface.) Thus a map may be said to give a bird's-eye view of an area.

It is, however, as if the bird were looking through a filter, because nearly all maps are restricted in their coverage. They show only certain natural and/or cultural features. For example, the typical road map shows only major roads, towns, and bodies of water and perhaps state and county boundaries. It gives no direct information about, for example, the location of hills versus valleys. Nonetheless, on the basis of what any map does show, one may locate himself with respect to some indicated feature(s) and, if he so desires, record something about that pin-pointed location. That it enables one to locate a specific place is, of course, one of the main values of just about any map.

The two kinds of maps of particular interest to geologists are the topographic map and the geological map. A good topographic map is the base map upon which the geologist generally prefers to record his field data. The geologic map thus becomes the geologist's data document.

Topographic Maps

The typical topographic map represents the relief—highs and lows—of the surface, roads, railroad tracks, power lines, buildings, other man-made structures and excavations, and gives political boundaries and geographic and place names. For Virginia the topographic sheets have been prepared and published by the U.S. Geological Survey and the Tennessee Valley Authority. These maps are printed in color with culture (man-made features) in black and red, contour lines in brown, and water in blue. Some maps are available with green overprinting that indicates the general distribution of vegetation. A few are available with shading, which aids some persons to perceive the relief better. Some of the map sheets have an explanation of their symbols printed on their reverse sides.

A booklet, *Topographic Maps,* which describes these maps, how they are prepared, the symbols used, and the like, has been prepared by the U.S. Geological Survey. This booklet and indexes indicating topographic map coverage for each of the states are available free of charge on request to the survey at either its Washington, D.C., or its Denver, Colorado, office.

Most of the symbols used on topographic maps are easily understood. Some beginners, however, have difficulty in understanding what the scale means and also in perceiving relief features by merely looking at the contour lines.

The scale is given as a ratio and/or fraction and is shown graphically. The ratio is between a unit on the map and the number of similar units on the surface represented. For example, the ratio 1:63,360 indicates that 1 inch on the map represents 63,360 inches, which equals 1 mile, on the represented surface of the earth. To put it another way, two points 1 inch apart on the map would be 1 mile apart on the ground. The graphic scale is particularly useful if the map, or part of it, is reduced or enlarged photographically; so changed, that scale may still be used to measure distances on the map.

The contour is the very essence of a topographic map. Contour lines indicate the relief of the represented surface. A contour is a line drawn to maintain the same elevation over its whole length (fig. B.1).

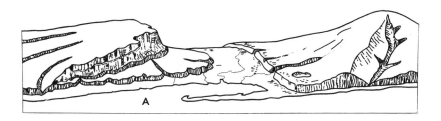

FIG. App. B.1. Contour lines: *A,* perspective sketch and, *B,* contour map of the same area. Notice that the steeper the slope, the more closely spaced the contour lines. (Reprinted, by permission, from C. R. Longwell, R. F. Flint, and J. E. Sanders, *Physical Geology,* © 1969, by John Wiley and Sons)

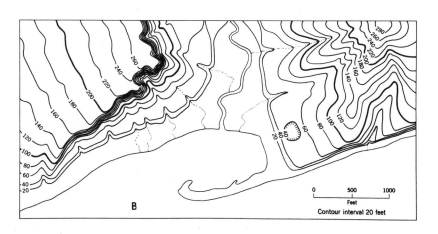

TABLE B.1. Common Geological Map Symbols

✗₂₅	Strike and dip of strata
✗	Strike of vertical strata
✗₂₅	Strike and dip of overturned strata
⊕	Horizontal strata
²⁰〰	General strike and dip of crumpled, etc., strata
✗₁₅	Strike and dip of foliation
✗	Strike of vertical foliation
✦	Horizontal foliation

A contour interval is the difference in elevation between adjacent contour lines. If the same contour interval—for example, 20 feet—is used, a relatively flat surface would have few contour lines whereas a hilly surface would have several. Additionally, the distance between contour lines varies inversely with surface slope: the closer the contour lines, assuming a constant contour interval, the steeper the represented slope.

Geological Maps

The typical geological map of a relatively small area of a few tens of square miles or less shows the nature and orientation of bedrock and other geological features. The different rock units are generally indicated in different colors and/or patterns; orientations (strike and dip) and structural features are usually indicated by more or less standard symbols (table B.1). In addition, some geological maps

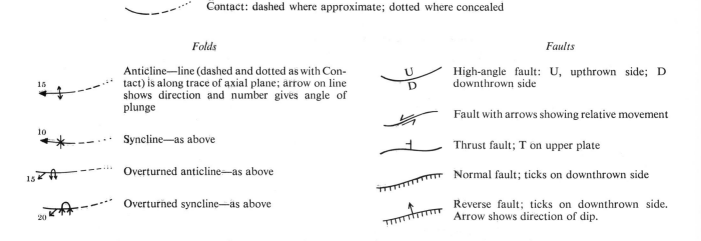

Contact: dashed where approximate; dotted where concealed

Folds

15 ↕ Anticline—line (dashed and dotted as with Contact) is along trace of axial plane; arrow on line shows direction and number gives angle of plunge

10 ✱ Syncline—as above

15 ↻ Overturned anticline—as above

20 ↻ Overturned syncline—as above

Faults

U/D High-angle fault: U, upthrown side; D downthrown side

Fault with arrows showing relative movement

⊥ Thrust fault; T on upper plate

Normal fault; ticks on downthrown side

Reverse fault; ticks on downthrown side. Arrow shows direction of dip.

show the locations and characteristics of certain surficial deposits.

Most geological maps of this general scale consist of an overprinting of the geology on the topographic base map of the area. This not only helps one to locate geological features but also permits him to ascertain relationships between topography and bedrock. It should never be forgotten that the topography and rock structure of an area may be quite different from each other—for example, a topographic basin may coincide with a rock structural dome (this is true of Burke's Garden in Tazewell County).

Geological maps of relatively large areas, such as states or countries, may be quite different. They are usually more generalized: only major rock units are differentiated, few if any structural symbols are given, and no topographic features are shown (see Appendix C). Limitations of space restrict such data; cluttering would lead to confusion.

Geological maps are often accompanied by structural cross sections (fig. B.2). These cross sections show how the rocks would appear if a deep vertical cut were made along the line of the section. Such sections almost always facilitate interpretation of the indicated relationships and sometimes permit the mapper to clarify his ideas.

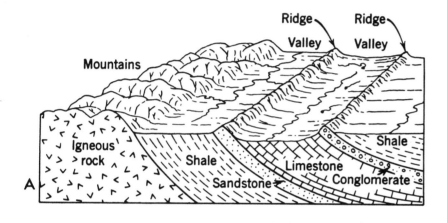

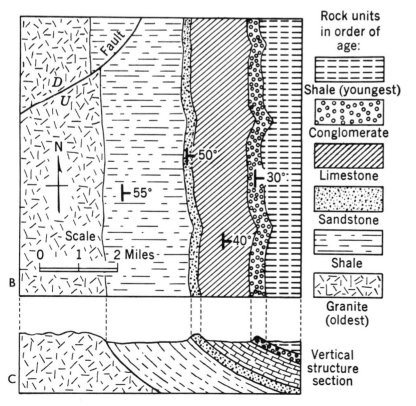

FIG. App. B.2.   *A,* block diagram; *B,* geologic map; *C,* cross section—all of the same area. (Reprinted, by permission, from A. N. Strahler, *Introduction to Physical Geography,* © 1965, by John Wiley and Sons)

Appendix C

Additional copies of this map
are available from

The Virginia Division of Mineral Resources
Box 3667
Charlottesville, Virginia 22903

COMMONWEALTH OF VIRGINI
DEPARTMENT OF CONSERVATION AND ECONOM
DIVISION OF MINERAL RESOURCES
James L. Calver
Commissioner of Mineral Resources and State

GEOLOGIC MAP OF VIRGI

Scale

| 0 | 25 | 50 | 75 | 100 |

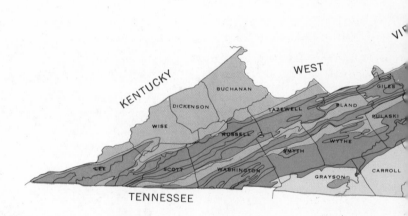

CENOZOIC   MESOZOIC

QUATERNARY   TERTIARY   CRETACEOUS   TRIASSIC
(0-1 million years) (1-70 million years)   (70-135 million years) (180-225 million
Sand and gravel.   Loose or partly in-   Partly indurated   years) Red and gray
Sand and gravel. durated sand, clay,   sand, clay, and   shales and sand-
                   marl, and diatom-   sandstone.   stones intruded by
                   aceous earth.   *Sand and clay.*   diabase; some thin
                   Sand, clay, marl,   coal layers.
                   and diatomaceous   *Crushed stone,*
                   earth.   *shale, and light-*
                                                             weight aggregate.

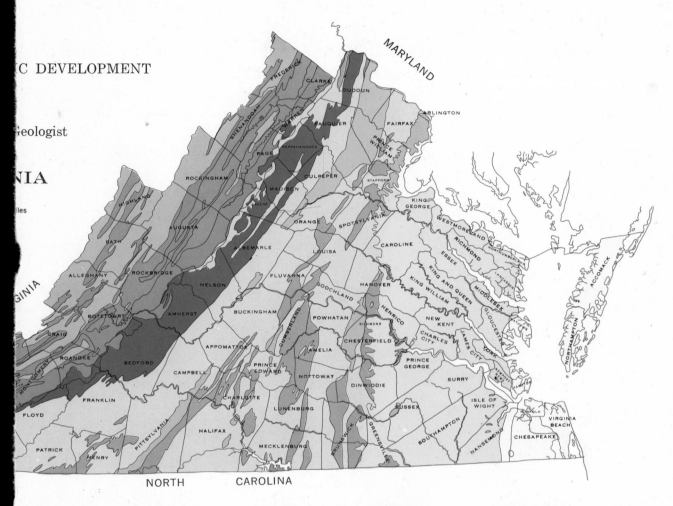

IC DEVELOPMENT

Geologist

NIA

iles

MARYLAND

NORTH CAROLINA

PALEOZOIC

PENNSYLVANIAN

(270-310 million years) Sandstone, shale, and coal. *Sand, coal, coke, lightweight aggregate, and natural gas.*

MISSISSIPPIAN-DEVONIAN

(310-400 million years) Sandstone, shale, limestone, gypsum, and coal. *Coal, coke, silica sand, gypsum, shale, cement, salt brine, and natural gas.*

SILURIAN-ORDOVICIAN

(400-500 million years) Limestone, dolomite, shale, and sandstone. *Lime, crushed stone, cement, shale, and petroleum.*

CAMBRIAN

(500-600 million years) Dolomite, limestone, shale, and sandstone. *Crushed stone, sand, zinc, lead, and shale.*

PRECAMBRIAN

VIRGINIA BLUE RIDGE COMPLEX

(Older than 600 million years) Granite and gneiss. *Crushed stone*

ROCKS OF UNCERTAIN AGE

GRANITE and GNEISS

Granite, granodiorite, augen-gneiss, granite gneiss. *Crushed stone.*

METAMORPHIC ROCKS and IGNEOUS INTRUSIVES

Schist, slate, phyllite, quartzite, marble, metamorphosed arkose and conglomerate; greenstone, diorite, and gabbro. *Crushed stone, soapstone, anorthosite, slate, dimension stone, kyanite, feldspar, aplite, and titanium minerals.*

Williams & Heintz Map Corporation, Washington 27, D.C.

Glossary

The following meanings are those implied by the word's use in this book; they should not be considered all-inclusive or hard-and-fast definitions. Mineral, rock, and fossil names are not included. Relatively common ones are described in chapters I, II, and III. For additional definitions of geological terms the reader is referred to the *Glossary of Geology and Related Sciences* published in 1960 by the American Geological Institute.

Absolute age, the age of a rock given in years; the age is generally based on isotopic data.

Abyssal zone, a deep-sea area.

Accessory mineral, in an igneous rock, a minor constituent that is disregarded in naming and classifying the rock.

Acicular, needlelike (said of crystals).

Adamantine, with a brilliant luster like that of a diamond.

Aggregate, the mineral and/or rock material mixed with, for example, cement to make concrete or mortar.

Alluvium, stream-deposited material.

Amorphous, having no apparent crystalline structure.

Amygdule, a filled vesicle, typically in basalt. (*adj.*—amygdaloidal).

Anthodites, aragonite, calcite, or gypsum in clumps of needlelike crystals deposited on a surface within a cave.

Anticline, a fold with its older strata nearer the center of the fold; typically, anticlines are upfolds— ∩.

Anticlinorium, a complex anticline that consists of subordinate folds, the whole having an archlike form.

Aphanite, crystalline rock in which the individual grains are so small that they cannot be distinguished by the unaided eye.

Arenaceous, consisting in a noteworthy part of quartz sand.

Argillaceous, containing abundant clay.

Asymmetric divide, a divide with streams on one side having steeper gradients than those on the other side.

Axes (*crystal*), see *Crystal axes.*

Axial plane, a plane that divides a fold into two equal parts.

Axis (*fold*), see *Fold axis.*

Bar, an offshore deposit, typically of elongate ridgelike shape, which is nearly always below water level.

Baselevel, the level below which stream erosion cannot take place.

Bathyal zone, the submarine continental slope between the continental shelf and the deep-ocean basin.

Bathylith (var. batholith), an intracrustal (=within the earth's crust) igneous mass having no known bottom and a horizontal plane intercept of greater than 40 square miles.

Bed, a stratum or layer; also the bottom of a stream channel.

Bed-load, the portion of a stream's sedimentary load that is rolled along the bottom of the stream channel as contrasted with the suspended load of finer particles.

Bedrock, the continuous solid rock that is exposed at the surface or is directly beneath soil or other unconsolidated deposits.

Bentonite, decomposed volcanic ash consisting chiefly of montmorillonitic clay. It commonly has the ability to absorb relatively large quantities of water and thus to swell.

Biochemical deposition, chemical precipitation promoted by some biological activity.

Biogeochemistry, a branch of geochemistry which deals with biological materials and processes.

Biostratigraphy, stratigraphy based on paleontologic data.

Cabochon, a polished gemstone with a smooth convex surface.

Calcareous, containing a noteworthy part of calcium carbonate.

Carbonaceous, containing a noteworthy part of amorphous carbon and/or some solid organic hydrocarbon(s).

Cirque, the head of a glacial valley that is shaped like a half cup.

Clastic, fragmental.

Cleavage, the tendency of crystalline substances to break, or split, along plane surfaces the positions of which are controlled by the substances' atomic structures.

Coal, a natural fuel consisting of solid hydrocarbons.

Colloform, having rounded or hemispherical prominences.

Colluvium, unconsolidated rock material that has moved downslope under the influence of gravity.

Column, a cave deposit formed by the merging of a stalactite and a stalagmite.

Conchoidal, relating to the smooth, concave, shell-like fractures characteristic of some materials—for example, quartz, glass, and some quartzite.

Concretion, an ellipsoidal or irregularly shaped mass, typically developed within sedimentary rocks by localized deposition around some nucleus.

Contour, an imaginary line on the earth's surface, all parts of which have the same elevation.

Crystal, a solid, bounded by plane surfaces, which is the outward manifestation of the regular periodic arrangement of constituent atoms, ions, or molecules.

Crystal axes, a convenient coordinate system used to characterize property functions of crystals.

Crystal habit, a crystal form that is typical for a given material.

Crystal structure, the periodic repetition of any certain arrangement of atoms.

Crystallography, the study of interatomic configurations within solids and the external forms that express those configurations.

Decomposition, the breaking down of rock that involves such reactions as solution and oxidation (=chemical weathering).

Dendrite, a mineral growth that branches irregularly like a tree.

Dendritic drainage, a stream pattern that branches irregularly like a tree.

Detrital, synonym for *fragmental.*

Diagenesis, changes that take place in sediments after their deposition but before, and commonly contributing to, their conversion to solid rocks.

Diaphaneity, the state or quality of transmitting light. Degrees of diaphaneity are described by terms like *transparent, translucent,* and *opaque.*

Differential thermal analysis, a method commonly used to determine the temperatures at which thermal reactions take place.

Dike, a tabular igneous mass that transects the bedding or foliation of the rocks adjacent to it.

Dip, the angle between the horizontal and a described plane.

Disintegration, the breaking down of rock that involves loosening and breaking up of large fragments into smaller ones without changing the composition of the original substances (=physical weathering).

Dissected, cut by erosion; said of surfaces.

Disseminated-type deposit, an ore deposit in which the desired mineral or minerals are more or less scattered throughout the ore.

Divide, the boundary line between two adjacent drainage basins.

Draperies, a cave formation that resembles window draperies.

Druse, an encrustation consisting of minute crystals.

Effervesce, to foam or bubble as gas escapes—for example, when hydrochloric acid is put on calcite.

Ejected, see *Extrusive.*

Element, any substance of fixed atomic composition that cannot be separated into substances different from itself by ordinary chemical means.

Eolian (or *aeolian*), relating to natural wind activities or deposits.

Erosion, the weathering and transportation of rock or unconsolidated materials.

Escarpment, a relatively long steep slope or cliff.

Estuary, the relatively wide downstream portion of a stream that is subject to the tidal activities of the ocean.

Eugeosyncline, a geosyncline containing notable quantities of volcanic rocks.

Extrusive, relating to igneous material ejected out onto the earth's surface, for example, volcanic rocks; synonym for *ejected* or, in part, for *supracrustal.*

Facies, rocks which have distinctive characteristics and are associated in space and origin but were formed in environments different from those of other parts of the same over-all rock unit.

Fault, a rock fracture with a lateral displacement of the rocks on one side of the break with respect to those on the other.

Flowstone, a cave deposit formed on a wall (as distinct from, for example, stalagmites, which may be termed *dripstone*).

Fluorescence, the emission of visible energy as a result of exposure of a material to ultraviolet light, *x*-ray beams, etc.

Fold axis, a line formed by the intersection of an axial plane and a surface of stratification.

Foliation, the streaked or banded appearance of a metamorphic or igneous rock that reflects a segregation and/or preferred orientation of platy or rodlike constituent minerals.

Foot wall block, a fault block beneath the fault zone of any nonvertical fault.

Fossil, a life form or evidence for life recorded in rock.

Fragmental, consisting of fragments of preexisting rocks; applied to sediments and sedimentary rocks or the rocks made up of such fragments (a synonym for *clastic* and *detrital*).

Geochemistry, the study of the abundances and distribution of elements in the diverse parts of the earth and its atmosphere.

Geochronology, the study of geologic time.

Geodesy, the study of the shape and size of the earth.

Geology, the over-all study of the earth.

Geomorphic province, a region characterized by a related group of landforms which are relatively distinct from those of adjacent provinces.

Geomorphology, the study of land forms.

Geopetal, of or relating to features useful in determining original tops and bottoms of rock units such as sedimentary layers.

Geophysics, the science treating the effects of natural or artificially produced seismic (earthquake) waves or electrical currents and of the earth's gravity or magnetism.

Geosyncline, an elongate belt in the earth's crust which subsided while great thicknesses (of several thousand feet) of sediments were accumulated within it.

Glass, a liquid with so high a viscosity that it appears solid. (The constituent atoms and ions do not have a regular arrangement like those of crystalline materials.)

Gouge, fine-grained material formed when rocks are ground up within a fault zone.

Groundmass, the finer grained matrix surrounding the larger phenocrysts in a porphyry.

Guide fossil, any type of organic remains useful in determining geologic age because it occurs in large numbers over a wide area within layers deposited during a relatively short period of time.

Hanging wall block, a fault block above the fault zone of any nonvertical fault.

Hardness, resistance to scratching.

Heave, the horizontal component of movement along a fault.

Helictite, a twiglike growth of calcite and/or aragonite which typically occurs in caves.

Hydrocarbon, a compound of hydrogen and carbon.

Hydrous, containing chemically combined water.

Ichnofossil, a fossil trail, track, or burrow.

Igneous rock, rock formed by the cooling and consolidation of magma.

Impoundment, an area of confinement—for example, of a stream behind a dam to form a lake.

Index fossil, a guide fossil.

Injected, see *Intrusive.*

Inorganic, containing no carbon of organic origin.

Intaglio, a carved gem with the carving incised below the main surface.

Intracrustal, relating to masses and processes occurring within the earth's crust.

Intrusive, commonly used as a synonym for *intracrustal* as applied to igneous masses (The term probably should be restricted to masses emplaced into preexisting rock.)

Invertebrate paleontology, the study of fossils of animals without backbones.

Iridescent, exhibiting multicolored reflections.

Isomorphic series, any pair or group of mineral compounds having the same structure and forming "solid solutions"; that is, the atoms, ions, and/or molecules of one may replace those of the other(s) without changing the basic structural arrangement.

Isotope, a name given to different forms of the same element which differ because of having different numbers of neutrons in their nuclei (and thus also different mass numbers).

Laccolith, a floored, lens-shaped igneous intrusive.

Lacustrine, pertaining to lakes.

Lagoon, a shallow part of a sea or ocean nearly surrounded by land.

Lamina, a thin sedimentary layer (typically less than 1 centimeter thick).

Lapidary, a gem cutter and/or polisher.

Lava, magma that is extruded onto the earth's surface.

Layer, a sedimentary stratum, bed, or lamina.

Levee, a bank that serves to confine a stream. There are both natural and man-made levees.

Littoral zone, an area near the shore of an ocean or sea which is not strictly marine or nonmarine. It includes the area between the levels of the lowest and highest tides. Also referred to as *strand.*

Luster, the appearance of a surface in reflected light.

Magma, molten or partially molten rock material.

Magnetism, the physical property rendering a substance capable of being attracted to a magnet.

Mantle, unconsolidated material atop bedrock. Also called *regolith.*

Marine, oceanic.

Mass wasting, downslope movement of material in response to gravity.

Meandering stream, a stream with a wandering course consisting of relatively regular curves.

Metamorphic rock, rock formed by the transformation of preexisting rock in response to changes in temperature and/or pressure, sometimes accompanied by changes in chemical environment. The process is called *metamorphism*.

Meteorite, a mass of natural material that has landed on the earth from outer space.

Meteorology, the science of the earth's atmosphere.

Microphanerite, a term applied to igneous rocks the specific minerals of which are distinguishable by the naked eye but which are less than about 1 millimeter in greatest dimension.

Migmatite, "mixed rock" consisting of different metamorphic or of metaphoric and igneous components, one of which apparently had at some time or times a greater mobility than the rest of the rock.

Mineral, a natural substance, generally inorganic, with a characteristic internal arrangement of atoms and a chemical composition and physical properties that are either fixed or that vary within a definite range.

Mineralogy, the study of minerals.

Miogeosyncline, a geosyncline containing *no* volcanic rocks.

Monadnock, an isolated mountain on either a mature erosion surface or a peneplane.

Monocline, a stairlike, one-limb fold.

Moonstone, feldspar that exhibits opalescence.

Mudflow, a flowage of debris with relatively little included water. This process is intermediate between a landslide and stream flow.

Native, relating to minerals, such as sulfur and gold, that occur as chemical elements in the pure state—that is, uncombined with other elements.

Neritic zone, a submarine, continental shelf area.

Nonclastic, nondetrital.

Nondetrital, of or relating to sedimentary rocks consisting wholly or chiefly of mineral grains that have been chemically or biochemically precipitated from aqueous solutions on or near the surface of the earth.

Nonfragmental, nondetrital.

Nonmarine, not of the sea or ocean.

Normal fault, a fault the hanging wall block of which moved down relative to the foot wall block.

Oceanography, the over-all study of the sea.

Octahedral, in the isometric crystal system, having eight triangular faces of equal size; used to describe a crystal or cleavage form.

Oölite, a small, nearly spherical mass which is typically calcium carbonate and may resemble fish roe; also, any rock consisting chiefly of such masses.

Ore, an aggregate of useful and worthless minerals from which the former can be separated at a profit.

Orogeny, mountain-building activities whereby geosynclinal sediments and/or volcanics are folded and faulted and in some cases metamorphosed.

Overturned (beds or folds), of or relating to a stratum with its original top beneath its original bottom; used to describe a fold one limb of which consists of overturned strata.

Paleobotany, the study of fossil plants.

Paleoclimatology, the study of ancient climates.

Paleoecology, the study of the relationships of ancient animals to their environments.

Paleontology, the study of fossils.

Palynology, the study of spores and pollen.

Parting, the tendency of certain minerals to break along composition planes of twin crystals. Sometimes the term is described as breakage along planes that are not cleavage planes, but, as is apparent from the preceding definition, parting could be parallel to cleavage.

Pedology, the study of the mineralogy of soils.

Pegmatite, any exceptionally coarse-grained igneous rock or multi-mineralic hydrothermal vein typically consisting chiefly of quartz, alkali feldspars, and mica.

Pelagic zone, the open-water part of the oceans; this "zone" is generally considered to be above the water depth of approximately 600 feet.

Peneplane, an erosion surface which is *almost a plane* and has been formed as a result of mass wasting and stream activity.

Permineralization, the adding of mineral matter to porous material, for example, bone or wood.

Petrography, the branch of petrology related chiefly to the description of rocks.

Petrology, the study of rocks.

Phanerite, an igneous rock in which the specific minerals are greater than 1 millimeter in greatest dimension.

Phase equilibrium studies, investigations of the actions of and reactions among different proportions of diverse phases (compositions) under controlled conditions of temperature and pressure.

Phenocryst, a relatively large grain surrounded by a finer-grained ground-mass (matrix) in a porphyry.

Phosphorescence, luminescence that continues after the source of excitation has been removed.

Phylum, a major division in the classification of both plants and animals.

Physical stratigraphy, stratigraphic studies based chiefly on petrographic data.

Pisolite, pea-sized oölite.

Plateau, an extensive, relatively high-level, flat surface underlain largely by horizontal strata.

Plunge, the dip of a fold axis.

Polymorphic, pertaining to different crystal structure forms of the same chemical substance.

Porphyry, igneous rock in which relatively large and conspicuous grains, phenocrysts, are surrounded by a finer-grained matrix, generally called the *groundmass.*

Pyroclastic rock, consolidated volcanic fragments extruded explosively and deposited like sediment—that is, by settling either on land or in water.

Radioactive, capable of spontaneous disintegration of an atomic nucleus with the emission of alpha or beta particles and/or gamma radiation.

Relief, difference in elevations on a surface.

Residuum, unconsolidated rock material which formed essentially where it now occurs—that is, it has not been transported.

Resinous, having a nonmetallic luster resembling that of freshly broken resin.

Reverse fault, a fault the hanging wall block of which moved up dip relative to the foot wall block.

Rock, a natural solid composed of mineral grains or natural glass or a combination of these.

Rubble, loose angular fragments, commonly colluvial.

Saprolite, mantle in which certain structures of the parent rock are still easily recognized.

Scarp, escarpment.

Sediment, chemically and/or biochemically precipitated minerals or fragments of preexisting rocks which have accumulated on the earth's surface.

Sedimentary rock, consolidated sediment.

Sedimentology, the study of sediment formation.

Seismology, the study of natural and artificial earthquake waves.

Silicate, any substance that contains the SiO_4 tetrahedron as an essential part of its structure.

Siliceous, consisting in a noteworthy part of silica (SiO_2).

Sill, a tabular, intrusive igneous mass that is concordant (parallel) with the bedding or foliation of the rocks adjacent to it.

Sink hole, a depression in the earth's surface formed by the collapse of the roof of a cave.

Slickensides, extremely smooth, slick surfaces along which movement has occurred. These are typically but not exclusively found to occur in fault zones.

Sliderock, rock that has moved by mass wasting.

Slip, the displacement along a fault.

Solubility, capability of being dissolved.

Solution sink, a sink hole.

Species, a biological subdivision based on the capability of its members to breed only with others of their kind and thereby produce offspring which, in turn, have that same capability.

Specific gravity, the ratio of the weight of a substance to the weight of an equal volume of water.

Specific mineral, in an igneous rock, the mineral or minerals required by the definition of the rock.

Stalactite, a cave "icicle" (hanging downward from the roof), commonly composed of calcium carbonate.

Stalagmite, an inverted cave "icicle," that is, one extending upward from the floor.

Stratification, the layering of sedimentary rocks.

Stratigraphy, the description of layered rocks.

Stratum (*strata* pl.), a sedimentary layer or bed.

Streak, the color of the powder of a mineral.

Strike, the compass direction of a horizontal line in a plane.

Structural geology, the study of deformed rocks.

Supracrustal, pertaining to rocks and processes that have been formed or take place on the surface of the earth.

Syncline, a fold with its younger strata nearer the center of the fold; typically, synclines are downfolds — ∪.

Talus, rock waste which has accumulated at the bottom of a cliff or steep slope chiefly as the result of physical weathering and gravity.

Tectonophysics, the study that relates rock deformation to physical principles.

Terrace, a relatively level-topped, elongate surface formed by stream, lake, or marine erosion.

Throw, the vertical component of movement along a fault.

Topography, the form and relief of a land surface.

Travertine, cave-deposited or spring-deposited calcium carbonate.

Trellis drainage pattern, a generally rectilinear pattern of streams.

Turbidity current, a high-density current that typically moves along the bottom of a lake, sea, or ocean.

Twinning, the distinctive characteristic of any crystal that appears to consist of two or more parts arranged so that the unit looks like two or more symmetrically united or intergrown crystals.

Unconformity, a surface marking a gap in continuity between rock units below and above. The gap represents a period of erosion and/or of nondeposition.

Unctuous, having a soapy feel.

Uniformitarianism, a principle which states that the present is the key to the past.

Upland, an area which has the general landform appearance of a plateau but which is *not* underlain by essentially horizontal strata.

Varietal mineral, in an igneous rock, any mineral that is commonly, although not necessarily, present. The names of varietal minerals are generally used as adjectives in the complete designations of the rocks containing them.

Varve, a sedimentary layer or combination of different layers deposited in one year.

Vein, a mineral-filled fracture in rock.

Vertebrate paleontology, the study of fossils of animals with backbones.

Vesicle, a small, typically spheroidal cavity which has been formed by the expansion of gas bubbles or steam during solidification of magma to an aphanitic or glassy igneous rock. (See *amygdule.*)

Vitreous, having the luster of broken glass.

Volcanology, the study of volcanoes and volcanic activity.

Weathering, pertaining to the processes and products of chemical and mechanical changes that take place as the result of exposure to the elements.

X-ray diffraction analysis, analysis whereby X-rays are diffracted through a substance in order to determine the internal arrangement of atoms, ions, and molecules within that substance.

Supplementary Readings

SELECTED references are listed here under headings corresponding to the titles of the chapters. General references and readings dealing with the historical growth of the geological sciences are listed in the first section. A book on reading maps is listed as section IX. Guidebooks and road logs pertaining to Virginia geology constitute the final group of references. The reader should also consult the *Encyclopedia Americana,* the *Encyclopaedia Britannica,* other encyclopedias, and the booklet *The Geology Merit Badge* used by the Boy Scouts of America. The Virginia Division of Mineral Resources (Box 3667, University Station, Charlottesville, Virginia, 22904) publishes several series of reports dealing with geological phenomena within the state.

Introduction

Adams, F. D. 1938 (repr. 1954). *The Birth and Development of the Geological Sciences.* New York: Dover. 506p.

Albritton, C. C., Jr. 1963. *The Fabric of Geology.* Reading, Mass.: Addison-Wesley. 372p.

Cloos, Hans. 1953. *Conversation with the Earth.* New York: Knopf, 413p.

Geological Society of America. 1941. *Geology, 1888–1938: 50th Anniversary Volume.* New York: Geol. Soc. America. 578p.

Gieke, Archibald. 1905 (repr. 1962). *The Founders of Geology.* 2d ed. New York: Dover. 486p.

Gilluly, James, Waters, A. C., and Woodford, A. O. 1968. *Principles of Geology.* 3d ed. San Francisco: Freeman. 687p.

Holmes, Arthur. 1965. *Principles of Physical Geology.* 2d ed. New York: Ronald. 1288p.

Howell, J. V. (coordinator). 1960. *Glossary of Geology and Related Sciences.* Washington, D.C.: Amer. Geol. Inst. With supplement. 325 and 72p.

Longwell, C. R., Flint, R. F., and Sanders, J. E. 1969. *Physical Geology.* New York: Wiley. 685p.

Longwell, C. R., Knopf, Adolph, Flint, R. F., Schuchert, Charles, and Dunbar, C. O. 1941. *Outlines of Geology.* 2d ed. 2 vols. New York: Wiley. 381 and 291p.

Mather, K. F., and Mason, S. L. 1939. *A Source Book in Geology.* New York: McGraw-Hill. 702p.

Merrill, G. P. 1924. *The First One Hundred Years of American Geology.* New Haven: Yale Univ. Press. 773p.

Moore, R. E. 1956. *The Earth We Live On: The Story of Geological Discovery.* New York: Knopf. 416p.

I. Minerals

Agfa-Gevaert (Incorp.). n.d. *The Structure of Matter.* Antwerp, Belgium: Agfa-Gevaert. 19p.

Berry, L. G., and Mason, B. H. 1959. *Mineralogy: Concepts, Descriptions, Determinations.* San Francisco: Freeman. 630p.

Deer, W. A., Howie, R. A., and Zussman, J. 1962. *Rock-forming Minerals.* 5 vols. New York: Wiley. 333, 379, 270, 435, and 371p.

Dietrich, R. V. 1969. *Mineral Tables (Hand Specimen Properties of 1500 Minerals).* New York: McGraw-Hill, 237p.

———. 1970. *Minerals of Virginia.* Va. Poly. Inst. & State Univ., Res. Div. Bull. 47. 330p.

Frondel, Clifford. 1962. *Dana's System of Mineralogy.* vol. III, *Silica Minerals.* 7th ed. New York: Wiley. 384p.

Liddicoat, R. T., Jr. 1966. *Handbook of Gem Identification.* 8th ed. Los Angeles: Gemological Inst. Amer. 361p.

Nassau, Kurt. 1964. Growing synthetic crystals. *Lapidary Jour.,* 18: 42–45, 313–17, 386–89, 474–77, 588–95, and 690–93.

Palache, P., Berman, H., and Frondel, C. 1944. *Dana's System of Mineralogy.* vol. I, *Elements, Sulfides, Sulfosalts, Oxides.* 7th ed. New York: Wiley. 834p.

———. 1951. *Dana's System of Mineralogy.* vol. II, *Halides, Carbonates . . .* 7th ed. New York: Wiley. 1124p.

Pauling, Linus. 1960. *The Nature of the Chemical Bond.* 3d ed. Ithaca, N.Y.: Cornell Univ. Press. 644p.

Pough, F. H. 1955. *A Field Guide to Rocks and Minerals.* 2d ed. Boston: Houghton Mifflin. 349p.

Sinkankas, John. 1955. *Gem Cutting: A Lapidary's Manual.* Princeton, N.J.: Van Nostrand. 413p.

———. 1966. *Mineralogy: A First Course.* Princeton, N.J.: Van Nostrand. 587p.

Zim, H. S., and Shaffer, P. S. 1957. *Rocks and Minerals: A Guide to Familiar Minerals, Gems, Ores, and Rocks.* New York: Golden Press. 160p.

II. Rocks

Bayly, Brian. 1968. *Introduction to Petrology.* Englewood Cliffs, N.J.: Prentice-Hall. 371p.

Daly, R. A. 1933. *Igneous Rocks and the Depths of the Earth.* 2d ed. New York: McGraw-Hill. 598p.

Dietrich, R. V. 1967. Gem-Rocks. *Rocks and Minerals,* 42: 340–43.

Folk, R. L. 1965. *Petrology of Sedimentary Rocks.* Austin, Tex.: Hemphill's. 159p.

Heinrich, E. W. 1956. *Microscopic Petrography.* New York: McGraw-Hill. 296p.

Huang, W. T. 1962. *Petrology.* New York: McGraw-Hill. 480p.

Pettijohn, F. J. 1957. *Sedimentary Rocks.* 2d ed. New York: Harper. 718p.

Pirsson, L. V., and Knopf, Adolph. 1947. *Rocks and Rock Minerals.* 3d ed. New York: Wiley. 349p.

Travis, R. B. 1955. Classification of rocks. *Quart. Colo. School of Mines,* vol. 50, no. 1. 98p.

Turner, F. J., and Verhoogen, Jean. 1960. *Igneous and Metamorphic Petrology.* 2d ed. New York: McGraw-Hill. 694p.

Tyrrell, G. W. 1929. *The Principles of Petrology.* 2d ed. New York: Dutton. 349p.

Williams, H., Turner, F. J., and Gilbert, C. M. 1954. *Petrography.* San Francisco: Freeman. 406p.

Wyllie, P. J. 1963. Applications of high pressure studies to the earth sciences. In *High Pressure Physics and Chemistry* (ed. by R. S. Bradley), 2:1–89. New York: Academic Press.

III. Fossils

Ager, D. V. 1963. *Principles of Paleoecology: An Introduction to the Study of How and Where Animals and Plants Lived in the Past.* New York: McGraw-Hill. 383p.

Andrews, H. N., Jr. 1961. *Studies in Paleobotany.* New York: Wiley. 487p. (With a chapter on palynology by C. J. Felix.)

Brenner, G. J. 1963. *The Spores and Pollen of the Potomac Group of Maryland.* Dept. of Geology, Mines and Water Resources of Md., Bull. 27. 215p.

Brown, Vinson. 1954. *How to Make a Home Nature Museum.* Boston: Little, Brown. 214p.

Buchsbaum, Ralph. 1938. *Animals without Backbones.* Chicago: Univ. of Chicago Press, 371p.

Butts, Charles. 1941. *Geology of the Appalachian Valley in Virginia.* Part II, *Fossil Plates and Explanations.* Va. Geol. Surv., Bull. 52, pt. 2. 271p.

Colbert, E. H. 1945. *The Dinosaur Book.* New York: Amer. Mus. Natural Hist. 156p.

———. 1955. *Evolution of the Vertebrates.* New York: Wiley. 479p.

Collinson, C. W. 1959. *Guide for Beginning Fossil Hunters.* Ill. State Geol. Surv., Educ. Ser. 4. 36p.

Delevoryas, Theodore. 1962. *Morphology and Evolution of Fossil Plants.* New York: Holt, Rinehart and Winston. 189p.

Faegri, Knut. 1956. Recent trends in palynology. *Bot. Rec.,* 22: 639–64.

Fenton, C. L., and Fenton, M. A. 1958. *The Fossil Book.* New York: Doubleday. 482p.

Kummel, B., and Raup, D. 1965. *Handbook of Paleontological Techniques*. San Francisco: Freeman. 852p.

Mathews, W. H., III. 1960. *Texas Fossils: An Amateur Collector's Handbook*. Texas Bur. Econ. Geol., Guidebook 2. 123p.

——. 1962. *Fossils—An Introduction to Prehistoric Life*. New York: Barnes and Noble. 337p.

Moore, R. C., Lalicker, C. G. and Fisher, A. G. 1952. *Invertebrate Fossils*. New York: McGraw-Hill, 766p.

Moore, Ruth. 1953. *Man, Time and Fossils*. New York: Knopf. 411p.

Muller, W. H. 1963. *Botany: A Functional Approach*. New York: Macmillan. 486p.

Ray, C. E., Cooper, B. N. and Benninghof, W. S. 1967. Fossil mammals and pollen in a late Pleistocene deposit at Saltville, Virginia. *Jour. Paleontology*, 41: 608–22.

Read, C. B. 1955. *Floras of the Pocono Formation and Price Sandstone in Parts of Pennsylvania, Maryland, West Virginia, and Virginia*. U.S. Geol. Surv., Prof. Paper 263. 32p. and 20 plates.

Rhodes, F. H. T., Zim, H. S. and Shaffer, P. R. 1962. *Fossils: A Guide to Prehistoric Life*. New York: Golden Press. 160p.

Roberts, J. K. 1928. *The Geology of the Virginia Triassic*. Va. Geol. Surv., Bull. 29. 205p.

Romer, A. S. 1966. *Vertebrate Paleontology*. 3d ed. Chicago: Univ. of Chicago Press. 468p.

——. 1959. *The Vertebrate Story*. 4th ed. Chicago: Univ. of Chicago Press. 437p.

Schenk, E. T., and McMasters, J. H. 1936. *Procedure in Taxonomy*. Stanford, Calif.: Stanford Univ. Press. 72p.

Seilacher, Adolf. 1967. Fossil behavior. *Scientific American*, 217: 72–80.

Shimer, H. W. and Shrock, R. R. 1944. *Index Fossils of North America*. New York: Wiley. 837p., 303 plates.

Shrock, R. R., and Twenhofel, W. H. 1953. *Principles of Invertebrate Paleontology*. New York: McGraw-Hill. 816p.

Vokes, H. E. 1957. *Miocene Fossils of Maryland*. Dept. of Geology, Mines and Water Resources of Md., Bull. 20. 85p.

Wilson, C. L., and Loomis, W. E. 1967. *Botany*. 4th ed. New York: Holt, Rinehart and Winston. 626p.

IV. Land Forms

Cotton, C. A. 1948. *Landscape, as Developed by the Processes of Normal Erosion*. 2d ed. Christ Church, New Zealand: Whitcombe & Tombs. 509p.

——. 1949. *Geomorphology*. 5th ed. New York: Wiley. 505p.

Dietrich, R. V. 1957. Origin of the Blue Ridge Escarpment directly southwest of Roanoke, Virginia. *Va. Jour. Sci.*, n.s. 8: 233–47.

——. 1970. V=f(S . . .). In *The Distributional History of the Biota of the Southern Appalachians*. Part II, *Flora* (ed. by P. C. Holt), pp. 66–99. Va. Poly. Inst. Res. Div. Monograph II.

Fenneman, N. M. 1938. *Physiography of the Eastern United States*. New York: McGraw-Hill. 714p.

Hunt, C. B. 1967. *Physiography of the United States*. San Francisco: Freeman. 480p.

Scheidegger, A. E. 1961. *Theoretical Geomorphology*. Berlin, Germany: Springer-Verlag. 333p.

Scorel, J. L., O'Brien, E. J., McCormack, J. C., and Chapman, R. B. 1965. *Atlas of Landforms*. New York: Wiley. 164p.

Strahler, A. N. 1965. *Introduction to Physical Geography*. New York: Wiley. 465p.

Thompson, H. D. 1939. Drainage evolution in the southern Appalachians. *Geol. Soc. Am. Bull.*, 50: 1323–56.

Thornbury, W. D. 1954. *Principles of Geomorphology*. New York: Wiley. 618p.

———. 1965. *Regional Geomorphology of the United States*. New York: Wiley. 609p.

U.S. Department of Interior—Geological Survey and National Park Service, 1970. *The River and the Rocks—The Geologic Story of Great Falls and the Potomac River Gorge*. U.S. Geol. Surv., Spec. Publ. 46p.

Wanless, H. R. 1965. *Aerial Stereo Photographs*. Northbrook, Ill.: T. N. Hubbard Scientific Co. 92p. (An inexpensive stereoscope comes with the book.)

V. Layered Rocks

Clark, T. H., and Stearn, C. W. 1960. *The Geological Evolution of North America*. New York: Ronald. 434p.

Dietrich, R. V., Hobbs, C. R. B. Jr., and Lowry, W. D. 1963. Dolomitization interrupted by silicification. *Jour. Sed. Petrology,* 33: 646–63.

Dunbar, C. O. 1959. *Historical Geology,* 2d ed. New York: Wiley. 500p.

Dunbar, C. O., and Rodgers, John. 1957. *Principles of Stratigraphy*. New York: Wiley. 356p.

Glaessner, M. F. 1945 (repr. 1963). *Principles of Micropaleontology*. New York: Hafner. 296p.

McAlester, A. L. 1968. *The History of Life*. Englewood Cliffs, N.J.: Prentice-Hall. 151p.

Moore, R. C. 1958. *Introduction to Historical Geology*. 2d ed. New York: McGraw-Hill. 656p.

Pangborn, M. W., Jr. 1957. *The Earth for the Layman*. 2d ed. Washington, D.C.: Amer. Geol. Inst. 68p.

Shrock, R. R. 1948. *Sequence in Layered Rocks*. New York: McGraw-Hill. 507p.

Simpson, G. G. 1953. *Life of the Past*. New Haven: Yale Univ. Press. 198p.

Tilton, G. R., and Hart, S. R. 1963. Geochronology. *Science,* 140: 357–66.

U.S. Geological Survey. 1970. *Geologic Time*. U.S. Geol. Surv., Pamphlet. 20p.

VI. Deformed Rocks

Badgley, P. C. 1965. *Structural and Tectonic Principles.* New York: Harper & Row. 521p.

Billings, M. P. 1954. *Structural Geology.* 2d ed. Englewood Cliffs, N.J.: Prentice-Hall. 473p.

Eardley, A. J. 1962. *Structural Geology of North America.* 2d ed. New York: Harper & Row, 743p.

King, P. B. 1959. *The Evolution of North America.* Princeton, N.J.: Princeton Univ. Press. 200p.

Lowry, W. D. (ed.). 1964. *Tectonics of the Southern Appalachians.* Va. Poly. Inst., Dept. Geol. Sci., Mem. 1. 114p.

Ramsey, J. G. 1967. *Folding and Fracturing of Rocks.* New York: McGraw-Hill. 568p.

VII. Geology and Man

Bateman, A. M. 1950. *Economic Mineral Deposits.* 2d ed. New York: Wiley. 918p.

——. 1951. *The Formation of Mineral Deposits.* New York: Wiley. 371p.

Bates, R. 1960. *Geology of the Industrial Rocks and Minerals.* New York: Harper. 441p.

Davis, S. N., and deWeist, R. J. M. *Hydrogeology.* New York: Wiley. 463p.

Dobrin, M. B. 1960. *Introduction to Geophysical Prospecting.* 2d ed. New York: McGraw-Hill. 446p.

Eckel, E. B. (ed.). 1958. *Landslides and Engineering Practice.* Highway Research Board Special Report 29. Washington, D.C.: National Research Council. 232p.

Eve, A. S., and Kerp, D. A. 1954. *Applied Geophysics in the Search for Minerals.* 4th ed. New York: Cambridge Univ. Press. 392p.

Flawn, P. T. 1966. *Mineral Resources: Geology, Engineering, Economics, Politics, Law.* Chicago: Rand McNally. 406p.

Gillson, J. L. (ed.). 1960. *Industrial Minerals and Rocks.* New York: Amer. Inst. Mining, Metall., & Petroleum Engrs. 934p.

Hawkes, H. E., and Webb, J. S. 1962. *Geochemistry in Mineral Exploration.* New York: Harper and Row. 415p.

Johnson, E. E. (Incorp.), 1966. *Ground Water and Wells.* St. Paul: Johnson Incorp. 440p.

Kazman, R. G. 1965. *Modern Hydrology.* New York: Harper and Row. 301p.

Krynine, D. P., and Judd, W. R. 1957. *Principles of Engineering Geology.* New York: McGraw-Hill. 730p.

Lahee, F. H. 1961. *Field Geology.* 6th ed. New York. McGraw-Hill. 926p.

Legget, R. F. 1962. *Geology and Engineering.* 2d ed. New York: McGraw-Hill. 896p.

Levorsen, A. I. 1967. *Geology of Petroleum.* 2d ed. San Francisco: Freeman. 724p.

McGuinness, C. L. 1963. *The Role of Ground Water in the National Water Situation.* U.S. Geol. Surv., Water-Supply Paper 1800. 1121p.

McKinstry, H. E. 1948. *Mining Geology.* New York: Prentice-Hall. 680p.

Moore, E. S. 1940. *Coal.* New York: Wiley. 473p.

Park, C. F., Jr., and MacDiarmid, R. A. 1964. *Ore Deposits.* San Francisco: Freeman. 475p.

Terzaghi, Karl. 1960. *From Theory to Practice in Soil Mechanics.* New York: Wiley. 425p.

Todd, D. K. 1959. *Ground-Water Hydrology.* New York: Wiley: 336p.

U.S. Bureau of Mines. 1960. *Mineral Facts and Problems.* U.S. Bur. Mines, Bull. 585. 1042p.

Virginia Division of Mineral Resources. 1963. *Mineral Industries and Resources of Virginia.* Charlottesville: Va. Div. Mineral Resources. Map.

Ward, F. N., Lankin, H. W., Canney, F. C., *et al.* 1963. *Analytical Methods Used in Geochemical Exploration by the U.S. Geological Survey.* U.S. Geol. Surv., Bull. 1152. 100p.

Watson, T. L. 1907. *Mineral Resources of Virginia.* Lynchburg, Va.: Bell. 618p.

VIII. Geological History

Butts, Charles. 1904. *Geology of the Appalachian Valley in Virginia:* Geologic Text and Illustrations. Va. Geol. Surv., Bull. 52, pt. 1, 568p.

Cederstrom, D. J. 1946. *Chemical Character of Ground Water in the Coastal Plain of Virginia.* Va. Geol. Surv., Bull. 68. 62p.

Dietrich, R. V. 1960. Basement beneath the emerged Atlantic Coastal Plain between New York and Georgia. *Southeastern Geol.,* 1:121–31.

Meyertons, C. T. 1963. *Triassic Formations of the Danville Basin.* Va. Div. Mineral Resources, Rpt. Inv. 6. 65p.

Roberts, J. K. 1928. *The Geology of the Virginia Triassic.* Va. Geol. Surv., Bull. 29. 205p.

Spangler, W., and Peterson, J. J. 1950. Geology of Atlantic Coastal Plain in New Jersey, Delaware, Maryland, and Virginia. *Bull. Am. Assoc. Pet. Geol.,* 34:1–99.

Virginia Division of Mineral Resources. 1963. *Geologic Map of Virginia.* Charlottesville: Va. Div. Mineral Resources. Map.

Wentworth, C. K. 1930. *Sand and Gravel Resources of the Coastal Plain of Virginia.* Va. Geol. Surv., Bull. 32. 146p.

IX. Maps

Lobeck, A. K. 1964. *Things Maps Don't Tell Us: An Adventure into Map Interpretation.* New York: Macmillan. 159p.

X. Guidebooks and Road Logs

Cooper, B. N. 1955. Geological Features along U.S. Routes 11, 29, and 250 in Virginia. Part I, U.S. Route 11 from Virginia-West Virginia Line to Bristol. In *Guides to Southeastern Geology,* p. 1–27. New York: Geol. Soc. America.

———. 1960. *The Geology of the Region between Roanoke and Winchester in the Appalachian Valley of Western Virginia.* Johns Hopkins Univ. Studies in Geol., no. 18, 84p.

———. 1961. *Grand Appalachian Excursion.* Va. Poly. Inst., Eng. Exp. Sta. Ser., Geol. Guidebook I. 187p.

Dietrich, R. V. 1962. *Southern Field Excursion Guidebook.* [Washington, D.C.:] Internat. Mineralogical Assoc., 3d Gen. Congr. 59p.

———. (ed). 1963. *Geological Excursions in Southwestern Virginia.* Va. Poly. Inst., Eng. Exp. Sta. Ser., Geol. Guidebook II, 99p. (Out of print.)

Dietrich, R. V., and Lowry, W. D. 1955. Geological Features along U.S. Routes 11, 29, and 250 in Virginia. Part II, Washington, D.C., and Point of Rocks, Maryland, to Staunton, Virginia. In *Guides to Southeastern Geology,* p. 28–43. New York: Geol. Soc. America.

Johnson, R. W., Jr., and Milton, Charles. 1965. Alkalic Complex and Related Rocks of the Central Shenandoah Valley, Augusta and Rockingham Countries, Virginia. 15p. (ditto). Field trip outline.

Ruhle, J. L. (comp.). 1962. *Guidebook to the Coastal Plain of Virginia North of the James River.* Va. Div. Mineral Resources Inf. Circ. 6. 46p.

Tillman, C. G., and Lowry, W. D. 1968. *Structures and Paleozoic History of the Salem Synclinorium, Southwestern Virginia.* Va. Poly. Inst., Geol. Guidebook 3, 21p.

Webb, H. W., Nunan, W. E., and Penley, H. M. 1970. Road Log—Storm-damaged areas in central Virginia. *Va. Minerals,* 16: 1–10.

Index

Numbers in *italics* give pages on which the terms are defined; numbers in **bold face** give pages on which there are pertinent illustrations. Entries are exclusive of animal and plant names given only on tables 3.2, 3.3, and 3.4 (pp. 56, 57, and 82-83); stratigraphic names given only on tables 5.1, 8.1, 8.2, and 8.3 (pp. 127, 168-69, 175, and 177); minerals given only on the Determinative Tables (Appendix A, pp. 179-81), and Glossary listings (pp. 187-95).